1. *Book on Paul Klee with student's binding showing use of appliqué and stitchery*

CREATIVE BOOKBINDING

By PAULINE JOHNSON

DOVER PUBLICATIONS, INC., NEW YORK

NOTE TO THE DOVER EDITION

For this edition, several outdated entries in the Supply Sources section (pp. 254–55) have been replaced with new information. The current availability of periodicals and products listed elsewhere in this book has also been checked as far as possible. However, readers should check with their dealers about the availability of any item or supplier named herein.

This Dover edition, first published in 1990, is an unabridged, slightly corrected republication of the 1973 edition of the work originally published by the University of Washington Press, Seattle and London (first edition: 1963). For this edition, several outdated entries in the Supply Sources section (pp. 254–55) have been replaced with new information. In addition, a few obvious typographical errors have been tacitly corrected throughout the book.

Manufactured in the United States of America
Dover Publications, Inc., 31 East 2nd Street, Mineola, N.Y. 11501

Library of Congress Cataloging-in-Publication Data

Johnson, Pauline, 1905–
    Creative bookbinding / by Pauline Johnson.
        p.   cm.
    Reprint. Originally published: Seattle : University of Washington Press, 1964, c1963.
    Includes bibliographical references.
    ISBN 0-486-26307-X
    1. Bookbinding—Handbooks, manuals, etc. I. Title.
Z266.J6 1990
686.3—dc20   90-3274
                                     CIP

Preface

Although the art of binding is rooted in the past, extending back for hundreds of years, it offers excellent opportunities as a means of expression today. This fascinating art is not widely known, and its potential as an educative medium as well as an amateur pursuit has not yet been fully explored. With bookbinding, in contrast to many arts, much can be achieved with a limited amount of equipment, and this is an advantage in the classroom or home where extra space is not available. Simple books can be constructed with only cardboard, paper, cloth, and paste. The worker can secure a few essential items, improvising when necessary by substituting weights for presses, and so forth; or he can build up a completely equipped workshop with expensive tools and equipment if he so desires. Older students can construct much of their own apparatus either in the school shop or at home.

This book presents bookbinding as an art form to be experienced and enjoyed. Procedures have been simplified for the use and understanding of the beginner to assist him in finding a means by which he can grow expressively through art. In combining the work of his hands with a sensitivity for art quality, he can experience the visual delight of his product and also derive much from the possession and use of a book that he himself has made.

Most manuals on bookbinding are confined to technical information and instruction and are prepared primarily for the use of the professional binder. Artistic standards are neglected in many cases, and sometimes stereotyped, repetitive patterns are employed. The material here presented does not attempt to replace the technical text, needed in professional work, but has for its aim the promotion of personal values for the child and beginner adult. The range includes all ages from the first grade through high school, the college student preparing to teach, or anyone who just wishes to bind his own books. Adults interested in this craft may start on a limited scale at first in their own home workshops, later progressing toward more ambitious efforts leading into the field of the expert. Some may find outlets for their services in the mending departments of libraries and universities, or in commercial binderies. Additional sources of help with regard to important details for those wishing more information than is included here will be found in the texts of Douglas Cockerell, Edith Diehl, and others, listed in the Bibliography.

Bookbinders of the past were devoted to their craft and went through long and exacting periods of training in preparation for their work. They stressed perfection and ideal craftsmanship with the result that the books they bound by hand were practically faultless in construction. Some of the books produced were great works of art, full of spirit and vitality, while others were only technical achievements following established traditions and duplicating styles of the past.

There are a number of hand binders in this country who work on special commissions when a particularly fine piece of binding is required. Every book they bind is a special problem to be considered individually. These binders, to be successful in their trade, must devote most of their time to it. In the United States, few binders now practice the craft as an expressive art; in Europe, there are guilds that encourage the designer and promote exhibitions of his work.

The less skilled person cannot expect to rival the craftsmanship of the binder who has devoted his life to this field of work, but even with a limited background of knowledge he can experience a great deal of enjoyment in binding his own books and building up a distinctive and personal library of which he can be proud. Each product can be an artistic creation to be cherished for many years. The same pleasure and satisfaction that the devoted binder experiences can be shared by others, whether in the classroom or in amateur endeavors.

Teachers have many opportunities for introducing this age-old art to children, particularly while studying ancient and medieval cultures through literature and history. Interest aroused in bindings and the art of the book can be applied to the making of attractive notebooks and portfolios for classroom or personal use.

The value of learning to use the hands in a thoughtful, constructive manner as a means for carrying out artistic concepts should not be overlooked. As in many crafts, patience is a virtue that comes naturally as the student becomes absorbed in the process. With the various steps laid out before him in logical order, he learns to carry through from a beginning conception to a completed goal, achieving satisfaction in both process and finished product. Not only does he gain technical experience, but he grows in his understanding and use of art as a personal experience. He learns about "fitness to purpose," "proportion," and "scale," through the principles of art. There is a merging of good design and careful craftsmanship, essential to book production and worthy goals to strive for. The increasing contact with and emphasis on design will enrich the student's background in art.

As the child constructs books his respect for them increases, and his discovery of how they can be made more beautiful may even stimulate his interest in reading. He becomes aware of the place of design in all phases of his daily life as he acquires the technique and knowledge to alter objects in his surroundings and make them more attractive. The fact that he can construct new objects that are both esthetic and practical in character helps to demonstrate the value of design as applied to functional articles. Parents who may not understand a child's sensitive, creative expressions are often more receptive to objects that seem to have a "purpose" and can be used and enjoyed in the home. In this way interest is aroused and approval gained, for the work is understood. Such support is very important and can lead the way to other expressive forms of art.

It is hoped that this neglected craft will be used more widely in schools for it fosters in the student important values of education and discipline. The art of bookbinding develops a feeling for good design combined with an appreciation for construction and craftsmanship. It is a rare accomplishment, but one which opens up new interests and a growing appreciation and awareness of one of the finest expressions in man's history.

Grateful appreciation is extended to those who have contributed in various ways to the production of this book. The author is especially indebted to Dorothy Macdonald, who provided personal inspiration as well as professional and technical knowledge related to binding. Miss Macdonald, an enthusiastic binder trained in Italy and California, generously shared her experience during several months of work in her studio.

The author's diagrams were inked by Robert Tsukui, a talented artist and teacher whose sensitive line and delicate control contribute a great deal to the character of the book.

The many photographs showing working processes and examples of student work were made with the cooperation of the Still Photography Production Unit at the University of Washington under the direction of E. F. Marten and William Eng. The expressive hands of Hazel Koenig, teacher of the children's creative art classes at the University of Washington, and those of Laurel White, art student, appear throughout the book in the demonstration photographs. The photographs showing the ink-and-fold process (figures 246-57), posed by Barbara White, appear with the permission of *Craft Horizons* and of Conrad Brown.

I wish to thank the following individuals and institutions who provided the photographs of rare books and bindings and granted permission for their use: Edgar Mansfield, president of the Guild of Contemporary Bookbinders in London, figures 30, 31, 261, 274, and 275; Trevor Jones, figures 34, 35, 36, and 37; Ivor Robinson, figures 32 and 33; R. Wright, figure 38; Arthur Johnson, figure 39; Mme Claude Stahly, figures 41 and 287; Pierre Martin, figure 42; Gerhard Gerlach, figure 43; Dorothy Macdonald, figures 284, 286, and 293; Dorothy Miner, librarian and keeper of manuscripts, and the Walters Art Gallery, Baltimore, figures 9, 10, 11, 13, 17, 22, and 23; Frederick B. Adams, director, and the Trustees of the Pierpont Morgan Library, New York, figures 12, 16 (courtesy of William S. Glazier), and 19; Karl Kup, curator of the Spencer Collection, and the New York Public Library, figure 22; Frederick R. Goff, chief of the Rare Book Division, and the Library of Congress, figures 11 and 40 (from the Lessing J. Rosenwald Collection); Robert Duane Monroe, curator of rare books, and the Library of the University of Washington, figures 18, 27, 28, and 29; Trustees of the British Museum, figures 3, 4, 6, and 7; the Victoria and Albert Museum, London, figure 15; Philip Hofer, of the Library of Harvard University, and Mrs. Hofer, figure 13; Arthur Rau, of Paris, figure 14; Julius Carlebach and the Julius Carlebach Gallery, New York, figure 8; Philip C. Duschnes and the Urs Graf Verlag Press of Switzerland, figures 20 (used by permission of the Board of Trinity College, Dublin) and 21; Bottega d'Erasmo, Turin, figure 5; Gilhofer and Ranschburg, Vienna, figure 24; Pageant Books, Inc., figure 25; Macmillan and Co., London, figure 26 (from *The Chained Library* by Burnett Hillman); Paul Hamlyn Publishers, London, figure 2 (from *Assyrian Palace Reliefs,* by R. D. Barnett); British Artist Craftsmen Ltd., London, figures 36 and 37; *Graphis,* figure 41; *Craft Horizons,* figures 42 and 246-57; Swedish Society of Industrial Design, figures 57, 285, and 298; Demco Library Supplies, figure 54. The Wadsworth Publishing Co., Inc., Belmont, California, gave permission for the use of a number of photographs from the book *Craft Design* by Spencer Moseley, Pauline Johnson, and Hazel Koenig.

Most of the examples of student work are from the author's classes; a few were supplied by Spencer Moseley and Marie Brown, fellow teachers at the University of Washington. Examples of junior and senior high school work are from Margaret Jane Seil and Dan Cannon, of the Seattle Public Schools.

PAULINE JOHNSON

Contents

INTRODUCTION   3

BOOK DESIGN   42

THE PARTS OF A BOOK   46

MATERIALS, TOOLS, AND EQUIPMENT   49

WORKING PROCEDURES   59

SIMPLE CONSTRUCTIONS AND BINDING PROCEDURES   84

DECORATED PAPERS   155

LEATHER   227

BOOK REPAIR   248

SUPPLY SOURCES   254

BIBLIOGRAPHY   255

INDEX   259

Creative Bookbinding

2. Cuneiform writing

Introduction

At one time well-constructed and beautifully embellished books were regarded as a major art form. They were produced by talented artist-craftsmen who were honored for their distinctive and original work. Books, which today are so common, were considered rare and precious objects, deserving the treatment and veneration accorded to great works of art.

The history of the book really reflects the history of civilization, for by means of books the records, sacred teachings, ideas, and experience of the past have been preserved and transmitted to the present. Through the ages, writings on stone, clay, papyrus, parchment, vellum, and paper have been a major instrument of cultural progress.

The earliest types of "written" communications were expressed through pictorial form, as in drawings on cave walls and the inscriptions on rocks, still used by primitive people today. There are, for example, the hunting episodes depicted in the rock paintings of African Bushmen and Australian aboriginals, and the symbolic picture writings of the American Indians, who drew pictographs on buffalo skins and birch bark as well as on rock cliffs. The Egyptians developed a form of picture writing called "hieroglyphics" in which symbolic interpretation of words was eventually simplified and reduced to a conventionalized system of writing, reading from right to left. The Chinese and Japanese evolved their calligraphy through similar means, by reducing to a few lines a pictorial element representing an object or idea.

The invention of writing, which Carlyle called "the most miraculous of all things man has devised," made possible the beginning of the book. The first true written language appeared about 3500 B.C. when the ancient Sumerians developed symbols called "cuneiform," which means "wedge-shaped," referring to the form of the letters (figure 2). These shapes, when considered as an allover design, produced a beautiful decorative effect, an example of which can be seen on the Babylonian clay tablets in figures 3 and 4. These tablets, similar to many produced by the ancient Babylonians as well as the Sumerians and the Assyrians, illustrate one of the

3. Babylonian clay tablet inscribed with events in the reigns of kings, 744-669 B.C. British Museum

4. Babylonian clay tablet inscribed with a letter from the governor of Tyre to the king of Egypt, c. 1450 B.C. British Museum

5. Inscription on stone

earliest means used for the preservation of records. The cuneiform inscriptions were incised with a square-headed stylus on damp clay and either dried in the sun or baked in an oven for permanence. For safekeeping the tablet was often inserted into an "envelope," like a hollow tube, also made of clay.

The royal library at Nineveh, capital of Assyria, contained thousands of these clay books dealing with astronomy, mythology, geography, and many other subjects. In fact the Mesopotamians had a wide and varied literature. In addition to the clay tablets, and little cylinder seals which they carried with them for signing documents, they left many inscriptions on stone, including those on the famous stelae in which pictorial forms were also carved in low relief.

Many records were engraved on stone, some of which still exist today (figure 5). Hammurabi, king of Babylonia, published an extensive code of laws that was chiseled on a block of black diorite 8 feet high, containing 44 columns and over 3,600 lines. The ancient Hebrews gave to the world the Ten Commandments engraved on stone. It was by the discovery of the famous Rosetta stone, found near Rosetta, Egypt, in 1799, that the written records of Egypt were revealed, for up to that time hieroglyphics were a mystery. This stone is inscribed in Greek, in Egyptian hieroglyphic, and in demotic, a later, simplified form of Egyptian writing. Molten lead was sometimes poured into incised letters that had been scratched in the stone with a hard instrument like an iron graver. In the Old Testament, Job exclaims: "Oh that my words were now written! Oh that they were printed in a book! That they were graven with an iron pen and lead in the rock for ever!"

The chief writing material of the ancient world was made of papyrus, a rushlike plant that grows along the Nile, by a method invented by the Egyptians. Strips from the stem of the papyrus plant were laid flat, one beside the other, with another layer placed on top, at right angles to the first, to form the sheets. These were covered with a gummed sizing solution, pressed, and pounded until the fibers were welded together. Afterward they were left to dry in the sun and were later coated with a preparation to keep them pliable.

These sheets, about 12 by 16 inches in size, were joined together with a paste into long rolls, and a

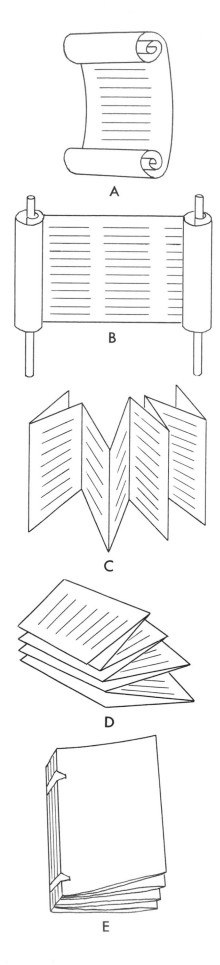

A

B

C

D

E

wooden stick was placed at either end for a roller (figure 6). The rolls generally contained about 20 sheets, although they varied from 15 feet to many yards in length. They were sometimes 12 inches in height but were often cut down to 6 or even 3 inches for easier reading. Pens of reed were used for writing. On the vertical scrolls the writing was continuous (diagram A), but on the horizontal ones it was broken up into columns, each column being the equivalent of a page in a book (diagram B). Later the sheets of papyrus were folded back and forth on the blank spaces between the columns, no doubt for easier storage (diagrams C and D), and kept flat with a board on top and bottom.

Before the method of folding the papyrus flat in a zigzag manner was devised, the scrolls were kept rolled up in jars holding about nine or ten rolls each. If the manuscript was too long for one roll it was continued on several others. The Latin word for one of these rolls is *volumen,* from which comes our word "volume." Papyrus was used in Greece and in Rome, and, along with parchment, it served the writing needs of the world until paper—invented by the Chinese about the second century B.C.—was introduced into Europe about the tenth century A.D.

Many of the ancient works produced on papyrus are in a remarkable state of preservation. One of the oldest books in existence is the Prisse Papyrus, now in the Louvre Museum in Paris. It is composed of eighteen pages of Egyptian hieratic writing of about 2500 B.C. and contains a treatise, thought to have been composed as far back as 3350 B.C., which includes the "moralizings of an aged sage" on how to behave wisely.

Other Egyptian books contained historical records and works of religion and philosophy, fiction, and magic, as well as funeral ritual. Probably the most famous, the Book of the Dead, included the formulas, hymns, rites, and directions to be observed in the passage of the soul through the underworld. Its 106 chapters deal both with funeral rituals and with Egyptian beliefs concerning events after death. They contain a collection of inscriptions from mummy cases and tombs, describing the adventures of the soul after death and the means of escaping torment. The book was written on papyrus and contained illustrations. The Egyptians had many such volumes, and soon there were enough collections to form libraries.

6. *Hebrew scroll containing the Book of the Law, fifteenth century B.C. British Museum*

Although papyrus continued to be in use for many centuries, the skins of animals also served as writing materials. Parchment is known to have been used as early as 500 B.C., but it did not become popular until a few centuries later. It was made from the skin of a sheep or goat but was not tanned like regular leather. When made from calf the material was referred to as vellum. Skins were cleaned and processed so that eventually texts could be written on both sides instead of just one. Parchment was used first for manuscripts written on scrolls and later as individual leaves bound into the form of a flat book.

The Romans used wax tablets for their personal correspondence and for records of business transactions involving sales and taxes. The tablet consisted of a wooden leaf somewhat similar in size and shape to the old-fashioned slate, with one side hollowed out and filled with a blackened wax upon which the text was scratched with a stylus, a sharp-pointed instrument usually made of iron, but sometimes of bone, brass, wood or bronze. Sometimes two tablets were hinged together with leather thongs to form a diptych, or as many as eight leaves might be so joined together. Books formed in this way were known as *pugillaria*.

The first public library appeared in Rome about 39 B.C. At this time books were more common than previously, and booksellers prospered. The earliest known work of the Latin period is a wax tablet found at Pompeii, from A.D. 55, and the oldest Greek literary manuscript has been dated 160 B.C. War and fire caused the destruction of many books, like those of the remarkable library in Alexandria, Egypt, which housed 700,000 papyrus rolls, many of which were destroyed at the time of the conquest by Julius Caesar.

Bookbinding as we know it today began in the Christian era. First the accordion-folded scrolls were flattened, and later they were turned into books with sheets tied together at one side through holes punched in the margin. In about the fifth century books with folded sheets of parchment were sewn together over leather thongs for more strength (diagram E, page 6), and thin wooden boards were placed on the top and bottom to protect the pages and make the curled edges lie flat. Eventually the protruding ends of the thongs were laced into the boards. As the art of binding developed, the back of the book was covered with leather to conceal the thongs, and finally the protective strip was extended over onto the surface of the boards far enough to cover the lacing-in of the thongs or bands. Later leather was used to cover the entire board area, setting the stage for the embellishment of covers and the development of the rich art of binding. The principles of construction remain the same today, although methods and materials vary, and paper has supplanted parchment.

7. *A monk copyist working in a monastery reproducing manuscript pages. British Museum*

The production of manuscripts and the binding of books became major art forms with the support of the church, wealthy patrons, and royal personages. Professional scribes were hired to make copies of books for private libraries, and educated slaves copied books for their masters. Monasteries established scriptoria where cloistered monks, carefully trained, worked painstakingly from dawn to dark for many months at a time reproducing manuscripts by hand for their own libraries and the use of scholars (figure 7). It often took from six months to a year to copy one book.

8. *Greek engraved book container, late Gothic, niello on silver. Carlebach Gallery*

9. *English book cover for the Gospels, silver ornamented with precious stones, c. 1040. Pierpont Morgan Library*

10. *German book cover for the Mondsee Gospels, silver, enamel, and ivory, late twelfth century. Walters Art Gallery*

11. *Core of a treasure binding for a lectionary of the Gospels, Rhineland, c. 1300. Library of Congress*

When boards were put on books for covers, there was opportunity for ornamentation in the form of casings made of precious metals, and later coverings of leather or cloth. These bindings had become more and more elaborate and sumptuously decorative by the time of the fourth century. Continuing through the Middle Ages and the Renaissance, binders of different countries vied with one another to produce the most beautiful results of which they were capable. The bindings were embellished in various ways, as in the example of figure 8, showing engraving on silver with niello, an ancient method of decorating metal with incised designs filled with a black alloy. The cover in figure 9 is made of thick wooden boards covered with plates of silver, ornamented with filigree, engraving, precious gems, and silver figures cast in full relief. In the upper part of the cover Christ is seated in majesty holding a book, while below he is shown on a rustic cross. In figure 10, heavy oak boards are covered with silver plates and a design made with silver filigree. The four gilt areas between the ivory relief carvings of the four evangelists in their studies form a cross at the center. Figure 11 shows a heavy wooden cover board nearly an inch thick, with cavities bounded by ridges of curving contours revealing the areas where decorative plaques of ivory, enamel, jeweled ornaments, or wrought metal were embedded. Holes for the attachment of the decorative units can be seen in the wood of the cover. Various sizes of nails were used to attach the leather to the board when the spine was re-covered in France about 1750.

Elaborate bindings were used because manuscripts were costly and the expense was justified by their importance. Under the Byzantine emperors, massive books were sometimes suspended from gold rods and paraded through the streets in public processions for all to see. Bookbinding attained its state of highest perfection in the fifteenth century.

Along with the use of gold and jewels came the decoration of leathers. These were often dyed brilliant red, blue, or yellow as well as the deeper shades of brown. Morocco, made from goatskin, became popular because it took color well, but other skins were also used. Designs were impressed on the surface of the leather with tooled lines and points, and stamped patterns were applied with heated, engraved metal dies or stamps. Earlier, in Alexandria, the Copts had been well advanced in the arts of writing, and bookbinding had flourished in the monasteries of the Coptic church as early as the second century. The Copts were familiar with the methods of blind tooling, either with heated tools or with metal punches, before the sixth century. In the Coptic binding of figure 12, the papyrus board is covered with dark brown leather to which was stitched an elaborate ornamental panel of red leather openwork tracery over a gilt parchment background.

12. Coptic binding of a Gospel book, seventh or eighth century. Pierpont Morgan Library

The design shows a central cross inscribed within a square and a border at the top containing rosettes, interlacings, and a Coptic cross. The technique of impressions on leather has generally been considered of much later English origin (figure 13).

In Morocco, the Arabs explored the use of the leathers for which they have become famous. The Moors introduced their patterns into Spain and Italy, and the Italians took gold tooling to France and England in the sixteenth and seventeenth centuries (figure 14). So the tradition continued to spread and be enriched. This type of decoration began to decline in quality, however, after the seventeenth century when patterns tended to become less vital and merely repetitious.

13. Romanesque binding of a processional manuscript, northern France or England, white deerskin on thin board covers with stamped imprints arranged in a narrow vertical plan, c. 1200. Collection of Mr. and Mrs. Philip Hofer

14. French binding by Padeloup, red, green, and citron morocco with flower, arch, and other impressions, c. 1725-30. Private collection

15. English embroidered book cover, silk on linen canvas, depicting the sacrifice of Isaac, and Jonah cast up by the whale, 1613. Victoria and Albert Museum

Cloth bindings came along some time after leather was introduced as a cover material. Velvet, silk, various other woven fabrics, and needlework were especially favored; Queen Elizabeth had books covered with embroidered cloth, some of which she had worked on herself. These were applied to boards made of a composition that took the place of wood (figure 15). Most present-day books are bound with a cloth that has been stiffened, calendered to give it a gloss, and embossed. This material serves a primarily utilitarian purpose and lends itself to mass production methods.

The art of illumination flourished along with the art of binding. Texts were elaborately hand-lettered and decorated with gold and color. The earliest manuscripts were relatively plain, but as more wealth became available the demand for beautiful books increased. The first letters of sentences were made larger and sometimes colored (figure 16), and often amusing sketches were added as in the tiny psalter of figure 17. The initial letter at the beginning

16. *Initial letter from manuscript of the Tollemache Bible. Collection of William S. Glazier*

17. *Flemish miniature psalter, c. 1300. Walters Art Gallery*

of the page became of great importance and was designed with flourishes and other decorative detail. These flourishes were eventually continued on into the margins and around the edges of the page. Elaborate borders followed, and color and gold were added so that the page took on a superbly rich appearance as in the Book of Hours shown in figure 18, which is written on vellum. The margin border is narrowest at the center of the book and wider on the other three sides. The Book of Hours, which contained prayers to be said at the canonical hours, was often commissioned by wealthy noblemen for personal use. Though generally small it was always richly illuminated, and it included a calendar illustrated with emblems or scenes suited to each month. The other manuscripts most often copied in Europe during the Middle Ages were the Gospels of the New Testament, church missals, and prayer books.

Small paintings illustrating the text of the manuscript were sometimes placed at the top near, or within, the main initial letter or at the bottom of the page. When these miniatures were done by artists of talent each page became a work of art, beautifully illustrated, with the text exquisitely lettered (figure 19). Miniature painting reached great heights of expression in Persian book illustrations, where

18. French Book of Hours, fifteenth century. Library of the University of Washington

19. French miniature painting of the nativity from an illuminated manuscript of the Hours of the Virgin, early fifteenth century. Pierpont Morgan Library

20. *Initial letter from the Book of Kells, Ireland, c. eighth century. Library of Trinity College*

enchanting detail and color were combined to produce great art. The calligraphy of the text was closely related to the illustrations, and these books are among the most beautiful ever made.

Although monasteries all over Europe produced a great many manuscripts, it was those of Ireland which, in the sixth, seventh, and eight centuries, yielded works that were most outstanding in workmanship and most skillfully executed. The majority of the bindings were plain, although some were elaborate, and the illuminated pages were unsurpassable in originality of design.

From the Irish monastery at Kells came the celebrated manuscript known as the Book of Kells, often called the most beautiful book in the world (figure 20). It was produced about the eighth century and contains the four Gospels, in Latin, written on vellum leaves that measure 13½ by 9½ inches. The illustrations represent various incidents in the life of Christ and portraits of the Evangelists, accompanied by formal designs. There are large initial letters, exquisitely conceived and richly ornamented. The book may now be seen in Dublin in the library of Trinity College. Unfortunately it was trimmed by a careless binder insensitive to the contents of the pages, and as a result parts of the illuminations were mutilated. Facsimile copies reproduced in entirety and containing 48 pages in full color and 630 in black and white have been published in Switzerland (see Bibliography), and are available in many of the larger libraries.

The Lindisfarne Gospels, second only to the Book of Kells in fame, represents one of the greatest achievements of Anglo-Saxon manuscript illumination (figure 21). The book was lettered in Latin in the seventh century by the monks at Lindisfarne Monastery in a British province at Holy Island, also called Lindisfarne Peninsula, off the Northumbrian coast. The monastery was founded in 635 and destroyed by the Danes in 793 and again in 833. The manuscript, now in the British Museum in London, includes purely abstract ornamentation, large decorative initials, portraits of the Evangelists, and many other decorative features. It, too, is available in a facsimile edition.

The oldest book known to be bound with ornamented binding is a little Gospel of St. John covered in red leather with skilled craftsmanship. It was found in the tomb of St. Cuthbert, who lived in the

21. *Initial letter from the Lindisfarne Gospels, England, c. 700. British Museum*

21

seventh century, and is known as the St. Cuthbert Gospel. It is now in the library of Stonyhurst College in England.

The girdle book, which appeared around 1350, remained in use about 150 years, primarily in Germany. The example in figure 22, one of the few in existence, is encased in wooden board covers over which is stretched a protective covering of soft doeskin extending over the sides and back and about a foot beyond the tail, where it is fastened in a knob. Thus protected from soil and the weather, the girdle books were suspended upside down from the belt or girdle of the monk, clergyman, or noble to whom they belonged, ready to be lifted into a reading position while the owner was strolling or riding, or wherever he might be (figure 23).

Connected with the history of the book is the art of the woodcut or wood engraving, which was developed to illustrate the books produced in the monasteries. The illustrations were cut with raised lines on blocks of wood, inked, and impressed on paper. They had a great deal of charm and vitality and are highly valued today for their originality. The Chinese printed illustrations from blocks in the ninth and tenth centuries, while in Europe the method was first used in the twelfth century and flourished through the sixteenth century, reaching its highest state of development in Germany (figure 24).

Wood-block illustration was a step toward the invention of movable type. Individual letters were cut on wood and grouped into words, sentences, and paragraphs. They could then be reassembled and used over again for the printing of other books. This technique revolutionized the production of books and brought within the reach of many knowledge previously available to only a selected few. The invention of printing with movable type was one of the greatest events in the cultural history of the world, for the power of the printed word provided mankind with the means for enlightenment and helped free him from ignorance.

Johannes Gutenberg has been credited with the invention of movable type about A.D. 1438, and no doubt he was the first in Europe to set up a press and develop the art of printing as we know it. He first designed and cut his type in relief in solid blocks of wood but later invented a movable metal type cast in molds with which he could make any combination of letters to form words.

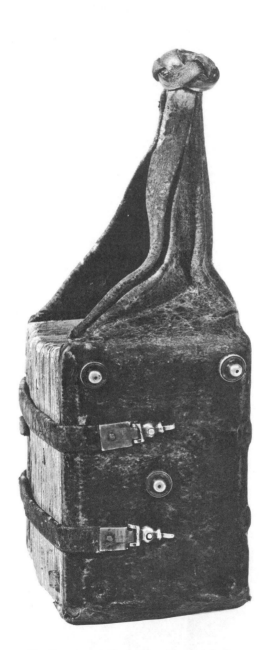

22. German girdle book with metal clasps, encasing a prayer book, 1454. Spencer Collection, New York Public Library

23. German girdle book, open

There is evidence, however, that engraved wooden plates composed of letters were used in China for the reproduction of books as early as the sixth century A.D. A complete printed book with a woodcut frontispiece was produced in A.D. 868, nearly six centuries before Gutenberg. The Koreans were printing with movable type in A.D. 1392, antedating Gutenberg by almost fifty years, and there are records stating that as far back as the first half of the thirteenth century they established a Department of Books whose duties included "the casting of type and the printing of books."

Gutenberg set up his printing press in Mainz, Germany, with the assistance of Johann Fust, a rich goldsmith who helped finance the venture. A number of

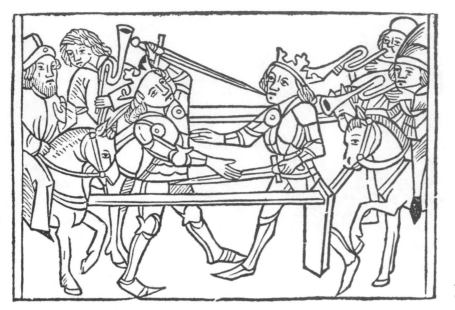

24. German woodcut illustration
of Alexander the Great, 1488

experimental printings were produced during the early stage of development, along with the *World Judgment,* a book of seventy-four pages. An astronomical calendar followed, and a grammar, the *Donatus,* printed on vellum.

The greatest masterpiece of all was the beautiful volume that became known as the Gutenberg Bible. Often referred to as the first printed book, it in any event marks the birth of printing. It was begun in 1450 and took about five or six years to complete. As a specimen of the art of printing it has never been surpassed. The text is in Latin, printed in large, handsome Gothic type arranged in double columns of 42 lines each; for this reason the book is also sometimes called the 42-Line Bible. A specimen page with text and illumination is shown in figure 25. Although it is believed that 200 copies were printed, 165 on paper and 35 on vellum, only 47 are known to exist today. Fourteen of these are in the United States, and the last one sold brought $511,000 at auction. The book was printed on 1,282 pages, 12 by 18$\frac{1}{2}$ inches in size, with space left so that the owners of copies could employ artists to illuminate them with religious miniatures, decorations, and initial letters. Thus no two copies were exactly alike.

A full-size, full-color facsimile edition of one thousand copies, in two volumes, has been published by Pageant Books in America. The copy is as close to the original as possible, with many colors and gold used to convey the richness of the original German volumes. The book is bound in top-grade leather stamped with gold and has marbled end papers. The printed sheets are folded and hand-

25. Illuminated page from the Gutenberg Bible, 1455

sewn onto tapes inserted in split-board covers by master craftsmen.

The character of the book changed when the development of printing methods permitted quantity production. Wooden board covers with their rich ornaments and clasps were no longer feasible. Leather and parchment continued to be widely used, however, and books with simple geometric interlacing designs on their covers became popular. The rapid spread of the art of papermaking was an important contribution to printing, since it made available an inexpensive material in the quantities needed for the multiplication of books.

Although books became more plentiful after printing was invented, they were often chained to shelves and reading desks in libraries to prevent their being taken away (figure 26). Bibles and prayer books were chained to the backs of pews as well as to pulpits. Examples of these old chained libraries can still be seen today in England at Hereford Cathedral and Wimborne Minster. The largest collection of chained books is found in the Laurentian Library of Florence.

26. *Chained books in the library at Hereford, England*

A charming version of the book, whose history extends back several hundred years, is the little hornbook, found almost exclusively in England and the United States (figure 27). This was a child's primer usually made of wood, but sometimes of ivory, metal, leather, or cardboard, and shaped like a paddle so that it could easily be held in the hand. The little books varied in size, but most were around 2¾ by 5 inches. The lesson sheet, containing the alphabet in upper and lower case, the vowels in combination with the consonants, the nine digits, and the Lord's Prayer, was fastened to one side of the piece of wood. Over it, for protection, was placed a sheet of horn, held in place with brass strips fastened to the wood by hand-forged tacks.

Horn sheets were made from the horns of sheep, goats, or cattle and formed a transparent covering. Lesson sheets were written by hand on vellum or parchment, later on paper. Still later they were printed with type. A hole was bored through the handle, and a cord was inserted so that the paddle could be hung from the neck, wrist, or waist. Some of the hornbooks were beautifully decorated on the back with carved wood, tooling, or embossing, while others were fairly plain.

Although many of the world's great achievements in the arts of the book were produced by anonymous craftsmen and designers, a number of individual printers, binders, and artists of various kinds have become known for their special genius. One of the first binders was Phillatius the Athenian, of the fifth century B.C., who embellished rolled books that were similar in style to those of the Egyptians. Bookbinding as we understand it was not known to the Greeks. Giulio Clovio and his pupils are known to have done the illuminations for such books as the Towneley Lectionary, written in Italy in A.D. 1540. Benvenuto Cellini (1500-71) made a book with a gold cover carved and enriched with jewels for the Cardinal Giulio de' Medici as a gift to Charles V.

Among the early printers one of the most famous was the Venetian Aldus Manutius (1450-1515), who, with his family, printed mostly small editions of Greek and Roman classics. He designed and cut his own type and made his own ink. His trademark, a dolphin entwined round an anchor, has been copied

27. *American hornbook. Library of the University of Washington*

27

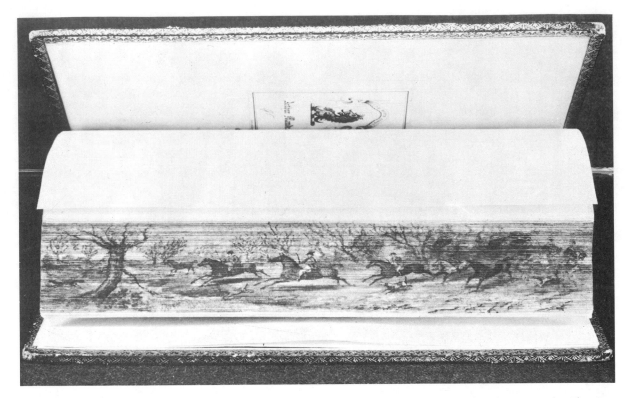

by modern publishers. Aldus was a binder as well as a printer.

In England, masters of the craft carried on the early traditions and added their contributions to the history of the book. William Caxton, the first English printer, learned the printing art in Cologne and established a press at Westminster Abbey in 1477. He designed and cut the first English type and in 1477 produced the first book printed on English soil, *The Dictes or Sayengis of the Philosophres.*

Charles and Samuel Mearne, binders to Charles II in the seventeenth century, invented a type of decoration called "cottage" style. Many of their books also had fore-edge paintings of picturesque scenes which were revealed when the pages were fanned out, but invisible when the book was closed. The example in figure 28 has a double fore-edge painting. When the pages are spread in the opposite direction, a different scene is viewed. Goffered edges were also used in this period. A decorative design was impressed on the edges of a closed book and covered with gold foil (figure 29).

In 1768 Roger Payne set up a small workshop in London, where he became known for the excellence of his gold tooling and for his creative ability. He designed and cut his own tools and created the designs for his bindings.

At the end of the nineteenth century William Morris published exquisitely printed editions of his own and other writings. Most valued by collectors is his Chaucer edition, beautifully bound in pigskin. Morris founded a private printing establishment called the Kelmscott Press, where he issued books of fine format, using types, papers, and decorative material that he himself had designed. His artistic genius raised the standards of British printing to a level of outstanding merit.

Thomas James Cobden-Sanderson (1840 - 1922) gave up a career in law to become a bookbinder. Although his work was very restrained, he contributed to bookbinding new forms of design, freeing it from obedience to classical traditions. He used simple stamping tools of flower, leaf, and bird motifs in well-chosen combinations. Like William Morris, with whom he was associated, he had a scholarly appreciation of the methods of the past and wanted to bring bookbinding back to the basic principles upon which it had been established. These men used little more than the simplest equipment, but they produced work that has been preserved in museums throughout the world.

Douglas Cockerell, the famous pupil of Cobden-Sanderson, helped carry on the revival established in England. He has become the authority to whom present-day bookbinders go, for his books on the techniques of binding are among the binder's best reference materials.

29. Goffered edges, English, early nineteenth century. Library of the University of Washington

English bookbinding has held a high place among the European nations for hundreds of years. Expert craftsmen used numerous small engraved blocks to decorate beautiful leathers and produce books of lasting quality. There were periods, however, when binders limited themselves to faithfully copying past styles, using metal stamps with dots, circles, crescents, and sprigs of flowers, combined with gold tooling on leather. These become lifeless when they are used only to reproduce the best of earlier periods. In this kind of copying the spirit of the original is lost, and there is no new vitality produced.

The Solander case or book box is named for its inventor, Daniel Charles Solander, a Swedish botanist. This box, shaped like a book, is made of cardboard in two parts, with a cover removable from the top.

30. Leather binding by Edgar Mansfield, natural morocco inlaid in greens with yellow circle, English, twentieth century

A deep interest in the art of the book led to the formation of the Grolier Club in New York in 1884. This organization of booklovers and bookmakers, both laymen and professionals, is devoted to "promotion of the arts pertaining to the production of books." The members share an interest in every phase of bookmaking, including the work of the printer, the engraver, and the binder. The club was named for Jean Grolier de Servières, a French booklover of the sixteenth century, who did much to promote the art of binding by having his books bound under his own supervision by the best binders available. He was famous for his collection of three thousand "rare and curious" volumes.

Among contemporary binders, some have continued to use traditional forms and techniques, preferring to be safe and restrained. Others, showing

31. Leather binding by Edgar Mansfield, deep crimson Niger morocco inlaid in white, black, gray, light and dark blue, yellow ocher, and bright red, English, twentieth century

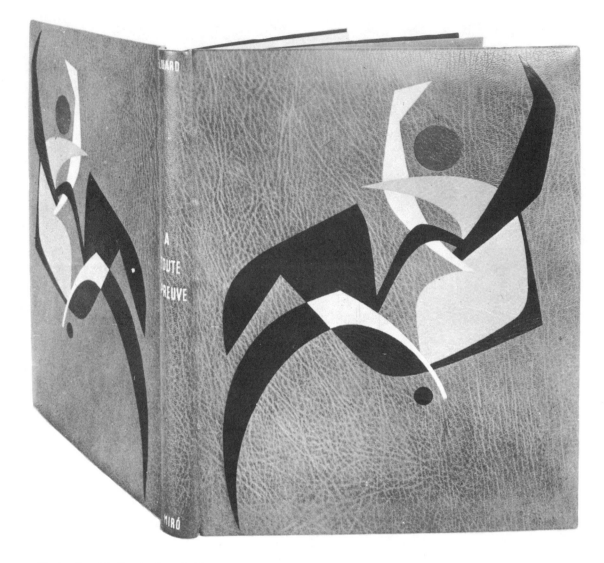

32. Leather binding by Ivor Robinson, gray Niger morocco inlaid with black, yellow, vermilion, and turquoise, English, 1959. Collection of Maurice Goldman

the influence of modern painting and of abstract art, are exploring new directions in the design and treatment of surfaces and the use of materials. This is true of Edgar Mansfield, of the London School of Printing and Graphic Arts, whose work is shown in figures 30, 31, 261, 274, and 275. Mansfield was a painter and sculptor before specializing in the craft of binding, and this training has undoubtedly influenced his concept of form and space, contributing to the emotional content of his creative work. He believes that technique in a craft is inseparable from its expression, and that where the binder is both designer and craftsman such direct contact, as in painting and sculpture, allows him to discover new technical possibilities and extend his range of expression. He achieves a penetration of areas with numerous moving and counteracting lines, and a wide range of

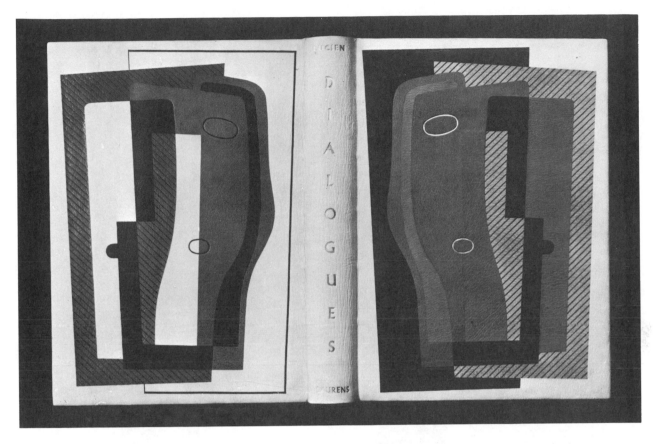

33. *Leather binding by Ivor Robinson, natural Niger morocco inlaid with turquoise, terra cotta, black, yellow, and gray, English, 1958. Collection of Maurice Goldman*

different textures by the use of straight and curved lines and dots in various combinations and thicknesses.

Examples of the work of Ivor Robinson, another English binder, are shown in figures 32 and 33. He, too, employs a contemporary treatment in his covers and builds spatial patterns of solid areas with inlay of various colored leathers. The shapes are derived from natural forms such as the human figure, but are modified to produce structural elements expressive of the content material of the books. His value tones are strongly contrasted and forcibly conceived, so that dark-light contrasts become fundamentally important. Texture is produced by the types of leathers used and by tooled versus plain areas.

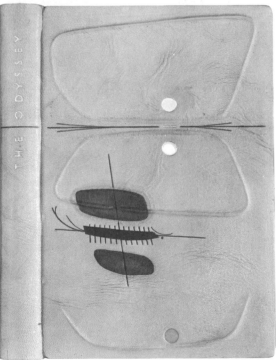

34. *Leather binding by Trevor Jones, rust native-dyed Niger goatskin with blue onlay, English, 1960*

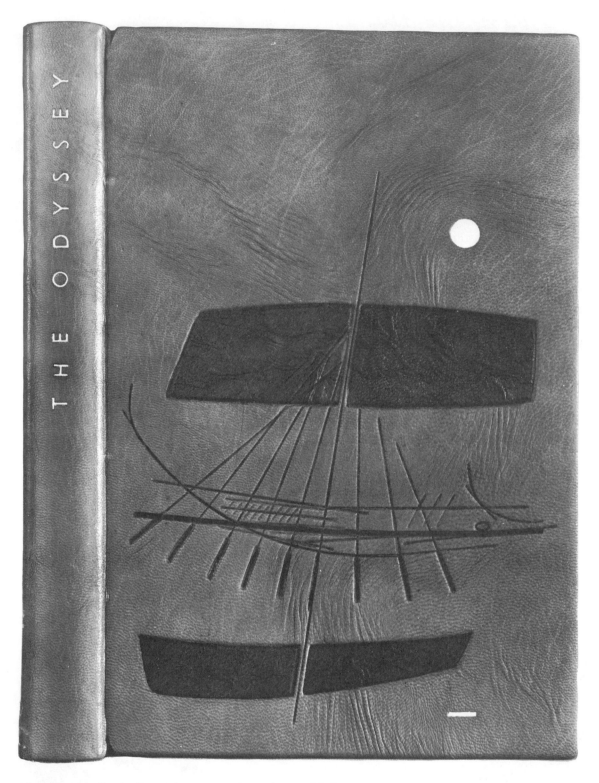

35. *Leather binding by Trevor Jones, natural goatskin modeled,*
with orange and black onlay, English, 1960

The work of Trevor Jones shows originality and versatility as in figures 34 and 35 where he has given two interpretations for *The Odyssey*. Casual and free forms and lines relate sensitively to the space to be filled. Subtle movements and delicate detail contribute to the aliveness of the conception. Mr. Jones carries out all stages of the binding himself, evolving the designs as he works. The two Bibles in figures 36 and 37, however, were commissioned works and of necessity are more formal in plan. They are designed with dignity and restraint, with emphasis on vertical and horizontal movement. In one the cross is defined by blind- and gold-tooled lines, while in the other the same symbol is formed and supported by colored inserts, which are repeated down the spine of the book.

36. *Leather binding for a Bible by Trevor Jones, English*

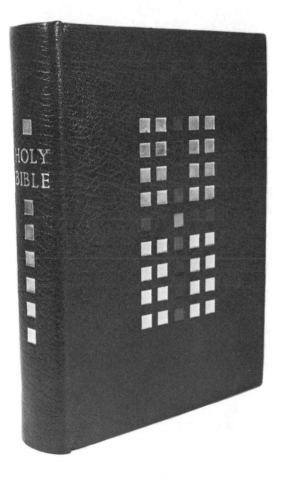

37. *Leather binding for a Bible by Trevor Jones, English*

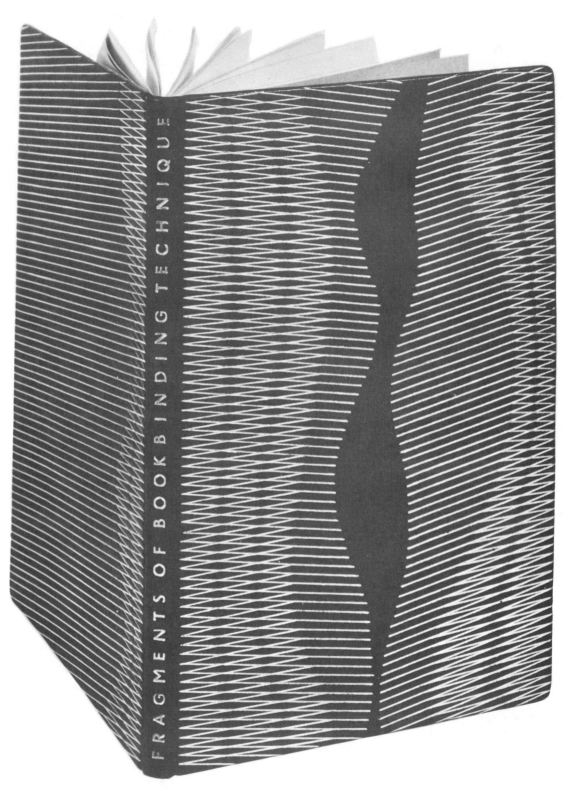

38. *Leather binding by R. Wright, English, twentieth century*

The binding by R. Wright in figure 38 is dramatic, yet simply conceived. Value changes of lights and darks, and movement, are created by the intersection of straight gold-tooled lines, producing a dazzling result. The effect is of a built-up, curvilinear pattern. The area of dark on the front cover is repeated in the dark tone of the spine, relieving the monotony of the tone produced by the line groupings.

Arthur Johnson uses a symmetrical design in his binding for *The Conservation of Antiquities and Works of Art* (figure 39). His conception, reflecting the nature of the subject in its formal arrangement, relies for movement on the intersecting curves and linear directions, which relate the front of the cover to the spine. Dark-light contrast and textural interest are produced by the use of leather inlay.

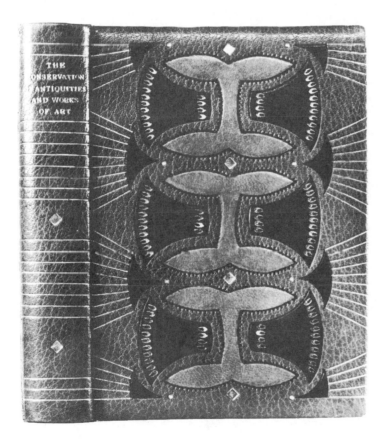

39. Leather binding by Arthur Johnson, crimson levant morocco with onlays of colored leathers, English, twentieth century

The work of French binders is daring and original, showing a structural use of forms. It is not unusual for designers to employ several craftsmen to execute their designs. In France, well-printed books are sometimes produced without covers so that the purchaser may choose his own bindings. The books are boxed rather than bound, and many are left with loose sheets to permit the removal of single plates or pages at will—a process that has been used by publishers since the Middle Ages.

A sculptured binding by Paul Bonet for the book *Calligrammes* by Apollinaire is shown in figure 40. The cover is of citron crushed morocco, and the design is based upon a theme using a combination of the letters of the author's name and the title. On the front cover the title appears in large letters and the author's name in multiple units stamped in an allover plan on various raised and sunken panels. The back cover reverses this idea, using the author's name in the large letters and the title in the small,

40. *Leather binding by Paul Bonet, French, 1943. Lessing J. Rosenwald Collection, Library of Congress*

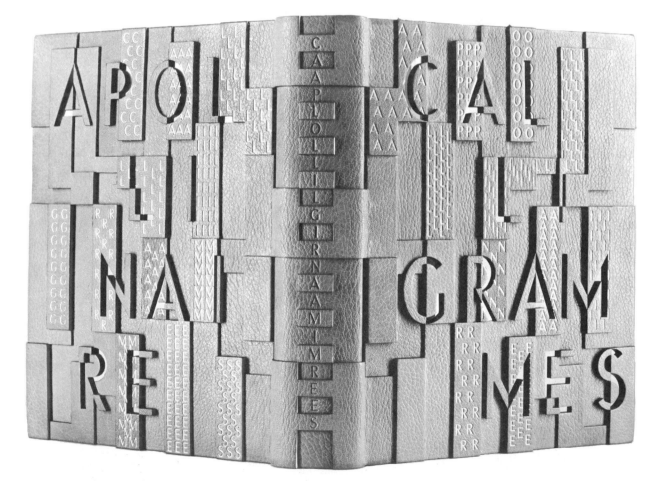

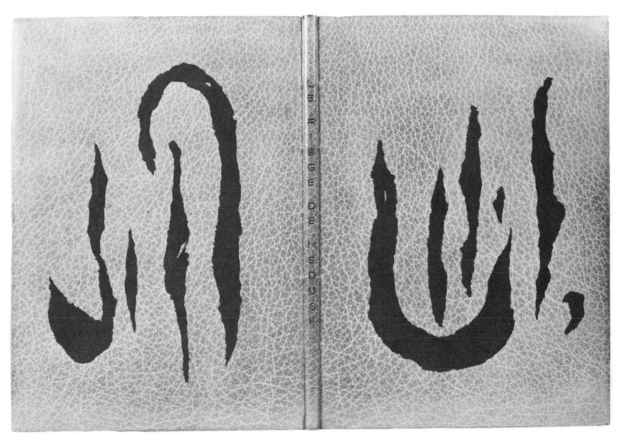

41. *Leather binding by Claude Stahly, French, twentieth century*

multiple, stamped ones. The author's name and the title alternate down the spine. On the inside, stripes of blue, white, and black calf are arranged to show through the openwork of the cover.

The bindings of Claude Stahly, wife of the French sculptor, François Stahly, are very experimental and fluid in style, as shown in the example in figure 41 where a method of "leather mosaic" has been used. Other examples have depressed designs made first in relief on copper that is heated and applied to the leather with pressure. Then, as the material cools, the pattern becomes permanent. Mme Stahly makes her own end papers to relate to her covers, using water-color brush strokes or oil paint on water, and also makes the boxes in which her books are cased, covering them with the material used in the end papers. She has done various bindings in collaboration with Georges Braque, Joan Miro, and other artists of the modern period.

42. *Leather binding by Pierre Martin, black calf with inlaid mosaic of red calf, French, 1961*

The cover binding by Pierre Martin (figure 42) is a good example of the use of counterchange design, which is explained on page 208. Martin, recognized as one of the few master binders in France, makes use of simple geometric forms in his designs. This direction has provided for him a means of liberation and personal expression. He believes that "the first law in binding is solidity. The architecture of a book comes first of all."

Imaginative contemporary binding is also being done in Italy and Sweden. The work of the late Ignatz Wiemeler, who was considered the greatest binder in Germany, was shown at the Museum of Modern Art in New York City in 1935. One of the best-known binders in the United States is Gerhard Gerlach, sometimes called the dean of American hand bookbinders. He has bound many books for private collectors and has made cases to hold unbound copies of limited editions (figure 43). The late Marguerite Duprez Lahey, who was trained as a binder in Paris, worked exclusively for many years at the Pierpont Morgan Library. Herbert and Peter Fahey, well known in San Francisco, have been described as "having enthusiasm that lifts the process of hand bookbinding into the sphere of poetry, music, and painting."

Students should avail themselves of every opportunity to see original manuscripts and bindings of the past. Collections are to be found in the libraries of most large universities, particularly those at Harvard and St. Louis universities, as well as in the New York City Public Library, which has the famous Spencer Collection; the Library of Congress; and numerous galleries and museums. The Walters Art Gallery in Baltimore has sponsored important exhibitions of bindings and published two impressive catalogues.

The greatest private collection of manuscripts is in the J. Pierpont Morgan library, in New York City, built in 1905. During Mr. Morgan's lifetime the library was accessible only to his friends, business associates, and a few scholars, but it was opened to the public in 1929.

Occasionally one can have the thrill of discovering a beautifully bound old book or an individual manuscript page in an antique or used book shop in this country or abroad, if only he is aware that such treasures exist.

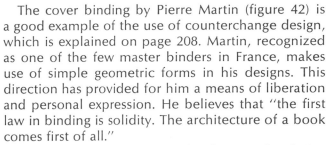

43. Leather binding by Gerhard Gerlach, dark gray spine and yellow sides, American, twentieth century

Book Design

The subject of bookbinding includes more than the knowledge and application of binding techniques, for the matter of personal taste in the selection and use of materials enters into consideration. The structuring of a book, whether conceived in its entirety or limited only to the application of the cover, should be approached as a problem in design to be solved by the application of the principles of art. It takes more than functional considerations, skills, and the following of rules to make a good binding. It takes emotional involvement, followed by the release of creative energies thoughtfully and sensitively employed. In a successful design there is more than mere technical achievement; there is a relation of good craftsmanship with fine feeling.

The designing of a book should be considered from the standpoint of the total production, for out of the assembling of the parts grows the harmony of the whole, down to the last detail. This includes the selection of the paper for pages and the establishment of their size and proportion, the choice and use of colors and textures, and the appropriate combination of materials. All the parts should be unified, and no ornamentation should be added as a separate or unrelated element, for a good decoration must support the total plan.

There must be a relation not only of the parts to the whole, but of the whole to the purpose, so that the result

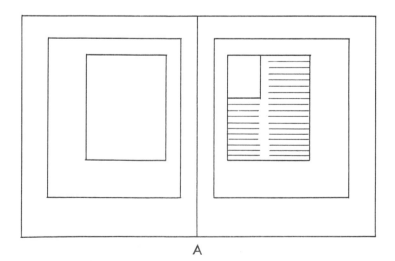

A

is an artistic production, uniting form with content. The trend today is away from thinking of binding as decoration only but rather toward considering it as related in some way to the character and intent of the book.

The medieval designers worked for fine space relations both on the covers and on the inside pages of their books. They were sensitive to the relation of page margins to the text area and carefully laid out their page designs with much thought and feeling for proportion and shape. Two pages seen together, facing one another, were a problem in balanced relationship, and the designer sought to unify them. The Persians were particularly successful in bringing all the parts of the book—binding, writing, and illustration—into an orderly, balanced harmony.

Every page can be viewed as a space in which text, illustration, and margins are rectangular shapes to be related to one another in good proportion. The text appears as a gray tone, formed by the black lines of type merging with the white spaces between. When seen through half-closed eyes, this gray contrasts with the lighter tone of the surrounding margin. It should be considered as an area to be positioned. To study various arrangements one can place on a sheet of white bond or typing paper a smaller contrasting sheet, gray or off-white, about 6 by 9 inches or less in size, and move it around to form various margin widths. It can be centered first, pushed upward to reduce the space above and widen the space below, and then shifted toward one side or the other. In this way the darker paper is seen as text or illustration related to the total page area. It is also helpful to study well-designed book pages for their page plans and observe each in relation to its facing page.

All written and printed medieval books followed established traditional margin spacings which varied in width but usually followed the plan of having the inner margin the smallest, the top larger, and the bottom the largest of all (diagram A). The Greeks arrived at a formula for pleasingly proportioned rectangles based on the golden oblong, which varied in size but always had the same proportion of approximately 5 by 8. They usually avoided such obvious proportions as a rectangle made of two full squares or a square and a half, preferring one of a square plus an unequal division of a square.

Most books are proportioned as rectangles in pleasing shapes and sizes to fit the purpose for which they are intended. When a square is selected, all parts of the book should be adjusted to this proportion so that its structure is dramatized. Whatever the shape, all lines when possible should conform to the horizontal and vertical directions of the outer frame to maintain balance and unity; diagonal placements are generally avoided because of their disturbing influence, unless they are structurally related to the cover or the page.

The modern designer is concerned with problems of space division and layout, and he experiments with various arrangements by shifting shapes about the page, manipulating them for balanced relationships of line and tone. He often places illustrations against outer edges, eliminating restrictive margins entirely, but always leaves supporting space for text to facilitate reading. Reference to magazines like *Domus, Graphis,* or *Print,* which contain page and cover designs from contemporary sources, will be of great assistance to students in enlarging their concepts of book design and will stimulate them in their own creative work.

The type selected is an important part of the total design, and its shape and weight have a considerable effect on the general tone value of a page. These factors should be studied for readability and appearance. Many modern types are designed without serifs, while others have simple modifications of them. The hand-constructed letters on illuminated manuscripts were carefully drawn and thought of as artistic forms. Type also must be designed and carefully drawn before it is cast in metal. Many type faces are named for their designers.

Nowhere in book design does the creative mind have more opportunity to function than in the planning and construction of the cover, for here the artist-craftsman is able to employ line, area, texture, tone, and color with imagination and forceful command of structure. He has the choice of following established concepts, where decorative pattern favors static symmetry and enclosure, or he may be experimental and daring and venture into new directions involving open design as influenced by the abstract. The newer approach affords more freedom in the manipulation of spatial relationships, resulting in a flow of movement and creation of dynamic forms.

The designing of a book can be a thrilling and adventurous experience. When color nuances of cover, lining, and page, as well as textural qualities of papers, are considered, and decorative features of cover and lining are related, the resulting harmony can be a pleasing work of art.

PROPORTION AND SIZE OF BOOKS

A great deal of flexibility is possible in determining the format and structure of a book. Children and other beginners will gain a concept of proportion and find freedom for choice within broad restrictions by folding a sheet of paper in various ways.

A 12-by-18-inch piece of newsprint is convenient to use since it is thin and can be folded a number of times (diagram A). When this is folded once, the result is 9 by 12 inches (diagram B). If it is then folded horizontally, it produces a 6-by-9-inch shape which can be turned vertically (diagram C) or horizontally (diagram D).

If the 9-by-12-inch shape (diagram B) is folded in half vertically, it will result in a narrow shape (diagrams E and F).

When the 6-by-9-inch folded sheet is creased in half the short way, the result is 6 by $4^1/_2$ inches (diagrams G and H). When it is creased the long way, the resulting form is 3 by 9 inches (diagrams I and J).

Thus a sheet of paper can be folded in many different ways, producing a variety of sizes and shapes that can be used in designing a book. This provides a structural basis for establishing a book size and proportion, while allowing considerable freedom of choice.

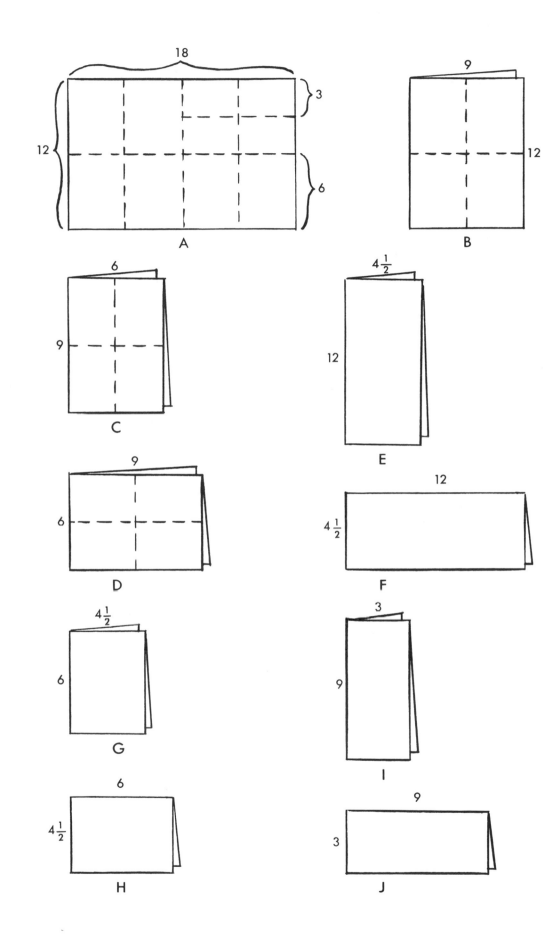

The Parts of a Book

A book is composed of contents enclosed within a hard or soft cover. The contents are the main body of the book, made up of sections called signatures fastened together at the spine. These signatures are formed by folding a sheet of paper one or more times. A paper folded once makes a folio; twice, a quarto; three times, an octavo; and four times, a sextodecimo. Beginners may want to cut separate sheets, fold them once, and assemble two or more, one inside the other. The number of sheets in a single signature will depend upon the thickness of the paper. If too many are used the result will be thick and awkward. The paper is always cut so that the grain will run vertically, parallel with the back of the book.

End papers are folded sheets placed on either side of the assembled signatures to form a lining for the inside of the cover board, and also a flyleaf.

The super is a mesh cloth or muslin placed across the spine, extending out on either side to form a hinge for joining the cover to the book. The joint comes at the edge of the board covers where they meet the back of the book.

Headbands and tailbands are applied at the top and bottom of the spine to produce a more finished appearance. The term "headband" is often used to refer to both. They are also called bandstrips.

The fore edge or front edge is the side opposite the back or folded parts of the book. The back of a book, including the part where the folded and sewn sections are glued together, is also called the spine.

The boards are the cardboards placed on the outside of the book to form the cover.

Familiarity with the parts of a book and the terminology associated with them will be of help in understanding the directions that follow. These parts can be seen in any well-bound commercial book, and if the book is falling apart there is an opportunity to get a clear view of the actual construction.

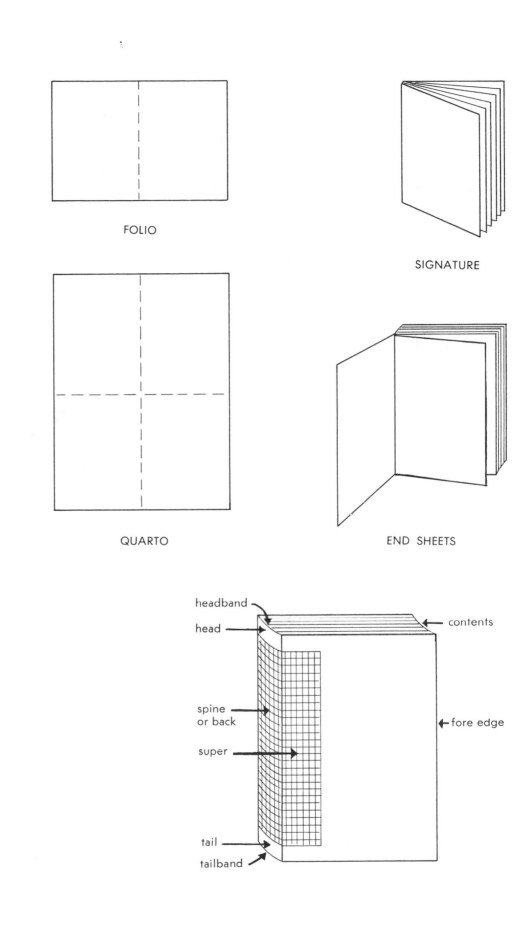

FOLIO

SIGNATURE

QUARTO

END SHEETS

headband

head

contents

spine
or back

super

fore edge

tail

tailband

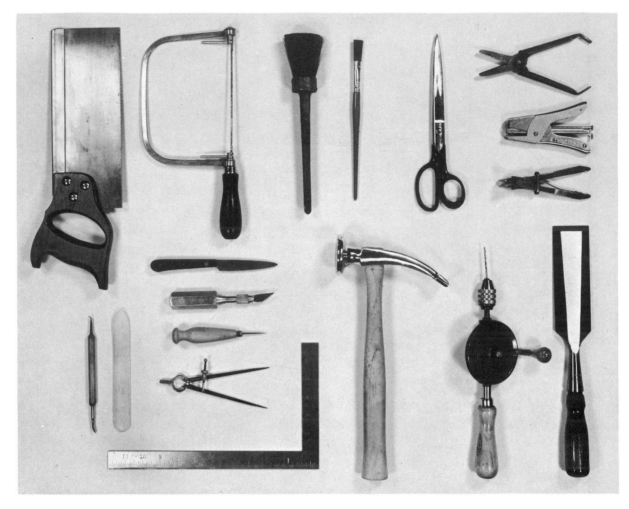

44

Materials, Tools, and Equipment

The amount and kind of equipment used in the making of books vary with the extent to which the binder intends to carry his work. Many simple forms of books can be produced with a limited amount of materials. Some projects require very little in the way of tools and can easily be adapted to classroom situations or to home workshops. The beginner interested in trying this fascinating craft can often make substitutions or improvise in various ways to accomplish results within his limitations. Although books can be made without the convenience of a sewing frame or press, items of this nature can be constructed along modified lines in the school shop or home workshop. Lack of expensive equipment need not prevent anyone from experiencing the pleasure of binding books.

The serious craftsman will find it of advantage to provide himself with presses and cutters, as well as the various tools necessary for advanced work of a professional nature. If he plans to work with leather, use gold-leaf printing, or put on titles, he will find that special types of equipment will be needed. The professional binder often has a considerable amount invested in his workshop, as large, heavy equipment is costly. This fact need not frighten the beginner, however, for he can start simply and add on as he wishes. The important thing is that he should respect his tools and use them to the best advantage.

A list of materials, tools, and equipment commonly used in this craft follows, with a brief description of each.

Materials	*Tools*		*Equipment*
Papers	Knife	Drill	Sewing frame
Mending tissues	Bone folder	Punch	Presses
Book cloth	Steel square	Awl	Vise
Leather	Ruler	Chisel	Pressboards
Cover boards	Needle	Band nippers	Tin sheets
Adhesives	Brushes	Spring dividers	Backing boards
Tape	Shears	Staple extractor	Cutting boards
Cord	Tin snips	Pressing iron	Sewing clamp
Thread	Hammer	C clamps	Cradle
Super	Mallet	Type and pallet	Cutters
Headbands	Saw	Finishing tools	Gluepot
Paste cloth			Hot plate
Sandpaper			

MATERIALS

A variety of papers is needed in making selections for use as book pages, covers, and lining sheets. Common and easily available papers like bond, white drawing, cream manila, colored poster and construction, charcoal, water-color, and Japanese rice paper are suggested possibilities. Inexpensive papers that come in rolls like kraft (which is generally available in schools), butcher, and heavy brown wrapping paper are convenient for general types of work. These will be referred to in the text as kraft papers.

Some companies have large assortments of domestic and foreign imports and issue sample sheets or booklets from which selections can be made. Colorful and unusual papers can be found at Japanese stores. It is advisable to check all local sources to discover what might be available in the immediate environment.

Tough, flexible papers used for soft covers on Bibles, notebooks, or wherever limp bindings are required can be obtained from bookbinding companies.

Wax paper for pasting operations is available in flat sheets or rolls; flat sheets are preferable when they are obtainable. Wax paper is used to protect the book and keep it clean and to prevent the moisture of the paste from going through the book while it is being pressed.

Disposable paste papers can be made by cutting old newspapers into quarter-size sheets, which are thrown away after being used.

MENDING TISSUES

Strips of thin paper about $^5/_8$ inch wide are used for mending tears and weak places in the folded parts of pages when doing rebinding. Japanese mending tissues can be purchased in strips or rolls, or tissues can be cut from very thin papers like onionskin.

BOOK CLOTH

Book cloth is the material used over the cardboard covers of a book. It may be any fairly heavy fabric, like linen, sailcloth, burlap, denim, light tapestry, brocade, or woven strawcloth, which has a pleasing textural quality. One can be imaginative in making selections. Suitable pieces can sometimes be found at remnant or upholsterers' shops. Hand-woven strips are also effective if they are not too bulky.

Book cloths referred to in the trade as "vellum" and "buckram" are available from bookbinding supply houses. They are made from cotton cloth that has been sized and are produced in various qualities, weights, and colors by the yard or bolt. Samples are usually available upon request. This material is very strong and durable and is used quite extensively on machine-made books. Many of the examples shown in this book are bound with a combination of vellum and patterned papers.

Trimmings from window shades thrown away in trash bins in stores have a quality similar to that of vellum book cloth and can be obtained without cost. They are limited in colors, however, and less durable than the vellum.

An adhesive-backed cloth tape up to 4 inches in width is obtainable in rolls from stationery stores and bookbinding supply sources.

LEATHER

Various domestic and imported leathers, available by the whole or half hide (or skin) as well as by the foot, can be used to cover books. These are discussed in the section on leather techniques.

COVER BOARDS

Cardboards of various kinds, used as covers for books, portfolios, and similar constructions, are generally referred to as "boards." Davey boards, obtainable from binders or through catalogue sources, are available in a variety of weights. Professional hand binders generally use a binder's board called tarboard, which is tough, strong, and very rigid. This type of board is recommended for books sewn on cords where the cord is laced into the cover. A board 1/16 or 3/32 inch thick is suitable for most work. Ordinary chip board can be used when a cheaper, more easily available board is desired, especially for school work; it is, however, less rigid and more likely to warp. It is available in several different thicknesses in sheets about 24 by 36 inches in size. Other boards, like Photomount, poster board, illustration board, and mat board can also be used. Heavy tagboard is satisfactory for school booklet covers and for pamphlet covers.

Tablet backs, shirt cardboards from laundries, and discarded advertising display cards are sources to consider. If the cardboard is too thin and flimsy, two or more pieces can be glued together and pressed to form a good, rigid board.

ADHESIVES

Paste for book work can be either bought or made by the binder as needed. Cooked flour paste, wallpaper paste, laundry starch, cornstarch, and rice flour paste are all suitable for use. Recipes for these will be found in the back of the book. Library paste is generally available in schools but proves expensive when large quantities are needed. Rubber cement can be used and is less expensive when purchased by the quart or gallon than when bought in small amounts. There are a number of milky latex rubber-base glues available on the market. Certain casein glues will stick even to book cloth that has a glossy treated surface. Some binders use a strong vegetable glue that can be thinned with water to the desired consistency. Librarians use a creamy white plastic adhesive, a polyvinyl acetate, sold under a trade name, which can be diluted with water for lighter consistencies.

It is desirable to use flexible glue on the spine of a book to hold the sewn sections together in order to keep it from drying out and prevent cracking when the book is opened. This glue can be purchased as a liquid or in gelatin form from a bookbinder who makes his own glue or from a bookbinding supply company. The gelatin glue must be kept wrapped in heavy wax paper so it will retain its softness. Some glues are used hot, and others are applied cold. Glues may also be used wherever paste is needed except on leathers, where paste is generally desirable.

Padding and tabbing cements, rubbery compounds used commercially in making scratch pads, have a great deal of strength and can take the place of strong glue when a series of magazines are bound together. They are available as a white or red liquid from bookbinding supply sources.

TAPE

The signatures that make up a book are sometimes sewn on tapes, which help to hold them together and secure the contents to the cover. Unbleached or white twill cotton tape is available from bookbinding supply sources in $3/8$-, $1/2$-, or $5/8$-inch widths. Twill lingerie tape found at notion counters makes a satisfactory substitute.

CORD

Book sections can be held together with cord as well as tape. The cord looks like a hemp rope and comes in different thicknesses, rolled in a ball. A thick cord is used when raised effects are desired on the spine, while a thinner cord will lie flat or can be sunken in. If regular bookbinding cord is not available, any cord that is not twisted too hard and can be frayed out at the ends, such as hempen cord, light rope hemp, or thick string, will suffice. Cord is available from bookbinding supply companies.

THREAD

An unbleached linen thread is used by binders to sew signatures. For average work size 16/2 is recommended. This comes in cones or in $1/2$-ounce skeins. Strong cotton thread about number 10 to 12, button thread, cotton crochet, or embroidery silk can serve as substitutes. If a book has thin sections and thin paper, a very fine linen or silk thread is recommended.

SUPER

Super is a material used on the back of a book, after the signatures have been glued together, in order to help form a hinge. Bookbinder's super is sold by the bolt, either narrow or wide. The kind used for average book jobs is a thin, stiffened mesh that looks like cheesecloth. Other materials that can be used for this purpose are cambric, unbleached muslin, crinoline, buckram, or tarlatan. A stronger super similar to outing flannel is used for binding heavy books or magazines. Regular outing flannel can also be used.

HEADBANDS

Commercially made headbands, placed at the top and bottom of the book to give it a tailored finish, are available in different colors by the yard or bolt about $1/2$ inch or less in width. The professional binder makes his own headbands directly on the book, generally with a silk floss.

PASTE CLOTH

Work areas and tools need to be kept clean during pasting operations. A soft cloth made from an old shirt or a piece of sheeting, cheesecloth, or something similar will suffice. This can be kept dampened to remove paste from fingers.

SANDPAPER

A medium or fine sandpaper wrapped around a block of wood can be used to even up slightly irregular pages when a book is being repaired and trimming is not advisable.

TOOLS

KNIVES

A special bookbinding knife with a long pointed end is helpful when taking a book apart for rebinding. A kitchen paring knife can be substituted if necessary. A knife with a sharp blade like an X-acto knife or mat cutter is needed for cutting cardboard and some leathers.

BONE FOLDER

A bone folder is used for folding and creasing paper, smoothing pasted surfaces, turning paper over the edges of the cover board when pasting, and pressing the hinges of a book to define the groove. This is a flat object with blunt edges, round on one end and pointed on the other, about 7 inches long, made of bone, ivory, or plastic (figure 51). Usable substitutes are a tongue depressor, the spine of a plastic comb, a heavy smooth letter opener, or a ruler.

STEEL SQUARE

This is an L-shaped measuring device made of steel, used both for measuring and for obtaining square or right-angle corners (figure 46). If a steel square is not available, a carpenter's try square or a ruler with a metal edge can be substituted.

NEEDLE

Regular bookbinding needles with slightly blunt points are available. A long needle with a small head, an ordinary darning needle, or a blunt-pointed tapestry needle is also satisfactory for use.

BRUSHES

Stiff, flat brushes about ¾ inch or 1 inch in width are used for pasting (figure 50). Regular paste brushes are available, or ten-cent-store varnish brushes can be substituted. A large, round, stiff brush, available from bookbinding suppliers, is used in the gluepot for general gluing purposes (figures 52 and 98).

SHEARS

Serviceable bookbinding shears can be obtained from a bookbinding company for general purpose work in cutting cloth and paper. Regular scissors of average or larger size can also be used.

TIN SNIPS

Tin snips are useful for roughing out cover boards from large pieces of cardboard. These are later trimmed more closely with a knife or cutter.

HAMMER

A hammer with a large, round face, available from bookbinding companies, is used for rounding or backing a book (figures 99 and 100). Any ordinary hammer, or the kind used by shoemakers, will also serve the purpose.

MALLET

A mallet can be used in place of a hammer for rounding a book. It is also used in stamping designs on leather.

SAW

A panel or back saw, or any small saw like a coping saw or hack saw, serves the purpose of cutting through the signatures for sewing sunken cords and making kettle stitches (figure 97).

DRILL

A hand drill, with assorted drill points, is needed for drilling holes through the pages of a book for side sewing (figure 120).

PUNCH

A hand punch is used to make holes for fastening scrapbook papers together.

AWL

An awl is used for piercing holes when sewing signatures or making holes through the paper for side-sewn books. It is also sometimes useful for taking out the stitches in a book being prepared for rebinding. An ice pick or compass point can be substituted (figure 121).

CHISEL

A sharp chisel can be used to trim the pages of a book (figure 47).

BAND NIPPERS

Band nippers are needed for adjusting bands on the spine, when making covers of leather, or for pressing corners of books after they have been glued.

SPRING DIVIDERS

Spring dividers are used in outlining leather covers and backs for tooling or stamping, and for all work where dividing and measuring space is involved.

STAPLE EXTRACTOR

A staple extractor is of great assistance when one is taking magazines apart for binding.

PRESSING IRON

An old, discarded electric iron is handy for pressing decorative papers on which starch paint or hot wax has been used, or for smoothing out pasted vellum book cloth that tends to wrinkle.

C CLAMPS

When no press is available, C clamps can be used to clamp the book between two boards (diagram D, page 69).

TYPE AND PALLET

Type of brass or lead for printing titles can either be purchased mounted individually with a wooden handle for holding, or assembled and held together in a tool called a pallet. A set $3/8$ inch high is recommended as a good size to start with. Other tools for printing using lines and designs are available.

FINISHING TOOLS

A fillet—a brass wheel attached to a wooden handle—can be rolled across leather to make a continuous line. Other tools, which produce straight lines of various lengths, can be used together with gouges, which produce segments of circles. Combinations of these make designs or letters on leather covers.

EQUIPMENT

SEWING FRAME

A frame is used to hold the signatures while they are being sewn. Professional frames have parts that screw to control the tension of the cords (figure 110). A simple frame can be constructed like the one shown in figure 96. All that is needed is a flat wooden surface on which to lay the book and an upright structure from which to stretch the tapes or cords. The upright part can be hinged, if desired, to make the frame easier to store. Among other possible substitutes for a frame is a box with tapes stretched across the opening, as shown in diagram C, page 125. Books can be sewn, however, without the convenience of a frame at all.

PRESSES

Several types of presses are available for use in bookbinding. The essential ones are the lying or finishing press for general purpose work (figure 111 and page 67), the plow and press for cutting and trimming (figures 48 and 49), and the book press for finished work. For pressing finished books, presses can vary from a simple one made of two boards bolted together at the four corners (figure 47), to those available from bookbinding supply firms, such as the one with a clamp on top (diagram C, page 69), a letter or nipping press (figure 55), or a standing press (figure 54), which holds more and larger books.

A narrow gluing press can be used along with the lying press (figure 53). This is constructed of two boards held together with a bolt at each end.

All these presses can be made in a workshop; directions will be found in technical books on bookbinding.

VISE

A woodworking vise fastened to a work table will hold a book between two wood or masonite boards for gluing jobs when a lying press is not available.

PRESS BOARDS

Boards that will not warp are needed for pressing books. If several books are pressed at once, a board is placed between every two books. Recommended are 1/4-inch masonite, three-ply wood, or laminated boards. A few boards with brassbound edges are desirable for casing work and for pressing books with rounded backs. Several sizes should be provided to accommodate books of various sizes, such as 7 by 10 inches, 10 by 14 inches, and larger.

TIN SHEETS

Pieces of tin cut from sheets to book sizes are used in pressing books to keep the dampness that results from pasting from penetrating through the book. A piece of wax paper folded in half or wrapped around a piece of tagboard can also be used for this purpose.

BACKING BOARDS

Backing boards can be of metal or of wood with a metal edge. They are used on top of the lying press for backing books (figure 100).

CUTTING BOARDS

Cutting boards are wedge-shaped boards placed on each side of a book that is being trimmed in a press (diagram C, page 63).

SEWING CLAMP

The sewing clamp consists of two narrow metal pieces with small holes spaced about an inch apart, clamped together at either end and secured to a table or bench edge. By this means books, magazines, pamphlets, or papers are held firmly while holes for sewing are drilled by a hand drill through the openings in the metal clamps (figure 120).

CRADLE

The cradle, made of two wooden boards arranged at a 45-degree angle to form a trough, is used in piercing holes through signatures or pamphlets preparatory to sewing them. The boards are about 12 inches long and 1/4 inch apart. They are supported with boards secured at each end and are lined with a strip of cardboard (figure 125).

CUTTERS

For the beginner, large paper cutters like those used by schools and photographers are adequate. One cutter can be reserved for cutting paper and another for rough work such as cutting cardboard. Commercial binders use large, heavy, guillotine-type cutters which are capable of doing production jobs with great accuracy. School shops that have cutters must see that they are well guarded. The plow of the plow and press is used both for cutting cardboards and for trimming books. Cutters of various types and prices are available on the market, some of them using small pointed blades or attachments. The Ku-trimmer, obtainable from Gane Brothers and Lane (see Supply Sources at back of book), is highly recommended for school and general use.

GLUEPOT

Electric gluepots equipped with a copper lining for keeping the glue hot are available with or without automatic controls. Nonelectric gluepots with a lower section for holding hot water can be kept warm on a hot plate. A double boiler will also serve the purpose (figure 52).

HOT PLATE

A single plate is sufficient for most purposes. It is used for heating water, making paste, heating glue, melting wax, and printing titles or doing gold tooling on leather.

45. *Student trimming a book with the plow and press*

Working Procedures

Although the artistic value of a book is determined by its design qualities, even a good design that reflects the originality and creative ability of the designer is rendered ineffective by poor craftsmanship. The reverse is true also, for all the technique in the world cannot substitute for inspiration. Technique, unless accompanied by artistic form, is lifeless and has no real appeal. Craftsmanship and design are both essential to the success of a book, and one depends upon the other. Sometimes the designer and the craftsman are the same person, but often a book is planned by one person and bound by another.

Even with simple book problems there are principles and procedures to be grasped, and children as well as adults can learn these with a little practice. The standards of craftsmanship should be raised with increasing experience. In all problems it is desirable that thought and care go into the execution. Paper should be cut as straight as possible, and paste applied with a minimum of confusion. These are things that can be learned. They require patience and persistent effort, but the results are rewarding, and the pride experienced from a thoughtfully produced book is well worth the effort.

Older children and adult beginners can learn to make various types of books with hard covers, miter corners, attach end papers, and do other things connected with book production. A number of the basic procedures and processes used in making books are presented in this section. After one has become familiar with them he can apply them to the many problems described later in the text. Such information is important and necessary to book construction and in no way hinders the expression of ideas. In fact the reverse is true, for if one is lacking in technical knowledge his accomplishment is limited.

The methods described include ways of cutting cover boards so that the corners are square, processes of trimming book pages, the manipulation of pastes and glues, various means for pressing books so they will remain flat when dry, a description of the usefulness of a "finder," ways of applying cover material, the mitering of corners for neat results, the attachment of end and lining sheets, and the making of headbands. Some of these operations require skills that are developed with continued application.

It is helpful and advisable to prepare some materials ahead of time before carrying out the various procedures so that they will be immediately available and there will be no delay in the construction of problems. The following items can be assembled and kept together in a box for easy accessibility: paste papers; paste cloths; brown paper strips 12 by 1 inches or more wide; wax paper; book vellum in 12-by-4-inch strips; super strips 4, 5 and 6 inches wide. If the supplies are to be used by a whole class, the various items can be separated so that they are more easily accessible.

High standards of excellence must be the aim not only in the finished product but in every part of the operation, for it is the striving for accuracy at each step that contributes to the total achievement.

CUTTING AND TRIMMING

Cardboard used for book covers must be cut to exact measurement with all corners at right angles and edges perfectly straight. This process, referred to as "squaring," is accomplished with a steel square, a carpenter's try square, or a T square. If a square is not available, a sheet of paper or stiff cardboard known to be square can serve as a guide for the corners, with a ruler being used to establish the width and length of each board. A well-sharpened pencil makes for more accuracy in the measurement of all lines that are to be drawn.

An aluminum gauge provides another way of measuring boards and securing square corners (see diagram A). It is adjustable by means of screws on either end and is particularly helpful in making cases for books, or in making portfolios where boards must be lined up evenly across, as in diagram M, page 76.

When boards are cut from large pieces of cardboard they can first be roughed out with tin snips or large bookbinding shears. They are then cut to exact size with a sharp knife, such as a heavy X-acto knife or mat cutter, guided by a steel square or metal-edged ruler (figure 46). A scrap piece of cardboard should always be placed underneath to facilitate the cutting and protect the table surface. If they are not too heavy, boards can be cut with a regular paper cutter reserved for rough use, or a sturdier table cutter for use with cardboards can be obtained from bookbinding supply firms. Large power cutters are regular equipment in newspaper offices and binderies but are not frequently found in schools or in individual binderies because of their size, cost, and associated hazards if not guarded. If there is a print shop in the school, a cutter will probably be available. Such cutters can also be used for trimming the pages of books that are uneven along the edges after the signatures have been sewn and glued.

Although slower in achieving results, a sharpened chisel or sharp knife blade can be used to cut off the edges of the pages while the book is held in a press similar to the one shown in figure 47. Two boards are bolted together through holes drilled at the four corners. The upper board should be thicker than the lower in order to help guide and support the chisel as it is pulled across. A metal strip fastened to the side of the cutting edge prevents the wood from being nicked each time the chisel moves across. The lower board should be at least 1 inch wider than the upper to provide space for the part of the book that projects. To protect the cutting surface underneath, a piece of cardboard is placed under the book.

46

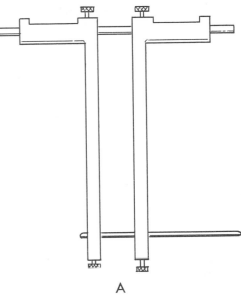

A

47

If clamps are used instead of bolts (diagram B), the lower board must be propped up to allow room for the clamps to fit underneath. For this purpose two pieces of wood, 2 inches wide, 1 inch thick, and the length of the press, can be glued as supports at either end under the baseboard to raise it up from the table top.

Before the cutting is begun, a pencil line is drawn on the top sheet of the book indicating the exact part to be trimmed. Care must be exercised to keep the book exactly square.

The worker pulls the chisel firmly toward him across the book, which is tightly clamped in the press. The chisel is held upright and braced against the upper board with the weight or pressure on its corner. This operation is continued until the book is cut entirely through. It is well not to try to cut more than one page at a time. If the pages are left slightly rough from the cutting, they can be sanded gently with fine sandpaper, but it is better to keep the cutting edge sharp than to rely upon sanding.

The plow and press, another means of cutting boards and trimming books, has been used by individual binders and craftsmen for many generations. It consists of a movable part, containing a sharp blade, that slides on guides on a cutting press. The steady rhythmic movement in the operation makes the cutting an enjoyable experience. Such a cutter can be seen in operation in figures 48 and 49. The blade must be kept sharp at all times so that it will not chew or rough up the cut edges of boards or papers. After considerable use it must be annealed, that is, tempered by heat.

When cardboard is cut, a pencil line is drawn to indicate where the blade is to cut. Several boards can be cut at one time, but an extra scrap of waste cardboard must always be included as a buffer so that the blade will come to rest against it when the cutting is completed, thus preventing damage to the wood of the press. When the cardboards to be cut are inserted into the press, it should be screwed and adjusted until it touches the cardboard (figure 48). The plow is moved forward so that it starts to cut, and the wrist turns slightly back (figure 49) as the plow is pulled backward, releasing the tension for cutting which is done on the forward stroke only. A steady rhythmic movement is kept up as the plow moves forward and back.

A book with uneven edges can also be inserted in the press and trimmed with the plow in the same manner, or it can be held in the press while it is trimmed with the chisel.

Books with rounded backs should be placed between wedge-shaped wooden boards for trimming (diagram C) when the book is thicker at the spine edge because of the sewing on the signatures. One board is level with the top of the book, above the press, and the other is level with the line drawn on the book where it is to be trimmed.

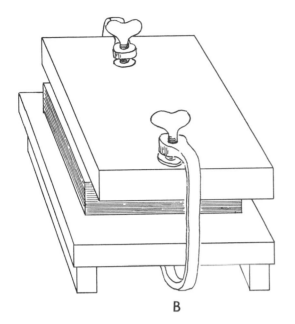

B

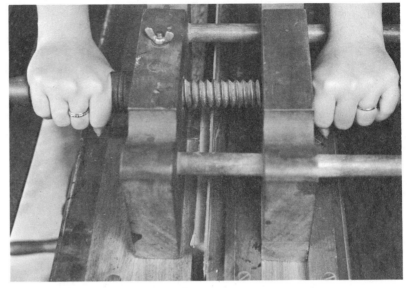

48. The knife blade projects from beneath the section that has the screw on top, with its point touching the paper or cardboard to be cut. The cutter is grasped lightly in the hands as it is moved forward.

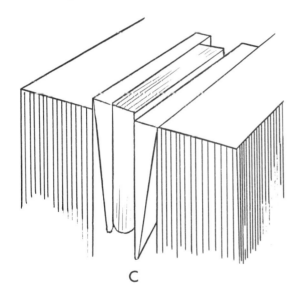

C

49. The worker bends over the plow while moving it back and forth. Wrists are relaxed as the cutter is pulled back.

PASTING

The various adhesives available for use in making books have been discussed under "Materials." In working with paste it is advisable to use it sparingly as too much will make the object stiff. If it is kept thin it is less likely to shrivel or wrinkle the paper. When paper is wet with paste it expands, and when dry it contracts. Most workers use too much glue and use it too thick. If it is too thin, however, it will not adhere or serve as a bind. Care is needed also to see that all lumps are eliminated.

Some binders prefer to apply paste to the cardboard rather than to the paper when pasting paper to boards or when pasting lightweight book vellum, which wrinkles easily when wet and must therefore be handled with care. The dampness of the paste will cause the material to stretch if it is pulled even slightly. Sometimes a slightly warm iron is helpful in smoothing out bumps and wrinkles while the paste is still damp. In another method the vellum is dipped in water before being pasted to the board so that it tightens as it dries, eliminating the wrinkles.

Pasted cardboards must be pressed before the paste dries to prevent warping, unless rubber cement is used. When a board has been pasted on both sides, the pull from each side will serve to equalize the tension. This is a basic rule to remember. Keeping the paste thin will help reduce the power of pulling. Glue warps boards less than paste. Paste is better than glue for leather covers, however, as it softens the leather and dries more slowly. It should also be used more thickly on leather than on paper. A paste made of starch is recommended for leather. Glue can be used on limp leather covers since they are put in casings.

Have the grain of the paper run up and down when it is pasted, since paper curls in the direction of the grain, and the grain of the paper should follow the grain of the board.

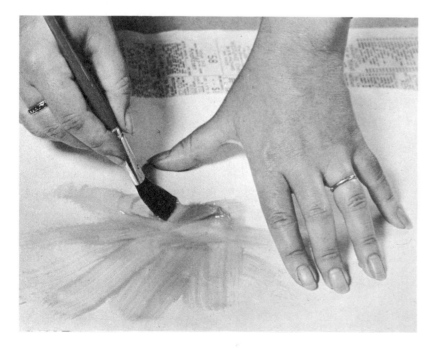

50. The paste mixture is put in the middle of the paper and spread quickly to the edges before it dries, either with a stiff brush or with the fingers. A supply of paste sheets, made by tearing newspaper pages into fourths, can be kept on hand to keep the table clean while working. A sheet is placed under the material being pasted and discarded immediately after it is used.

51. Papers can be smoothed with the fingers or a crumpled piece of wax paper immediately after they are pasted, and then rubbed gently but firmly from the center outward with a bone folder or dry cloth to remove air bubbles and push out wrinkles. A plain protective paper put over the pasted area will prevent the wet surface from tearing while it is being rubbed. Paste is removed from the hands with a damp cloth or sponge kept within convenient reach.

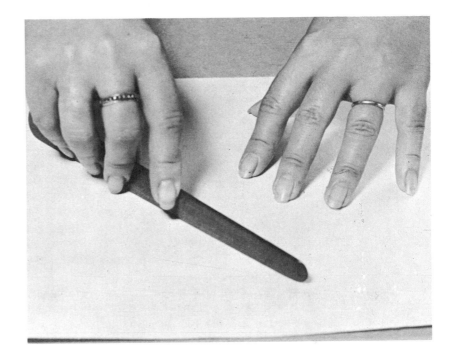

52. Flexible gelatin glue is cut into small chunks and melted in hot water in a gluepot. The dissolved glue should be thin and slightly tacky. If it is overheated or singed at any time, it cannot be used again. The glue brush is kept in a jar of water when it is not in use to keep the glue from hardening in it.

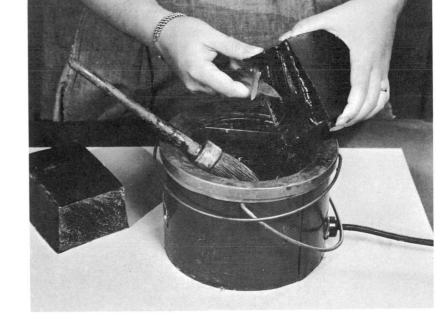

65

For pasting operations involving the spine of a book it is most convenient to use a press. A simple gluing press can be constructed with two pieces of wood, 2 by 16 by 1 inch in size, screwed together with a bolt at each end, as shown in figure 53. The press will sit more level when it is on its side if the head of the cylindrical screw rod is embedded even with the surface of the wood.

A book or group of signatures is lowered into the upright press until the spine touches the table (diagram A). The press is then screwed tightly and turned on its side to provide access for gluing. The pages of the clamped book can also be dropped down into a finishing press so that the spine is held upward for work. If two rulers or flat sticks are put across either end of the finishing press so that the gluing press rests upon them when it is placed on the finishing press (diagram B), the finishing press can be tightened, the rulers removed, and the gluing press loosened and dropped until it touches the finishing press, leaving the back of the book slightly protruding above (diagram C). This is especially desirable when glue is being worked down between the folded signatures.

In another method, two book boards are placed upright within the finishing press and clamped in position with the book protruding between them (diagram D).

These presses are also used for sawing and other book processes described below.

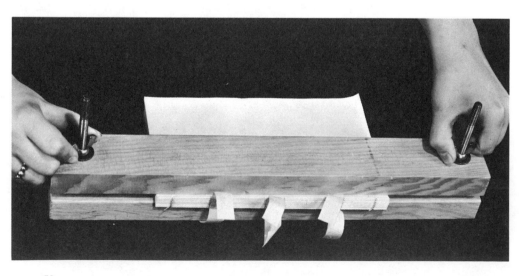

53

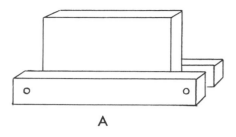

A

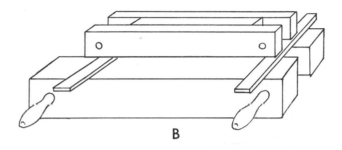

B

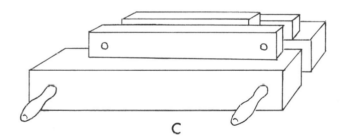

C

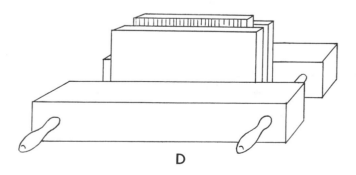

D

PRESSING

54

55

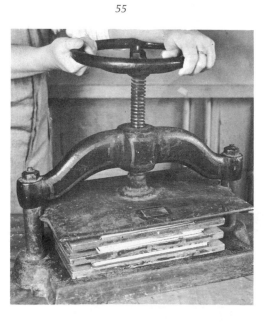

All bookbinding projects, immediately after being pasted, should be put to press and left to dry. This keeps the cardboard flat and prevents it from warping. The length of time for pressing depends upon the kind and amount of paste used, but finished problems are usually left overnight or for twenty-four hours.

When a book is pressed the dampness of the paste in the lining sheets will penetrate through the pages and cause them to buckle unless they are protected. Tins covered with wax paper, placed in the front and back of the book just inside the covers (diagram A), will prevent this buckling. If these are not available wax paper alone, blotting paper, or stiff pieces of oak tagboard enclosed in a folded sheet of wax paper can be substituted.

Books can be pressed under a weight like bricks (diagram B) or other books that are large and heavy. If bricks are placed directly on top they should be neatly wrapped in newspaper or a piece of flannel to protect the book from rough edges.

Other presses can be devised with smooth boards of hardwood, masonite, or plywood, held together by C clamps (diagram D) or bolts. A wood vice fastened to a work table, in which pressing boards are inserted upright, is another means. Several books can be pressed at a time if press boards or pieces of chipboard cut to size are used to separate them from one another.

Two or three strong rubber bands placed around the book can be substituted for other types of pressing.

Small book presses like the one shown in diagram C can be purchased. They have a screw top which is attached to the lower board at the rear and fits into a metal jog on the top board. Since they are adjustable, more than one book can be pressed at a time.

An iron nipping or letter press with a wheel on top will also hold several books (figure 55). This is a very heavy press that can be fastened down to a table.

The tall standing press will hold a greater number of books, or books of larger size, than the other types mentioned. It is capable of enormous pressure (figure 54). In the example shown, the backs of the books alternate, and knitting needles have been laid in the hinges to keep them from being flattened.

Press boards are made of solid or laminated wood about 1/2 inch thick. Boards with metal edges are used for pressing a book with a rounded back. The metal fits into the ridge or groove along the spine, and the spine projects outside the press. Boards should be a little larger than the books, and a number of assorted sizes, such as 8 by 12 inches, 10 by 16 inches, and 18 by 24 inches, will prove to be useful.

Tins or wax papers are placed between the cover boards and the contents when the book is being pressed.

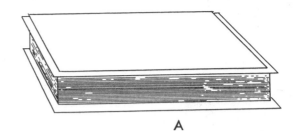

A

The book is placed between boards which are weighted on top with bricks.

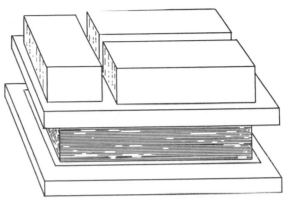

B

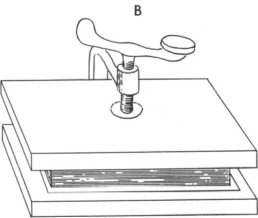

A press with a screw top is attached to the lower board. The upper board lifts off.

C

The book is placed between two boards held together with C clamps.

D

56

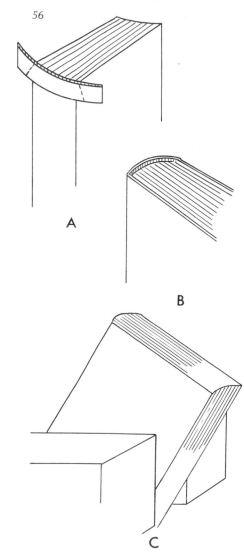

A

B

C

APPLYING HEADBANDS

Headbands are used on many commercially made books. Although not an absolute necessity, they add to the appearance of a book, giving it a tailored finish and providing some support and protection when it is being handled or left standing on the shelf. The headband on a book today is mostly a decorative unit unless it is made directly on the book by hand, in which case it becomes a part of the structure.

Commercially made headbands can be purchased by the yard or bolt in the form of a tightly woven cloth tape, about 1/2 inch wide, edged with a decorative colored thread. They are cut in pieces only slightly wider than the spine and attached to the book with glue, with the right side of the tape facing the book (figure 56). The ends are then trimmed even with each side so that they are the exact width of the book at the edge but wider at the base (diagram A). When the super is put on, it overlaps the edges of the headbands as in figure 101. Diagram B shows the headband as it appears when the cover boards are on.

Headbands can be constructed by tightly wrapping silk or linen thread of any desired color around rolled-up paper strips that are first pasted flat and shaped. The floss can also be wrapped around two strips of tagboard, about 1/4 inch wide, glued together, or around two strips of vellum glued together. Thick string soaked in glue can be wrapped after it is dry. Using the buttonhole stitch to wrap the floss, with the loops placed on the edge, gives the decorative effect.

Another method uses a cord or heavy string of any length tied taut to a nail at either end of a board. A piece of cotton cloth with a narrow stripe, such as might be used for shirting, is cut an inch wide, brushed with hot glue, and folded in the center lengthwise over the cord so that the cord rests inside the cloth within its fold. When this is dry, any length of head-band can be snipped from the strip, all ready for use. The bands are then glued to the top and bottom of the book as previously explained.

In many professionally hand-bound books with leather covers, the headband is made directly on the book as shown in diagrams D through I. Silk floss, buttonhole twist, linen, or heavy cotton thread is used to cover a band cut from vellum, leather, cord, or something similar. A very heavy silk floss has enough body to make it unnecessary to insert a strip or band. A color related to the leather should be chosen.

When a headband is made directly on a book, the book is held in an upright position in a press or vise and tipped forward toward the worker with the fore edge in front (diagram C). The threaded needle is inserted through the center of the first signature and pulled out at the back below the first row of stitches that hold the signatures together (diagram D), leaving half of the

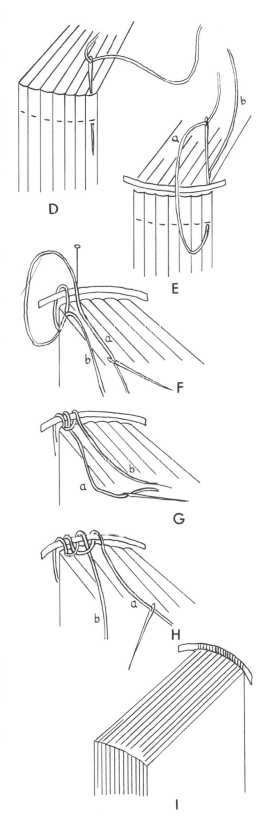

thread trailing behind and the other half on the side where the needle is. Thus two threads a and b become available for use in making the band. The needle and thread are brought back over to the front and again inserted through the same hole (diagram E), and the thread is pulled down until a small loop is formed. Through this loop is inserted the band of vellum, thin leather, cord, catgut, or heavy string, with a small amount left projecting at the ends (diagram F). The loop is then pulled tight so that it holds the band securely in place.

A pin stuck into the book vertically against the back of the band will help to hold it in place (diagram F). To continue the making of the headband, the needle thread a is again brought over the band to the front and shifted to the left hand, where it is held taut next to thread b. Thread b is lifted with the right hand, brought over thread a, slipped under the band, and brought back over it (diagram G).

The two threads exchange hands again, and this time the needle thread a moves to the right, crossing over the other thread b, goes under the band, and then over the top to the front again (diagram H). This process continues across until the band is covered, except that after every three or four stitches the needle thread is again inserted into the book between signatures or in the center of one, in order to anchor the band to the book.

When the stitching is finished (diagram I), the ends of the threads are cut to about 1 inch, frayed out, and pasted down on the back of each end signature. The finished band should be a little lower than the cover boards. After one band is completed, another is put at the other end of the book.

To vary the above procedure, two threads of different colors can be knotted together at one end, with one thread passing through the needle and the other remaining free. The process is the same, with a mixture of colors resulting as the threads cross each other.

The directions for making a headband may seem a little confusing at first but, if one follows along step by step, the rhythm of forming the stitches will soon be evident. A completed headband on a book is shown in figure 57.

57

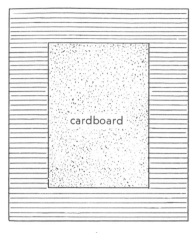

cardboard

A

B

C

USING A FINDER

The finder is a device used in working out the proportional design for the cover of a book and in the selection of the patterned area.

A section the size of the proposed cover is cut from the fold edge of a piece of plain paper (diagrams B and C), or one of the cover boards can be laid on the paper as in diagram A, traced around, and the paper cut so that the opening will be the exact size of the finished book.

If a decorated paper is to be used on the cover, this cutout frame or finder can be placed over it and moved around until the best portion is selected (diagram D). When a book cloth is used for the back, it is slipped under the finder and the desired proportion of cloth to paper determined (diagram E). In this way the finished cover can be visualized as it will look when completed.

D

An adjustable finder that is more flexible can be made by cutting pieces of cardboard, identical in size, with right-angle corners and with one side longer than the other (diagram F). These can be shifted to fit the size and proportion of the particular cover surface being planned (diagram G). When sections of the decorative paper are isolated in this manner they can be studied for scale and proportion to see if the pattern is too large or too small for the proposed area.

After the parts of the decorative paper are selected for the covers, an additional inch is added to three of the sides for overlap. The fourth side overlaps the book cloth about 1/4 inch.

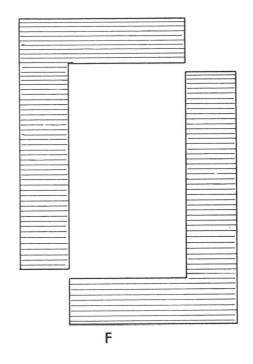

F

E

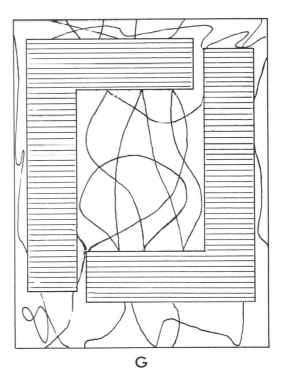

G

APPLYING COVER MATERIAL AND MAKING A CASE

FULL-BOUND

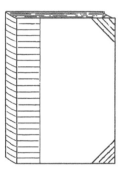

HALF-BOUND

HALF-BOUND

QUARTER-BOUND

The materials most generally used for covering books are cloth, paper, and leather. When the entire book is covered with one piece of material, it is referred to as full-bound. When it is covered around the back and at the corners or outside edge with one material, such as cloth or leather, and on the sides with another material, such as paper, it is called half-bound. In a quarter-bound book one material is used on the back and another on the sides. By combining materials in these manners pleasing relationships of texture, color, and pattern can be achieved.

For a full binding, the material to be used on the cover is cut so that when wrapped around the book it will project about $3/4$ inch beyond the edges at the top, bottom, and sides. A line is drawn down the center of the material, on the wrong side. Then a slip of paper is placed around the spine of the book, and the width of the spine is marked on it. This measurement is marked on the cover material, evenly spaced on either side of the center line. The position of the cover boards is drawn on the material, with the distance of the width of the spine of the book allowed between them. In applying the cover material to the boards, paste is put either on the board or on the material, the book is laid on the place marked (diagram A), and then it is turned over and rubbed carefully with a bone folder. Paste is put on the other board, the material is pulled firmly onto it, and this side is also well rubbed with the bone folder (diagram B). The book is opened and held upright so that the edges of the material can be turned in first at the top and bottom as in figure 106, and then on the sides. It may be necessary to slit the hinge slightly on each side of the spine in order to tuck the back part in (figure 104). The corners are then mitered (figure 58), and the book is completed.

For a quarter-bound book, a piece of material about $1\frac{1}{2}$ inches longer than the book is cut and fitted around the back according to the desired width. A pencil line can be used to indicate how far it is to extend over onto the cover board. Paste should be applied on one side of the book at a time. The material is laid on (diagram C) and pressed well with a bone folder, then wrapped around the spine and pasted to the board on the other side (diagram D). The book is opened up, and if necessary the material is slit on each side of the spine between the cover boards so that it can be tucked in (diagram E). The cover paper is cut so that it will overlap the back material at least $1/4$ inch and project about $3/4$ inch on the top, bottom, and fore edge (diagram F). The paper is pasted and well rubbed, the cor-

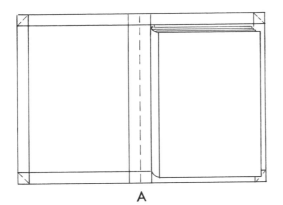

A

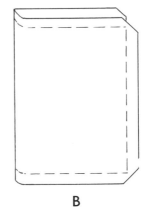

B

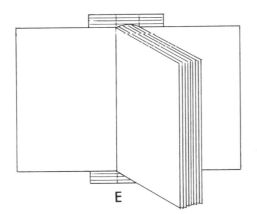

C

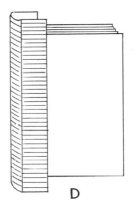

D

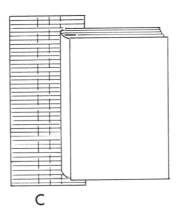

E

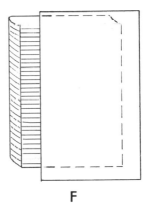

F

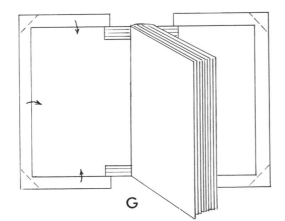

G

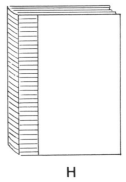

H

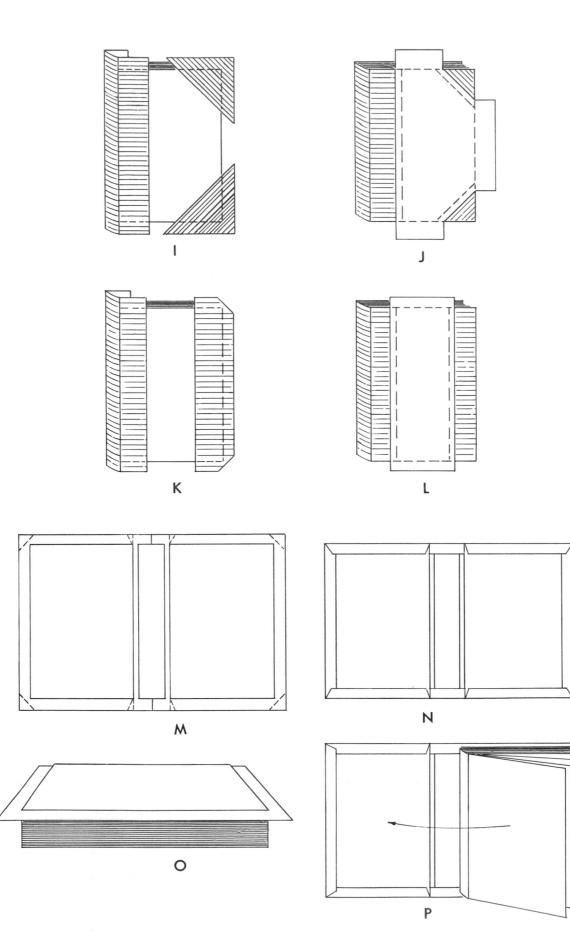

I

J

K

L

M

N

O

P

ners are mitered, and the edges are turned in (diagram G). The completed book is shown in diagram H.

A half-bound book is made like a quarter-bound one, with the addition of corners or fore edge of the same material used around the back (diagram I). When corners are used, a pattern of paper should be cut to determine the proportion and amount of material needed (diagram J). A straight or irregular cut strip may be used down the outside edge in place of corners (diagram K). The cover paper is cut to extend about $3/4$ inch at the top and bottom so that it can be folded over on the inside of the board, and $1/4$ inch is allowed for overlap on the material at each side (diagram L).

When a book is cased, the boards are pasted to the binding material, making the case, and the contents are pasted to the case by means of a hinge, or to the end papers.

To make a case, two boards are cut measuring $1/8$ inch wider than the sewn book, extending from the joint near the back to the front edge, and $1/4$ inch more than the height, so that the board will extend $1/8$ inch beyond the top and bottom. A strip of paper used as a measure is placed around the spine of the book, and the width is marked with a pencil. A lining strip is cut from a piece of thin card, tagboard, or kraft paper, $1/4$ inch less than the width of the spine and the same height as the boards. A piece of material is cut extending about $3/4$ inch beyond the top, bottom, and sides of the book. A line is drawn down the center of the wrong side of the material, and the lining strip is placed on it. The boards are put on either side of the lining strip, leaving a space of $1/8$ inch or more (diagram M). If the boards are unusually thick, it may be necessary to allow more distance. The location of the boards is marked with a pencil. The boards and the lining strip are glued to the cover material, which is then turned over and rubbed with a bone folder. For a smooth effect, or if the cover material is bulky, wedge-shaped pieces can be cut out at the top and bottom as indicated by the dotted lines in diagram M. To finish the case, the corners are mitered and the flaps are folded over and pasted down on the inside (diagram N).

When the book is to be put into the case, a paste paper is placed between the end sheets and the book, or between the super hinge and the book, at the front and at the back (diagram O). Paste is applied to one outside sheet, and the book is laid on its side on the casing and pressed firmly (diagram P). The casing is brought around so that it covers the whole book, and the other end sheet is pasted in the same way. Wax paper or tin should be slipped in at the front and back, and the book is then put into a press to dry.

MITERING CORNERS

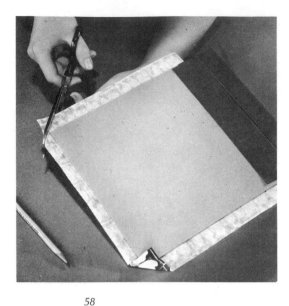

58

Mitering refers to the process of finishing the corners of a book when the cover paper or cloth is folded over the edges. Five ways of doing this are shown in the diagrams. The choice of method may be determined by personal preference, or it may depend upon the material used. If the covering material is a lightweight cloth that is likely to fray at the edges, one of the plans shown in diagrams B and E will the best choice since the cloth can be folded.

In diagram B the corner is folded over without any cutting and the overlaps are brought down and pasted to the board.

In diagram E the corner is cut from the outer edge of the paper or cloth to the corner of the cardboard and the divided corners are folded down until the edges are parallel with the edges of the cardboard. The overlaps are then folded over onto the cardboard and pasted.

In the plan shown in diagram A the corner is cut off straight across, leaving a space beyond the cardboard the width of the thickness of the board. The corner can be creased first, as in figure 58, before cutting. The top flap (overlap) is always pasted down first, the bottom flap next, and the side last.

Diagram D is similar to A except that the corner is cut at a slight angle rather than straight across. This permits a little more overlap of the edges. Even frayed edges of cloth can be turned under if they are cut this way.

When a book has been covered with leather, there is often a problem of added thickness and bulk at the corners unless the leather is a thin type like skiver. If the leather is thick and difficult to fold it will have to be skived first. For this purpose there are various types of knives called skiving knives, by which the leather is carefully scraped on the wrong side until it is thin and flexible enough to bend easily (figures 264 and 265). The leather can then be cut and the edges brought together as already explained, or they can be dampened and pulled over the edge of the board without being cut. The gathers that will form should be pressed as flat as possible with a bone folder when the leather is pasted down (diagram C). The corner will appear rounded.

The corners of a book should be made as neatly as possible. A little care and practice will give them a look of real craftsmanship. It is suggested that the beginner practice the methods described with scraps of paper and cardboard in order to study the results and work for improvement.

A

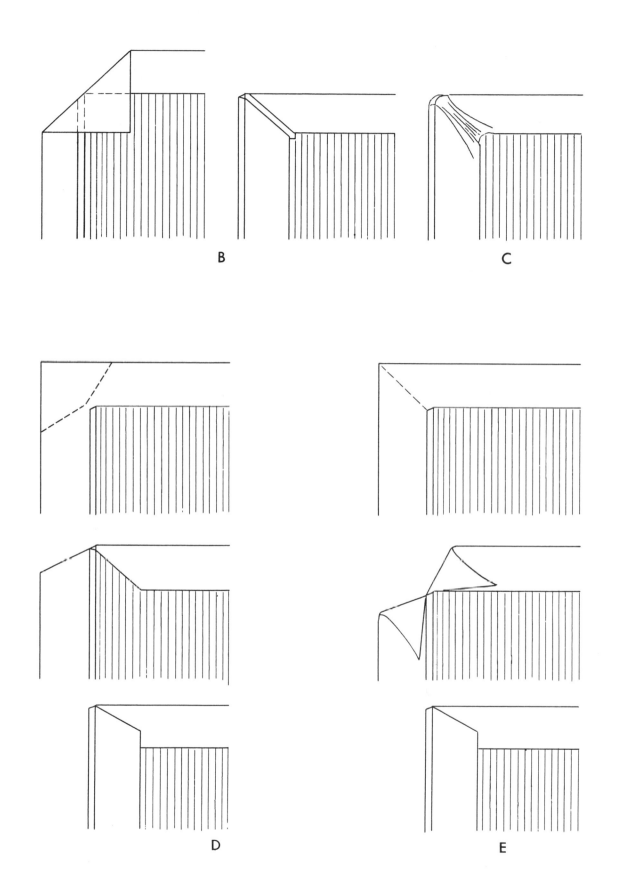

B   C

D   E

APPLYING END PAPERS

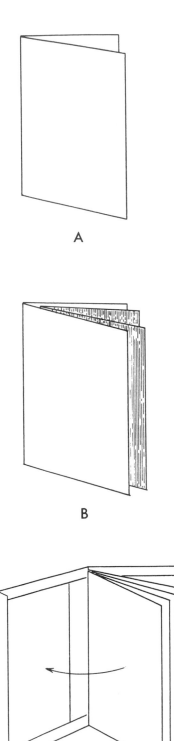

End papers are used inside the front and back covers of a book to help relate the contents to the cover (figure 59). They are folded so that half of the sheet is pasted to the inside cover board as a liner and the other half is left free as a flyleaf. In other words, the lining and the fly sheet are generally cut in one piece, with the grain of the paper running up and down to prevent curling. If desired, the liner and flyleaf can be cut separately of different papers or colors.

End papers can either be sewn in with the first and last signatures of a book or tipped in afterward. To provide a perfect fit, the flyleaf is cut the same size as the pages of the book, and the part that is pasted to the cover is cut the same height but $1/8$ inch or more wider to allow for the thickness of the board at the hinge. When the paper is pasted inside the cover board, it should be about $1/8$ inch from all the edges of the book.

One or several end papers can be put into the front and back of a book (diagrams A and B). When several are used they are inserted one inside the other to form a signature and are sewn in the same operation as the content signatures. The outer sheets at the front and back of the book are pasted to the inside of the cover boards after the cover paper has been applied and the corners have been mitered (diagram C). If only one folded end sheet is used, the sewing will show when the liner is pasted to the cover. This can be avoided by using at least two sheets to form a signature, or the folded end sheet can be tipped in instead of sewn.

When an end paper is to be tipped in, the cover is opened and a piece of wax paper is laid on top of the contents about $1/8$ inch from the hinge edge (diagram D). Paste is applied sparingly with a brush to the $1/8$-inch area of paper exposed; excess paste should go on top of the wax paper, which is then removed. The folded end sheet (diagram E) is laid on top of the contents over the pasted area (diagram F). A clean wax or paste paper is placed inside the folded sheet of the end paper, and thin paste is applied sparingly to the part that is to be pasted to the cover board. This must be done carefully so that the paper will fit straight when it is attached to the cover (diagram G). The surface is then rubbed gently with a crumpled piece of paper or a bone folder. The same process is repeated in attaching the back end paper, and this completes the making of the book (diagram H). If a patterned paper is used, the right sides are folded together so that when the liner is pasted down in the cover the pattern will be visible.

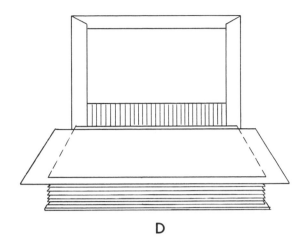

D

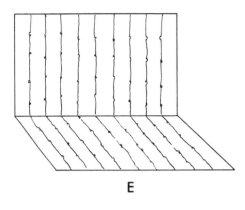

E

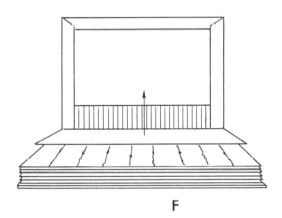

F

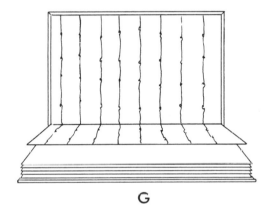

G

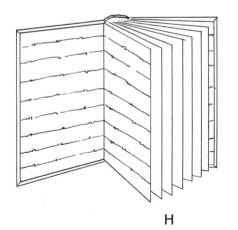

H

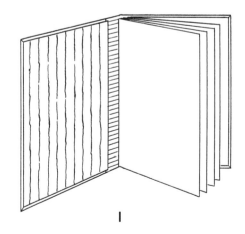

I

In books with side-sewn sheets, portfolios, and scrapbooks, the liner is cut without a flyleaf and is pasted to the inside cover slightly overlapping the cloth hinge (diagram I). If no cover paper has been used, or if it is not folded over the edges of the cover board, the liner may extend clear to the outside edge without leaving the customary 1/8-inch margin.

A method for making more durable end sheets, sometimes followed by professional binders, makes use of what are called accordion-pleated or zigzag sheets. This method is more complex, but it is not difficult if directions are carefully followed. The logic of the plan will be clearly comprehended if it is tried out first, step by step, with scrap papers.

A total of six sheets of paper is used, three in the front and three in the back. They are made into signatures and sewn in with the rest of the book material.

To make one of these signatures, two sheets of paper are cut the same height as the book contents but at least 1/2 inch wider than the pages of the book when they are folded. The third sheet should be about 1/2 inch wider when folded than the other two. All three sheets are folded in the center.

A line is drawn about 1/4 inch from the fold edge of the larger sheet (diagram A), now designated pages 1 and 2. Sheet *b,* one of the smaller sheets forming pages 3 and 4, is placed next to it with its fold edge back to back with the larger one. Paste is put on the 1/4-inch strip, and the fold edge of the smaller paper is laid over onto it (diagram B). These two sheets are put under a weight to dry.

Page number 1 is then folded back over page number 3, and page number 2 over number 4. Note that page number 2 must be pleated near the fold in order to be even with number 1.

The third folded sheet (diagram C) forms pages 5 and 6. It is inserted between pages 2 and 4, and it is through this part that the signature is sewn when the book is made.

Page number 1 is a waste or protective paper that is later torn off and thrown away. Number 3 is the real lining sheet, which is to be pasted to the cover, and number 4 is the flyleaf. Thus, if a colored or patterned liner and flyleaf are desired, these would be included as sheet *b.*

The signature is placed so that page number 2 faces the other signatures of the book. A similar signature is placed underneath at the back of the book in the corresponding position, where it will also be sewn in.

The biggest difficulty in pasting end sheets is to keep them from wrinkling at the joint. One way to help prevent this is to bend the covers straight back. The pasted sheet is brought over onto the board and rubbed well, especially at the joint. The book can be kept open in this manner for a half hour or so until it starts to dry. It should then be gently closed, with tins or wax paper inserted to keep the moisture from penetrating into the pages, and pressed only lightly.

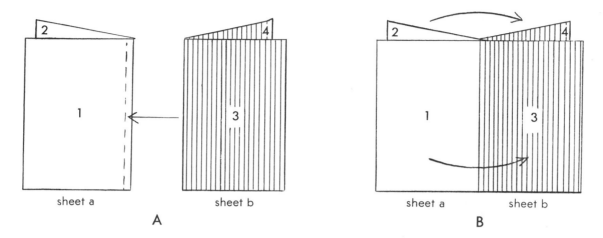

sheet a   sheet b

A

sheet a   sheet b

B

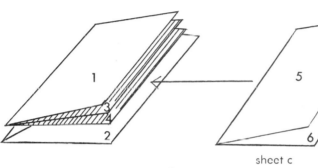

sheet c

C

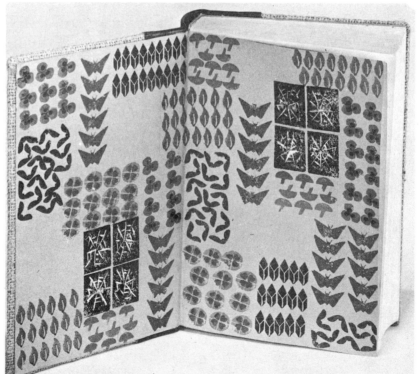

59

Simple Constructions
and Binding Procedures

60. Constructing an accordion-fold book

The problems presented in this section range from simple folders, files, note pads, scrapbooks, portfolios, boxes, and telephone book covers to books with sewn signatures and leather covers. Most of the problems can be adapted to any level, with the age and experience of the participants determining the degree of complexity.

Teachers can set up an environment in which the child can produce. The approach should be kept as imaginative as the process allows, avoiding detailed measurements, so that the experience will not become monotonous and uncreative, resulting in stilted products.

Processes should be kept quite simple for very young children. They can work on all kinds of little book problems that do not require a great outlay and yet provide them with the opportunity of being creative through art. Teachers will have to decide how materials should be arranged and organized in the classroom and how much preparation should be made ahead of time. For little children paper may be cut to the size needed, or they can learn to tear the paper along the fold if they are not yet ready for scissors.

As children mature they can be helped in applying the principles of art in the making of their products and to individualize many of the things they use in school every day. They can be encouraged in working out color and shape relationships and given freedom of choice in the selection of colors and sizes and in relating plain with patterned papers, to allow for originality. As the child works he will discover new ideas that may carry over into personal interests. Thus, he might make cards at holiday time or gifts of little books for relatives and friends; bind his own original stories, poems, and drawings; or cover his class papers attractively. Children in Oriental schools are taught to construct little notebooks like the examples shown on pages 144-47.

Older children can learn to bind books with one or several signatures in hard covers, and to construct large folders to hold their art work, as well as notebooks, sketchbooks, and scrapbooks in which to put sketches, diaries, recipes, poems, or clippings. They can bind artistically illustrated term papers that are worthy of preservation. They can also learn to care for and appreciate books by rebinding old ones in need of repair, to bind magazines, and even to mend their own schoolbooks. This work should not be allowed to become drudgery or too demanding, however, for too much stress on technique and measurement can destroy the personal satisfactions to be gained. They can be made aware of proportion and size by folding a sheet of 12-by-18-inch newsprint as described on pages 44-45. This will help them to establish the format of the book they wish to make and will give them a freer approach to book conception.

For group work a class can collaborate on a project by making a large scrapbook or accordion-fold book in which the work of the whole group—as for example drawings made from scientific material in class, or pictures gathered to illustrate a geographical unit—can be mounted. A class can also produce a sewn book for which each child writes one chapter or section. In a book about Europe, for example, illustrations, sketches, and page layouts can be arranged to form a unified whole with each child's section fitting into the common plan. When sewn together and bound, such a book makes a fine addition to the classroom library, to be studied and enjoyed.

Many of the procedures explained may not become clear until the worker is actually involved with them. As directions are followed a step at a time in logical order, meanings will be revealed. It is important not to become discouraged with technical failures; errors that occur can be either corrected or charged up to experience and avoided in future problems. Skills in pasting and cutting will improve with practice. The adult and older student will realize that continual striving for accuracy and neatness, without sacrificing personal expression, contributes toward a more satisfying product. A carelessly produced book does not provide great satisfaction, but one thoughtfully and carefully constructed is a real treasure. Although there are many restrictions and exacting demands in advanced problems, freedom comes in the selection and decoration of cover and lining, as well as in the choice of materials where it is advisable to experiment with a variety of different kinds of papers and book cloths.

Preparatory to working with binding procedures, a period of time can be spent in exploring various paper decoration techniques. The section on decorative papers includes many ways of producing such patterned papers. Young children can start with potato or eraser prints, or with little units made with crayons or paints. The best results should be kept to use later for cover material or end sheets on the appropriate projects, or new papers can be made as needed. Time should be provided for sufficient experimentation so that ideas for designs can be developed and improved. Little children will naturally work more casually and freely and be less concerned with exactness of spacing, but they are able to learn how allover patterns are produced by the repetition of shapes and colors.

The working procedures describing the processes of cutting, pasting, pressing, and so forth that are used in book construction should be studied and referred to as the information is needed when individual problems are worked on.

The operations involved in binding a book are of two kinds: forwarding and finishing.

1. Forwarding has to do with the actual making of the book, the collating (assembling of sheets), sewing, gluing, and attachment of the cover. This is the part that requires the work of the artisan and, according to Ignatz Wiemeler (German binding authority), "entails a wondrous sort of drudgery."

2. Finishing is concerned with the decoration of the outer part of the book, on the sides and back, after it has been covered. This requires the work of the artist.

There are two methods of attaching the covers to a book, casing and binding. In cased books, the covers are made apart from the book and fastened to it by means of the super and end papers which are pasted to the boards (see diagram M on page 76). This is the process used in machine-made books.

In bound books, the bands (tapes or cords) on which the book is sewn are laced into the board or pasted to them. This is the method used in the section describing books made on tapes and cords (although cased covers could also be used here).

The making of a book is a step-by-step process that can best be learned by following directions in a given order. Later, after one is familiar with the individual procedures and their purpose, the methods used can be varied.

The main steps in making a book are:

Folding the sheets

Gathering the consecutive signatures

Marking and cutting the backs for tapes or cords, and kettle stitch

Sewing the signatures to the bands
Gluing the signatures
Trimming the fore edge
Rounding the back
Trimming the head and tail
Putting on headbands and super
Attaching the covers
Covering boards with leather, cloth, or paper
Mitering corners
Pasting down end papers
Applying tooling, gilding, inlay, or other embellishment; printing titles.

SIMPLE FOLDERS AND FILES

Constructions like the folders and envelopes shown here can be made in any desired size to hold school-work or other material. Papers used should be flexible but tough enough to withstand strain; butcher paper and other wrapping papers that are light in weight and easy to handle are convenient for these purposes. Tagboard is somewhat heavier and must be scored with a bone folder or dull knife so that it can be folded without cracking where it is creased.

The simplest way to make a folder for holding flat material is to take a sheet of paper twice the length desired for the folder, fold it in half, and staple it several times on both sides. If the folder is to be pasted instead of stapled, it can be made as shown in diagrams A or C.

In diagram A the paper is creased down the center, and the shaded sections are cut away. The flaps on the left side and at the bottom, about an inch in width, are folded over and pasted, and the right-hand section is brought over on top of them. The flap at the top is folded down as shown in diagram B.

In diagram C the rectangle is creased in the center and the strips indicated by the shaded area are cut off. The remaining flaps on either side of the upper portion are folded inward, paste is applied, and the bottom half is folded up (diagram D). The folder can be decorated with an allover design as shown in figure 61, which was printed from an eraser.

An envelope-type folder is shown in diagrams E and F. The center and lower sections are made the same height, while the flap on top is shorter. The sides of the top and bottom flaps are cut on the diagonal, and all shaded portions are removed. The flaps on the sides are folded in, the bottom flap is folded up, and the top one is brought down.

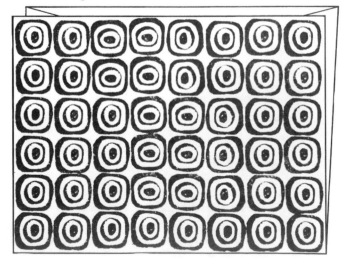

61

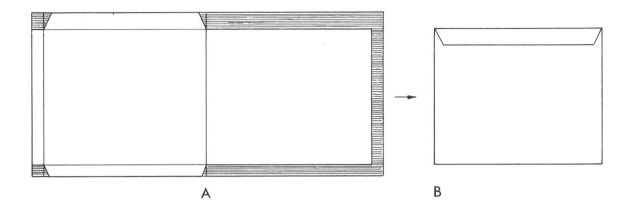

A

B

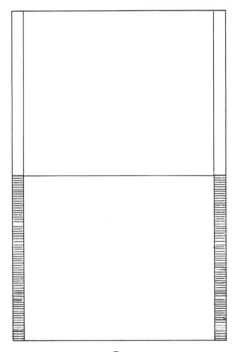

C

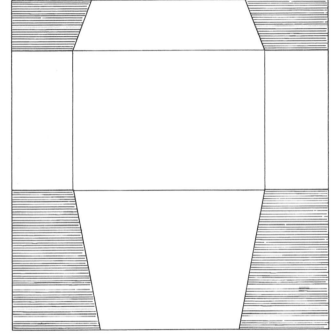

E

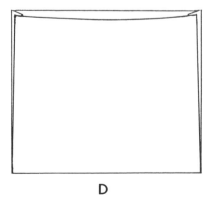

D

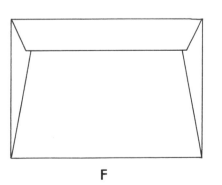

F

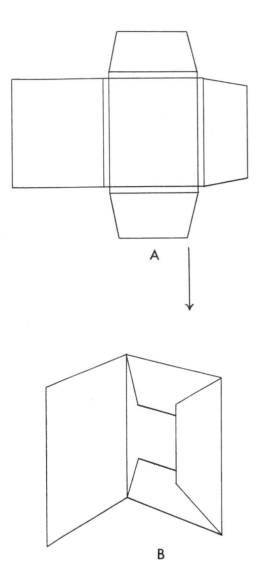

A

B

The folders shown here are cut with flaps on. These are folded over to make a case for holding stationery, loose papers, photographs, or other flat items. In diagram A, some allowance has been made for expansion by means of an extra crease, about $1/2$ inch from the fold on each flap. Three of the flaps are the same size, and the fourth is the size of the base. Diagram B is the same as diagram A but omits the extra crease for thickness.

In diagram C the folder is planned in a rectangle by dividing the space in the center and marking out the size of the two covers, which should be slightly larger than the material to be held. The flaps are the same width on all four sides, and the corners are cut out at an angle so they will fold more easily. The flaps on the left are pasted down, while those on the other side are kept free to hold the inserted material (diagram D). If the paper is light in weight, a thin piece of cardboard can be glued to the inside of the right-hand section to give it greater rigidity.

An attractive lining sheet can be applied to the inside cover on the left or to both sides if desired. It can be decorated with a repeat design, as explained in the section on decorated papers. A simple repeat pattern of pleasing colors is effective, especially if the folder is to be used for a gift. The outside cover can also be decorated. Folders like these can be made from colored construction papers or wrapping papers as well as lightweight tagboard or Bristol board.

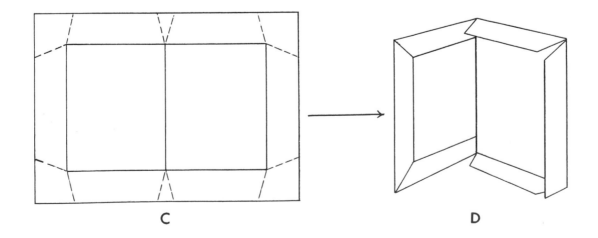

C   D

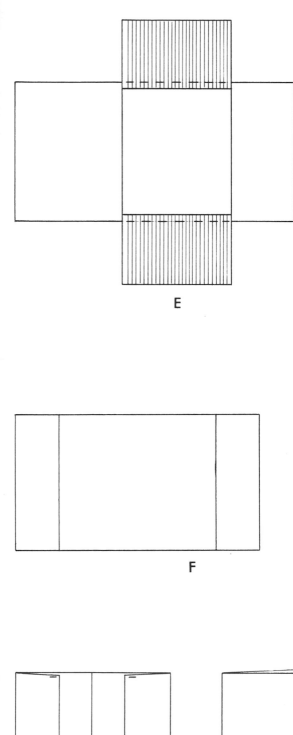

E

F

When a contrasting color or texture is desired the flaps are attached to the case as shown in diagram E. About ½ inch is allowed for overlapping on the back of the case, the flaps are pasted down, and when dry they are folded over. The flap on the right, which is cut in one piece with the folder, can be the same width as the added flaps, or a different width. The one on the left is the size of the center rectangle. Interesting effects can be obtained through the use of varied colors and kinds of paper; for instance, the lower flap could be a different color but related to the upper one.

The folders below are similar in construction. They are made from an extended rectangle with pockets folded over on either side and held in place with staples or paste. In diagram F a line is drawn at each end of the rectangle indicating the width of the pockets to be made by the folded paper. These can be identical in size, or one can be larger than the other. After the pockets have been folded and fastened, as in diagram G, the case is creased in the center and becomes a folder (diagram H).

The example in diagram I has pockets that have been shaped to provide variety, and the case is folded off center so that the top part is narrower than the underportion (diagram J). These cases can be lined if they are too thin. They can have a decorative design applied to the outside and the pockets.

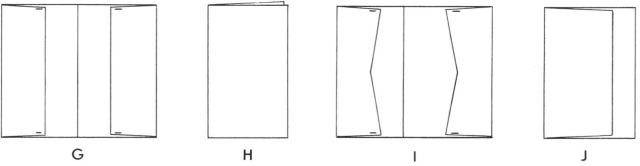

G   H   I   J

Two folders for holding note paper or stationery are shown in diagrams A and B. In one, the pocket flap is folded over at the side, while in the other a portion is folded up from the bottom and fastened with staples or paste.

To make a file that will allow for the thickness of inserted material, two vertical lines are drawn on each side of the center, and two horizontal lines are drawn a few inches from the bottom (diagram C). The distance between the vertical lines must be twice that between the horizontal ones to allow for the double thickness when the parts are folded. If cardboard is used, the lines will have to be scored for easier folding. The shaded portion shown in diagram C is cut out, and the lower parts are folded upward as in diagram D.

An expanding file is shown in diagrams E and F. The width of the base is established by drawing two horizontal lines through the center. Two vertical lines are drawn on either side at a distance from the edge at least twice as much as that between the horizontal lines through the center. The actual width depends upon the number of pleats desired. The shaded portions are cut away, the outside upper sections are folded into accordion pleats as indicated by the lines, the center horizontal lines are creased, and the file is held together by paste on the edge of the outside pleat.

The file in diagram I is made by folding a rectangle along two parallel lines through the center to form the base, as shown in diagram G. A smaller rectangle is folded into four parts and then into accordion pleats (diagram H). Paste is put on the outside pleats, and the section is inserted into the end of the larger folded rectangle. Another accordion-pleated rectangle is inserted into the other end to complete the file (diagram I).

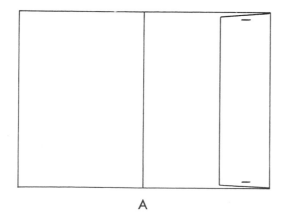

A

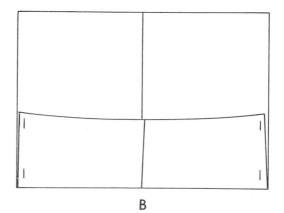

B

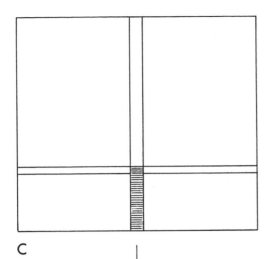

C

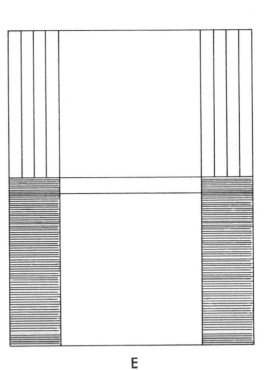

E

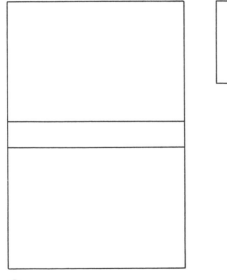

D

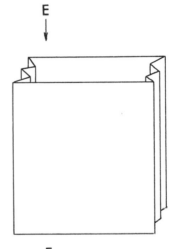

F

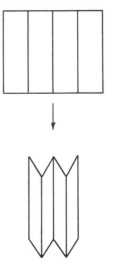

G

H

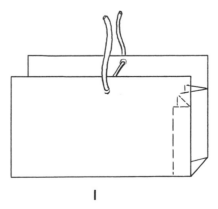

I

EXPANDING FILE

A flexible file can be constructed from any paper that is lightweight but strong, such as tagboard, thin cardboard or Bristol board, heavy wrapping paper, kraft paper, or butcher paper. Bookbinding supply companies have a tough, flexible, red-brown paper used for limp bindings that is also suitable.

The desired width and height of the front of the file are determined first. The example diagrammed is 5 by 11 inches in size. One inch is allowed for each pleat, which is then divided into 1/2-inch folds.

It is well to practice first with bond paper, newsprint, or kraft paper. The plan is laid out as shown in diagram A. If multiples of two, four, or eight pleats are used, they can be folded without drawing each line. Otherwise the space should be divided into 1/2-inch widths, and lines drawn to indicate where the creases are to be. When stiff paper is used, lines will have to be scored with a dull knife or similar instrument guided with a ruler. There should always be an even number of spaces, and lines should be continued all the way across the middle section, as shown in the diagram.

The corners are cut out on the dotted lines, leaving 1/2-inch flaps which will make the front and back overlap the sides when the file is completed.

The lines *aa* and *bb* are well creased, then opened again. The paper is folded in half so that *aa* and *bb* meet (diagram B). The rest of the lines indicated for pleats are folded until all are creased. The paper is again opened, and the creases are refolded into accordion pleats as in diagram C.

The end arms are bent straight upward so that they rest on top of the flat area, parallel to the edges on each side; they should be very well creased (diagram D). The arms are rebent so that they are on the back (diagram E) and are well creased again.

62

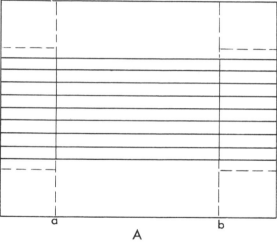

A

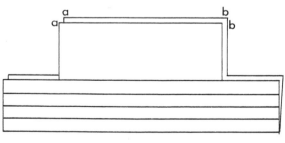

B

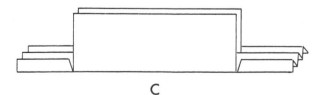

C

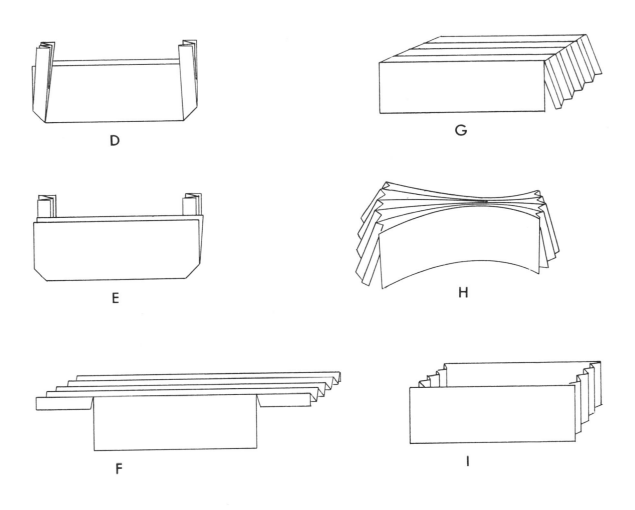

D

G

E

H

F

I

The entire structure is opened up flat with the two sides folded outward. It is then turned upside down (diagram F), and the two ends are folded down (diagram G). The end pleats are collapsed also and well creased where they join together at right angles with the side pleats (diagram H). This interlocks them. It is easier to work on the structure by having it upside down, and with a little patience the trick of making the pleats take their positions will soon be learned.

The end tabs are pasted to the inside of the front and back sections (diagram I). Decorative papers can be used to cover the sides as in figure 62 which has an eraser print design. A file made of tagboard and covered with book vellum is shown in figure 217.

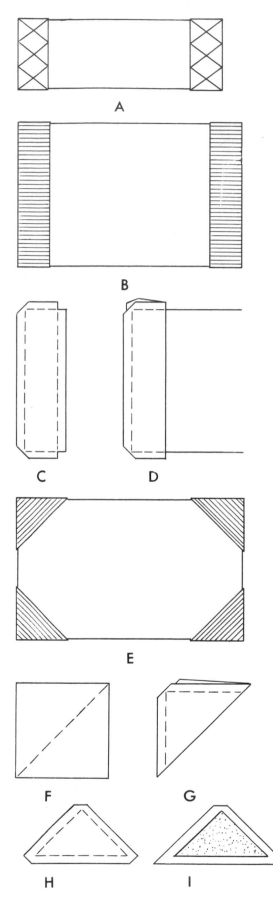

A

B

C   D

E

F   G

H   I

DESK BLOTTER

Desk blotters can vary in size from small ones about 3 by 8 inches up to large ones 18 by 24 inches (diagrams A and B). Stiff cardboard is used.

A piece of paper is pasted to the top surface of the board, with ½ inch allowed to overlap the edge. In diagrams A and B the paper need not extend clear to the end of the board because of the pockets. In diagram E the cover paper can be cut off slightly across the corners to reduce bulk. Instead of covering the entire board, strips 1 inch shorter than each side and about 1¼ inches wide are pasted over each of the four sides (see diagram C, page 115).

For the strip type of pocket shown in diagrams A and B, a paper pattern rectangle is cut first in the desired width, with ½ inch added to all four sides (diagram C). The dotted line represents the exact size of the pocket. The two outer corners are cut off on the diagonal, and the two on the inside edge are cut out at right angles. The top, bottom, and outer flaps fit over the edge of the board, while the inner flap folds under and makes a neat edge where the blotter slips under. This inner flap does not always have to be pasted. If the pocket is too flimsy, a piece of lightweight cardboard can be inserted. When leather is used, unless it is thin like skiver, the edges will probably have to be skived to make them thin enough to fold.

For a heavier, stronger pocket, the material can be doubled as in diagram D with the fold used inward, where the blotter is inserted, and the open sides folded over the edges of the board.

When triangular corners are used, a square is folded in half as in diagrams F and G, allowing a ½-inch flap to be pasted over the edges of the board, or the two squares can be cut in half to make four single corners as in diagram H. The dotted line indicates the part that is folded under. Corners are snipped out, and the base edge of the triangle is turned under. For more strength, a lightweight card or muslin can be pasted onto the corner material (diagram I).

When the corners are being put on, the blotter, with its corners snipped off, can be placed on the board at the same time to test for thickness. The lining sheet is pasted to the back about ¼ inch from each edge, and the finished construction is put to press.

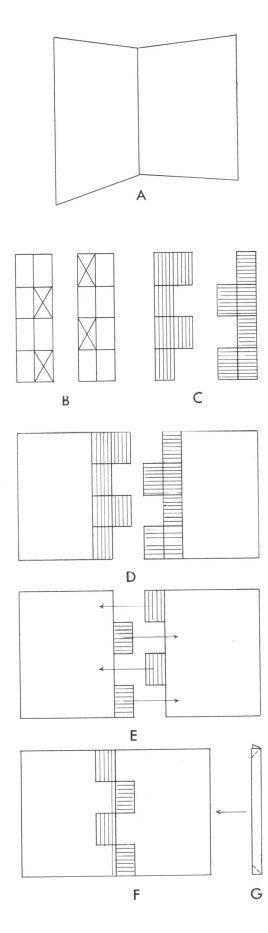

FOLDING SCREEN

A table screen suitable as a background for a flower arrangement, a plant, or a piece of sculpture is made with a flexible hinge that bends either forward or backward. Two or more boards rigid enough to stand upright, like beaverboard, heavy chipboard, Davey board, or stiff-backed corrugated board, are hinged together (diagram A). They may be equal in size or not, and either vertical or horizontal in direction.

Two pieces of book cloth are cut the height of the boards and 2 inches wide. They are divided in half vertically and folded into four even parts. The sections marked x are cut out (diagrams B and C).

The long, uncut half of each strip is pasted onto the edges of the boards with the cutout parts extending beyond them (diagram D). The boards are turned over (diagram E), the projecting sections are interlocked, and each is pasted to the opposite board (diagram F). The cutout pieces are glued to the open areas to fill in the gaps. To finish, the boards can be covered with a paper of interesting color or texture, one that has a pleasing decorative design, or one of the exotic Oriental metallic papers. The paper is cut to cover each board so that it extends across the cloth hinge to within $1/8$ inch of the edge and overlaps the other three edges about $3/4$ inch. The corners are then mitered (diagram I I). Another paper is put on the back, $1/4$ inch from each edge and $1/8$ inch from the hinge edge. If desired, all of the edges can be covered with pasted 1-inch folded strips of tape or vellum, with the corners cut as in diagram G. Paper can then be applied to the front and back, leaving a $1/4$-inch margin on all sides.

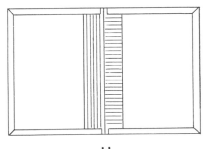

NOTE PADS

The pads shown on this page are simple enough in structure so that even a young child can make them, but they can also be produced by older students as attractive little gifts. Inside pages can be newsprint, bond paper, typing paper, or drawing paper, and colored construction papers are good material for the covers. Several plans are presented as suggestions.

In the example shown in diagram A, the colored paper used on the back is extended over the top about an inch and secured with staples, sewed, or punched and laced.

Diagram B is similar to diagram A with the addition of a front paper cover on which an allover repeat design has been made. The cover is tied in with the rest of the sheets by means of a cord. The two ends pass through the outer punched holes from the front to the back and are brought back through the center hole where they are tied together around the cord. They may also be extended into a loop for hanging.

The decorated paper of diagram C can be mounted on a lightweight cardboard or tagboard to make a stronger, more rigid cover. In diagram D the cardboard is folded at the top, and the decorative design is mounted on it.

The note pad in diagram E, page 99, is made simply by stapling several sheets inside a folded piece of paper.

When cover designs are made with thought and imagination the results can be very attractive, and the pad is a useful item for jotting down notes or making a shopping list. The design in figure 63 is made with a combination of hot wax crayon and paint. The one in figure 64, made with crayon, is the work of a young child.

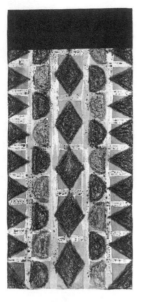

63

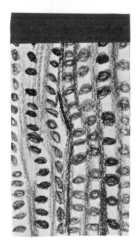

64

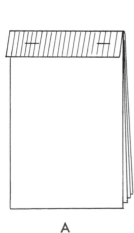

A

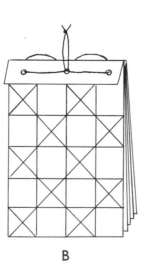

B

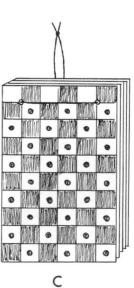

C

D

TAGS

Gift tags for packages present an opportunity to work out simple design problems without utilizing much material. Colored construction papers, lightweight colored card, tagboard, and papers of similar weight are suggested. Colorful designs can be applied with crayon, paint, ink, cut papers, or combinations of these. Luggage or name tags can be made this way also, with an eyelet punched to hold the cord (diagram F).

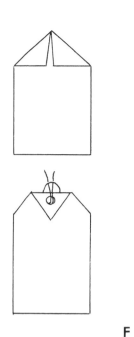 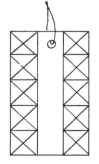

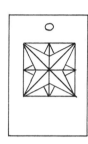

F

STAND-UP CARD

A card that will stand up on a table or shelf as a mounting for a calendar, photograph, or picture can be constructed of stiff paper or lightweight cardboard (diagram G). A strip of paper twice the size of the desired card is creased in the center (diagram I). A piece of cardboard half the size of the strip (diagram H) is pasted to the lower half. The upper part of the paper is then folded, with half of it pasted to the cardboard and the remaining part left free to be bent out as a tab (diagram J).

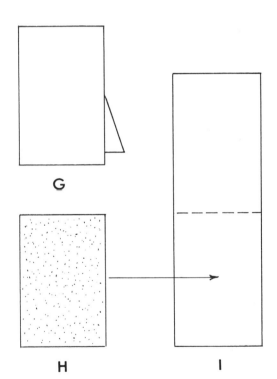

G

H   I

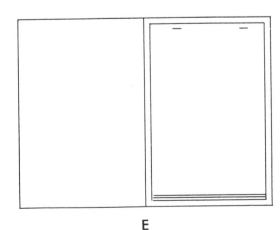

E

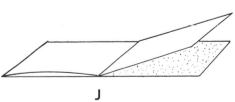

J

99

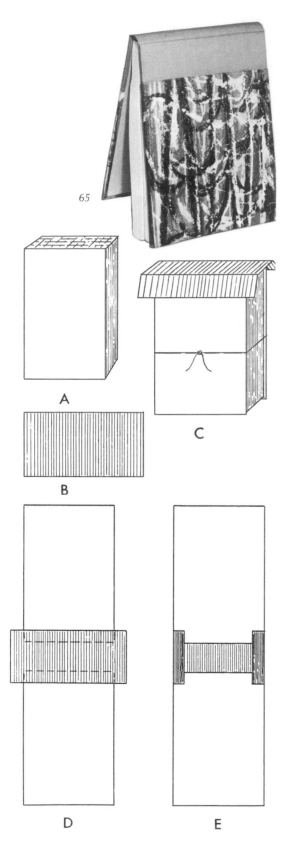

65

A

B

C

D

E

MEMO PAD

A memo pad holds scratch paper for use in jotting down notes. When the colors for the hinge, cover paper, and lining paper are chosen with an awareness of relationships, it can be an attractive little book (figure 65).

The scratch-pad filler (diagram A) is available in several sizes, from 3 by 5 inches up to letter size. For convenience, the size 4 by 6 inches is used in the following directions. Two pieces of cardboard are cut the same size as the pad or ¼ inch wider and ⅛ inch longer, in this case 4¼ by 6⅛ inches. If a pencil is to be attached at the side later, the board can be made slightly wider to allow space for it.

A piece of book cloth or tough paper is cut for the hinge strip (diagram B). It should be 1 inch wider than the cardboards (5¼ inches), and large enough to cover the top of the pad and extend over onto each board, that is, about 3½ inches wide (diagram C).

One of the two cardboards is placed in front of the scratch pad and the other behind it, even at the top edge. A rubber band or piece of string is put around the middle to hold them together. The hinge strip is laid over the top, and a pencil line is drawn along the edge where it touches the cardboard in front and in back.

The cardboards are then removed from the scratch pad, and paste is put on one of them in the space above the pencil line. The hinge strip is placed on the pasted area and smoothed down. The other cardboard is pasted, and the opposite edge of the hinge strip is laid on it, thus hinging the two boards together (diagram D). Care must be taken to line up the cardboards so that they are hinged directly opposite each other.

The projecting flaps are pasted down on the inside (diagram E) and can be covered with a lining piece of book cloth or paper cut to extend to within ⅛ inch from the edge at each side (diagram F).

The cardboard attached to the back of the scratch pad can be glued to the inside of the casing just completed, or a pocket can be constructed into which it is inserted. For the pocket, a piece of book cloth or tough paper is cut 1 inch wider than the cardboard and any desired length (diagram G). It is placed on the inside of the back cover near the top, and the extending parts are folded over onto the outside (diagram H). Only the flaps are pasted down; the rest is left free for the insertion of the pad. The pocket can also be added after the cover and lining sheets are on. In this case the flaps are folded under and pasted to the inside of the back cover as shown in diagram B on page 112.

The cover paper is cut from ¹/₂ to ³/₄ inch wider on each side and at the bottom of the cardboards to which it is pasted. It should overlap the hinge about ¹/₄ inch on the outside (diagram I). Corners are mitered, and the overlap is pasted to the inside of the covers (diagram J).

Lining sheets are applied on the inside of the cardboards ¹/₈ inch from each edge and level with the top of the pocket and hinge (diagram K). If a pencil attachment is desired, a strip of vellum can be looped and the ends inserted under the lining sheet.

To prevent warping, the casing should be spread out and put to press until dry before the scratch pad is inserted. As a substitute for a purchased scratch pad, several sheets can be put into a press and their top edges glued together, or sheets can be folded and sewn together through the center. Figure 66 shows a sketchbook made in the same way as the memo pad, but hinged at the side instead of at the top.

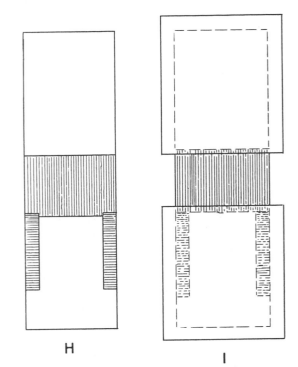

H   I

66

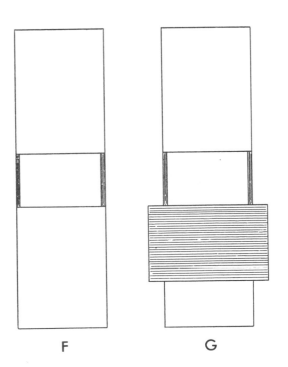

F   G   J   K

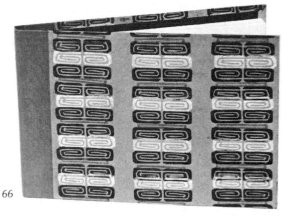

ACCORDION BOOK

The accordion type of book is composed of a continuous folded sheet of paper enclosed between two covers. It can either be expanded outward or kept flat (figures 67, 68, and 69). If used as a scrapbook, it will hold as much mounted material as desired without bulging at the open edge, as do scrapbooks that are tied at one side. Both sides of the pages are usable, and the book can be small and intimate in size or large and impressive. If the work of a whole class is to be mounted on the pages, the book will have to be quite large. It can be kept flat on the library table for leisure-time enjoyment, arranged to stand on a table for display, or spread out and fastened to a bulletin board. Tabs of cloth can be pasted after every four or five sheets so that the expanded pages can be hooked over pins when the material is displayed.

Paper used for the inside sheets can be of the weight of drawing paper, heavy wrapping paper, or colored construction paper, or it can be heavier, like tagboard or thin Bristol board. Two cardboards are cut for covers. The cover paper is cut about 1/2 inch wider than the boards on each of the four sides. The paper is pasted to the back of both boards, and the corners are mitered and pasted. If a tie is used, it is pasted across the inside of one of the boards before the lining is applied (diagram A). The inside paper, which is folded into sheets, may be the same size as the cover board or slightly smaller, leaving a 1/8-inch margin. If the book is to stand, stiff paper the size of the cover will work best. The inside paper can be extended by joining sheets with a small overlap (diagram B) or by pasting one page over the other (diagram C).

When single sheets are used, they can be joined together with strips of bookbinding tape or with pasted strips of cambric the length of the page and about 3/4 inch wide. Between every two sheets, 1/8 inch should be left for folding (diagram D). Another strip of cloth is pasted over the back of the joint. The two ends of the folded paper are pasted to the inside of the cover boards and can serve as lining sheets (diagram E), or contrasting papers can be pasted over these if desired as in figure 68, where strips of different colors are used.

This type of book comes to us from the Orient, and books made in this way are available in shops specializing in Chinese and Japanese products.

67

68

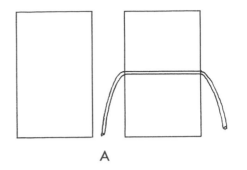

A

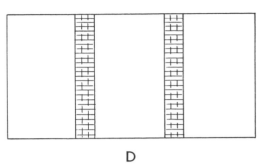

D

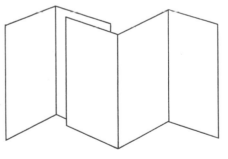

B

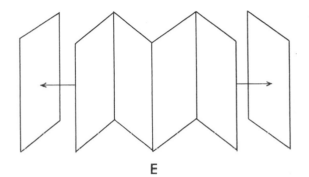

E

C

69

SCRAPBOOK

A scrapbook has many uses and is not very difficult to make. After the shape and size are determined, three cardboards are cut, one for the back and two for the front cover, providing a hinge so that the book can be opened. The hinge board is approximately 1 or 1½ inches wide, depending upon the proportion and size of the book. The hinge board and the other front cover board together, allowing about ¼ inch of space between them, should equal the total width of the board used for the back.

The two front boards are hinged together with a strip of book cloth cut twice the desired width and 2 inches longer than the boards. The cloth is creased in the center, and the boards are glued to it. The corners indicated by the dotted lines are then cut out (diagram A), the flaps are glued down (diagram B), and the other half of the cloth. is folded over and glued (diagram C).

Holes are made in the hinge board with a hand drill or punch. Cover papers are put on the outside of the boards, the corners are mitered, and lining sheets are pasted to the inside, leaving a ⅛-inch margin on three sides and overlapping the cloth lining ¼ inch.

Another method is shown in diagrams D and E. Both front and back covers are hinged, and the hinge is turned to the inside in order to conceal the fastening. It is necessary in this case to leave a wider space between the boards to allow for the turned hinge.

Filler paper of a heavy enough quality to support the work to be mounted on the pages is fastened between the cover boards. Stationery stores sell packages of scrapbook fillers in various sizes. Each page has one edge folded over about 1 inch on the side where it is tied into the book to allow for expansion when material is mounted on it (diagram F). For this same purpose separate strips of paper an inch wide can be inserted at the edge between every two sheets. The covers and the pages are held together with screw posts (figure 71), tied with cords, or laced as in Japanese binding (figures 70, 72, and 73; see pages 144-45). The holes in the paper are made to line up with those on the cover boards. If a hand punch is used, only a few pages should be punched at a time. The papers can be placed on the edge of a table with the ends extending over a heavy weight at the other end to hold them in position.

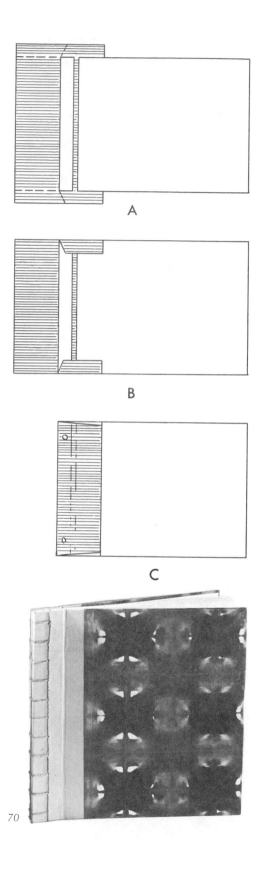

A

B

C

70

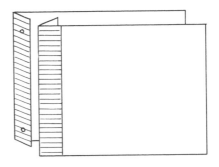

D

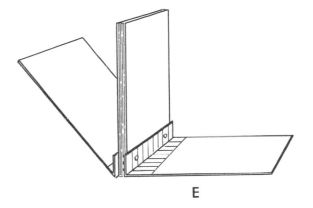

E

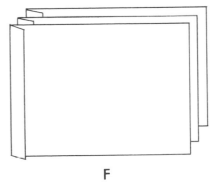

F

71

72

73

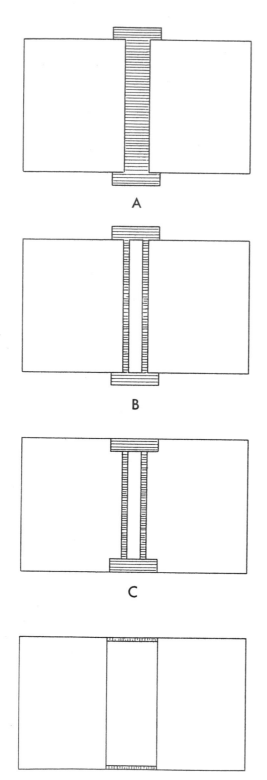

A

B

C

D

PORTFOLIOS

A portfolio is designed to hold loose papers and may serve as a carrying case or file for clippings, mounted pictures, photographs, paintings, and, when pockets are added, as a writing case (figure 81). It can be as small as 9 by 12 inches or less, or as large as the cardboard available, which may be as much as 24 by 36 inches. The use determines the dimensions. In its simplest version, it is composed of two identical cardboards hinged together with book cloth. The cloth is cut about 2 inches longer than the cardboard, a line is drawn or creased down the center, and the distance between the two cardboards is indicated by drawing two lines, one on each side of the center, as far apart as desired (diagram A).

The cardboards are laid on the book cloth, and a line is drawn at the top and bottom where they touch the cloth. Paste is put on one side of the marked cloth, and the cardboard is laid in place, turned over, and rubbed well with a bone folder to get out all the wrinkles. Then the other cardboard is pasted to the cloth. The boards must be lined up evenly across. When a book vellum is used, care must be taken not to stretch it while it is damp with paste since it wrinkles easily.

If a stiff back is desired, a cardboard strip is pasted down the center of the hinge, leaving a space of $1/8$ to $1/4$ inch on either side, depending upon the size of the portfolio and the thickness of the cardboard (diagram B). The top and bottom flaps are pasted down on the inside (diagram C), and a lining of cloth or heavy paper is put on top about $1/8$ inch from the top and bottom edges (diagram D).

A decorative design can be printed or painted directly on the cardboard, as in figures 74 and 75, or a cover of paper or cloth can be used either in combination with other material or all in one piece, as shown in diagram M on page 76. The portfolios in figures 77 and 78, by junior high school students, show original designs painted on paper.

If desired, ties may be used on the portfolio. Materials like tape, cord, yarn, raffia, shoestrings, trimmings or bands from fabric or yard goods centers, or whatever seems appropriate are cut to length, pulled through a slit made in the cardboard with a sharp knife or razor blade, and pasted to the inside (diagrams E and F). Another kind of fastening is shown in diagram H, which illustrates a method for

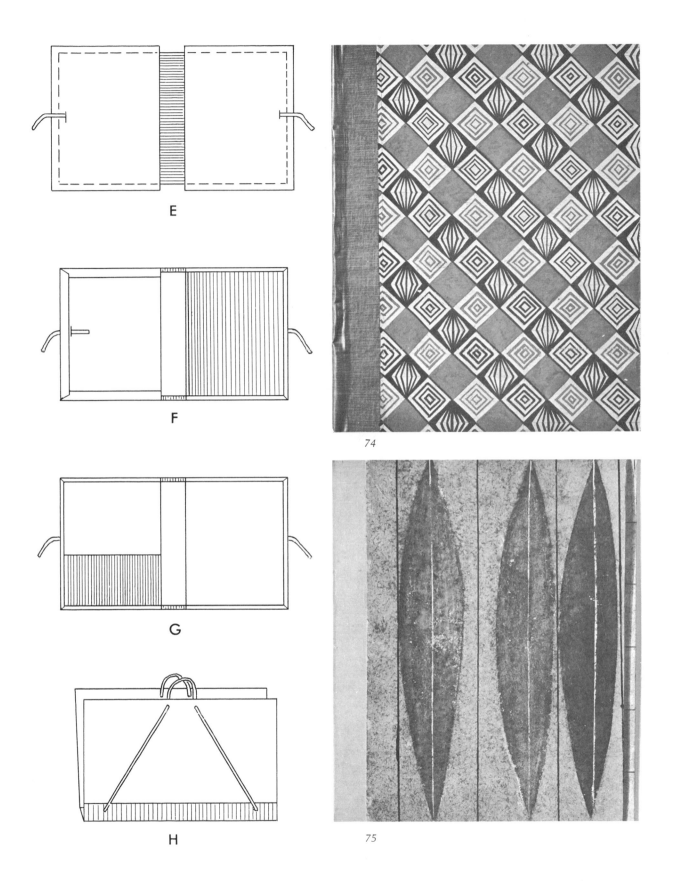

E

F

74

G

H

75

76

77

inserting cords to be used as handles. This is particularly good for carrying large folios.

To complete the job, lining sheets are pasted on, extending to ⅛ inch from the outer edges. If an inner pocket is added, as in diagram G, book vellum or tough paper can be used. Three ways of making this are shown in diagrams I, J, and K. The lines are creased, and the flaps are pasted either under the lining or on top of it.

A cover for a telephone book or magazine can be made like the portfolio, with the addition of a metal plate attached with rivets through the inside of the back. See figure 76, and refer to page 256 for the source of the metal plates.

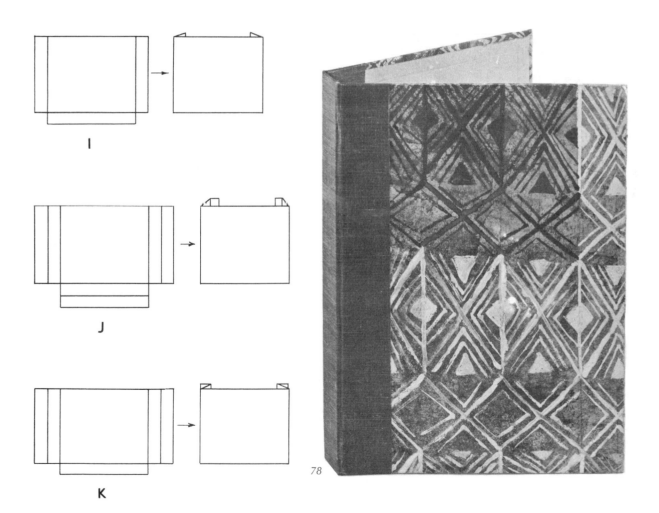

78

79

80

Flaps can be added to a portfolio by using the structural plan that has already been shown. After the boards are hinged together, the cover paper is applied, and the corners are mitered, the flaps are constructed and attached to the inside of the back cover. Diagram A shows such a plan.

The flaps are constructed of cardboard covered with book cloth or a tough, flexible paper. It is advisable to cut a paper pattern first in order to determine the size and proportions needed. The length of the flap is usually the same as that of the side of the portfolio to which it is attached.

Two cardboards are needed for each flap. The piece next to the portfolio should be the same width as the hinge between the two cover boards. Diagram B shows how the book cloth is cut from a rectangular shape, with corners x and y removed. A pencil line is drawn 1¼ inches from the bottom edge and 1 inch from the other three edges. Corners are cut out on the dotted lines indicated. Line ab is the same length as the side of the portfolio to which it will be attached. The cardboard strips are pasted to the book cloth, allowing ¼ inch of space between the pieces to permit bending (diagram C).

After the overlaps around the edge are pasted down (diagram D), a lining of the same material is applied with a ¼-inch margin at the top and sides and even across the bottom (diagram E). This can be put on either before or after the flap is attached to the portfolio. The flaps are pasted to the inside of the portfolio, overlapping the edges about 1 inch (diagram A). A lining paper is then pasted to the inside of both covers.

If more strength is desired, the flaps can be attached to the outside instead of the inside of the corner. In this case the edges are bound with strips of cloth cut 1 inch wide, as shown in diagram C on page 115. The cover paper is cut ½ inch shorter in length and width than the boards so that the bound edges of the cloth will show. The portfolios in figures 79 and 80 are made in this way. In figure 80 the hinge and flaps are covered with a dark red vellum, and the repeat design on the cover is painted with poster colors on drawing paper. The one in figure 79 has a fold-and-dye cover design.

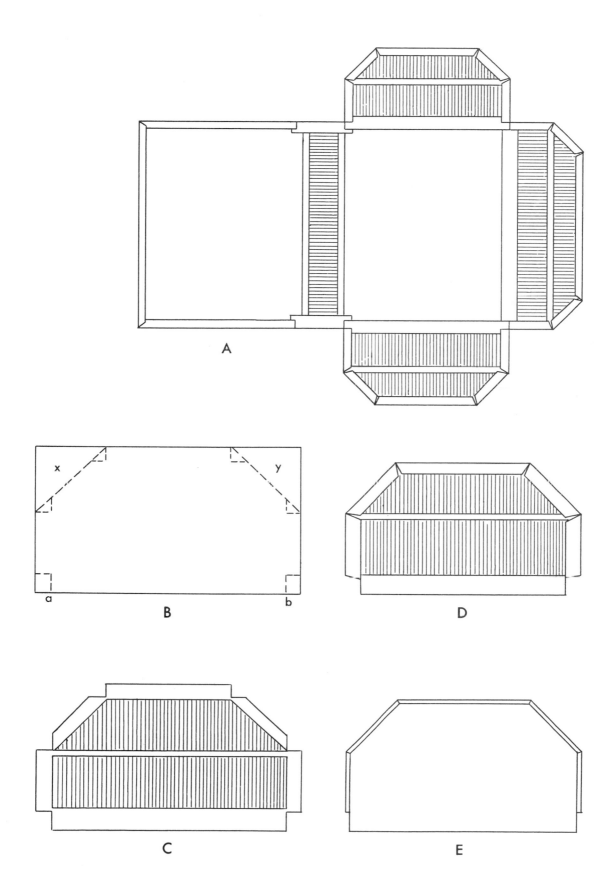

A

x

y

a

b

D

C

E

111

81

A folder to hold stationery and envelopes or loose-leaf papers is shown in figure 81. It has a cover in which pieces of brilliantly colored papers are inserted behind the areas cut out of the paper. The binding can be cut all in one piece of heavy paper or book cloth if desired, with an allowance of 1/2 inch or more for overlapping on the edges. Two cardboards are glued to this piece, leaving about an inch between (diagram A); the edges are turned over onto the boards; and the corners are mitered. To give added strength a strip of tough paper or book cloth is glued between the boards, overlapping them 1/4 inch and extending to within 1/8 inch from the top and bottom edges. A lining paper is pasted to each board, 1/8 inch from the outer edges and slightly overlapping the center strip.

Pockets to hold papers can be placed at the bottom of the case (diagram B) or down the sides. They are cut as in diagrams C and D. Two corners are removed, forming flaps that are folded under and glued to the boards.

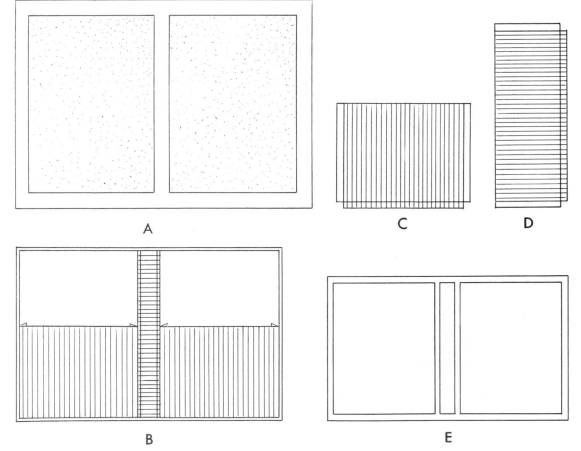

A

C

D

B

E

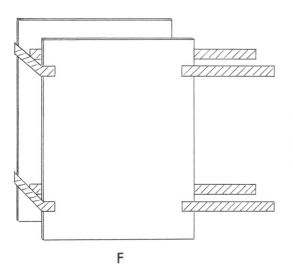

F

For a stiff back, a small strip of cardboard can be glued between the larger boards, with ¼ inch or more allowed on either side (diagram E).

A stiff folder that is adjustable is made from two pieces of cardboard held together with tapes. Slits are cut into the boards with a sharp knife, and strong tapes are inserted through them. These can be adjusted to fit the contents inside and will hold them firmly in place when tied (diagram F). The boards can be decorated or covered with a decorative paper.

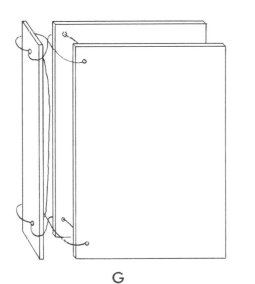

G

WOODEN BOOK COVER

Thin boards, such as plywood, are cut for the covers, including a narrow board for the back (diagram G). Holes are drilled at top and bottom, and a strong cord or thong is laced through according to the direction indicated in diagram H.

A book or pamphlet can be held in place by means of the vertical cord, or the cover can be used for a scrapbook by running the cord, at the top and bottom of the boards, through holes along the side of the paper.

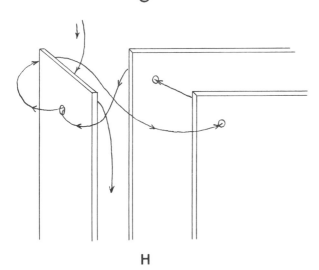

H

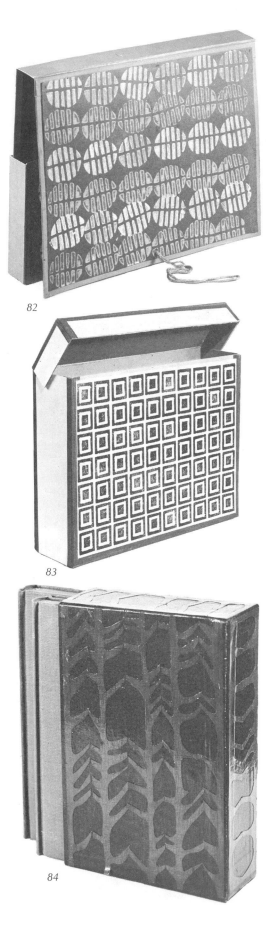

82

83

84

BOX FILES AND BOOK BOX

The box files shown in the examples were planned for holding reference material, mounted clippings, pamphlets, magazines, music, and so forth. The box in figure 84, with the vellum appliqué on the outside, was designed to hold two books. All of these boxes are constructed from pieces of cardboard taped together with strips cut from book vellum. Directions for figures 82, 85, and 86 are given on the facing page. Seven pieces of cardboard are hinged together. It is important that the boards be cut accurately with all corners square so that they will fit together.

The example shown is constructed to hold papers 9 by 12 inches in size. Boards 1 and 3 are $9\frac{1}{2}$ by $12\frac{1}{2}$ inches, board 5 is $5\frac{1}{2}$ by $12\frac{1}{2}$ inches, boards 2 and 4 are $1\frac{1}{4}$ by $12\frac{1}{2}$ inches, boards 6 and 7 are $1\frac{1}{4}$ by $5\frac{1}{2}$ inches.

Four pieces of book cloth are needed for the hinges. Those for boards 2 and 4 are 3 by $13\frac{1}{2}$ inches, and those for boards 6 and 7 are 3 by $6\frac{1}{2}$ inches. Boards 2 and 4 will each need a piece of cloth or paper 3 by 12 inches for a lining.

The boards and the cloth hinge pieces, cut to size, are laid out and assembled as in diagram A, which shows the inside of the box with the cloth strips underneath the cardboard strips. The boards should be lined up as evenly as possible. A space of 3/16 inch is left between every two pieces unless the cardboard is unusually thick, in which case $\frac{1}{4}$ inch should be allowed.

Before the box is assembled, cloth strips 1 inch wide are cut to be used as a binding to cover the three outside edges of board 1, the two outside edges of board 3, and the lower outside edge of board 5. These strips are creased down the center and pasted over the boards (diagram C). The corners can be cut on the diagonal for mitering.

Boards 2, 4, 6, and 7 are glued to the cloth strips under them. Then board 2 is attached to boards 1 and 3, and board 4 is attached to boards 3 and 5. The edges of the cloth extending out from boards 2 and 4 are pasted down to the inside, and a cloth or paper lining is put over them.

If a tie is to be used, holes or slits are made about $\frac{5}{8}$ inch from the edge of boards 1 and 3 where dots are shown in diagram A. Cords or tapes about 6 inches long are inserted, and the ends are pasted

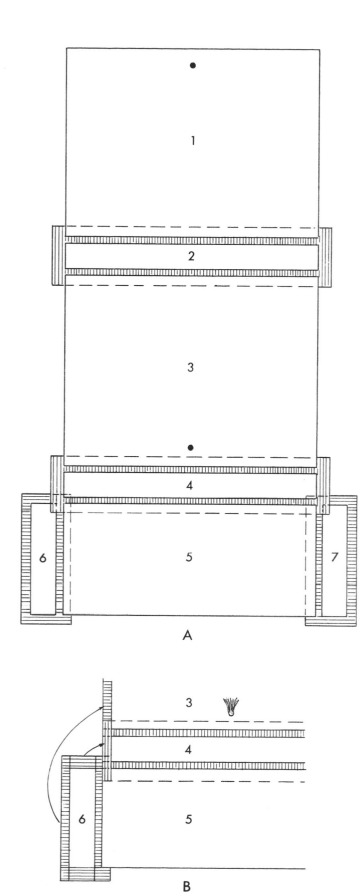

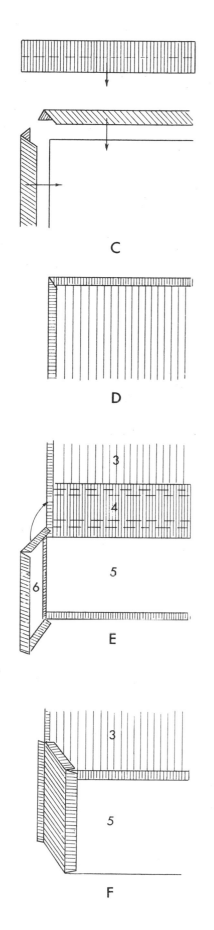

A

B

C

D

E

F

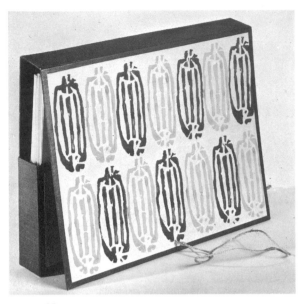

85

86

down to the inside of the boards (diagram B). A paper lining sheet is put on boards 1 and 3, extending to about ¹/₄ inch from each edge (diagram D).

Boards 6 and 7 are pasted to board 5, and the top and bottom corners of the cloth pasted to them are cut out. Board 5 is raised upward, parallel to board 3, and is attached by means of the flaps of boards 6 and 7. The top flaps of boards 6 and 7 are pasted to the inside of board 4 (diagrams B and E). The outside flaps wrap around board 3.

Outside cover paper is applied to boards 1, 3, and 5 to about ¹/₄ inch from each edge.

The boxes in figures 82, 85, and 86 are covered with papers decorated with patterns made from potato prints. The pattern of the cover on the box in figure 83 was made from an artgum eraser print, and the same shape is used again in figure 62 on page 95 and in figure 94 on page 120, with variations resulting from the manner of printing.

A larger box file, covered with red vellum and containing individual pamphlet file boxes constructed of thin cardboard, is shown in figure 87. The box in figure 88 was designed to hold a series of three classical fairy tales, the covers of which may be seen on page 215. Another box file, shown in figures 89 and 90, is tied with shoelaces on the sides.

87

88

Portfolio boxes for holding magazines or papers can be constructed in a similar manner by hinging boards 1, 2, 3, and 4, as shown in diagram A on page 115, but with board 1 cut about 1/16 inch wider on three sides. Additional flaps are hinged on the other two sides of board 3 and on the three sides of board 1. These are raised upright at right angles to the boards and hinged together where they meet at the corners, forming a box with a lid.

A box to hold letters or mounted material standing upright can be made of lightweight cardboard or tagboard. A shape is cut from a rectangle (diagram A), with the size of the bottom established by the center rectangle *(bdjh)* and the height at the back by the rectangle *cfdb*. The front *(ljhi)* can be lower than the back if desired. The length of *ab* is the same as *bc,* and *de* is the same as *df*. The length of *gh* is the same as *hi,* and *kj* is the same as *jl*.

The front, the back, and the sides are folded upright and are held together by 1-inch strips of tough kraft paper, book vellum or other cloth, or tape, folded and pasted to the edges (diagram B).

The matchbox in figure 91 is covered with a decorated paper in which the design is derived from a matchstick shape.

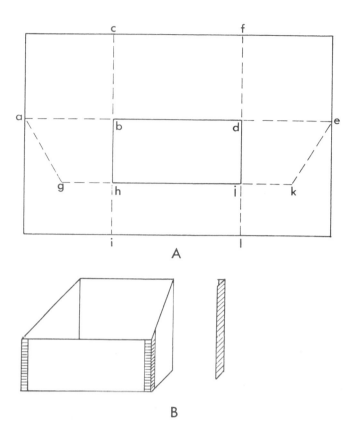

A

B

89

90

91

117

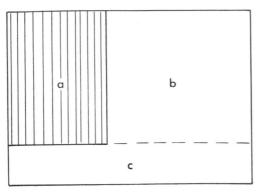

A

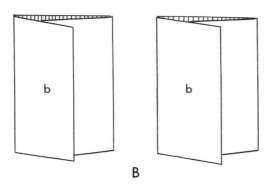

B

BOOKLETS

A simple book requiring no sewing or pasting can be made with limited materials and equipment. It is formed of two pieces of cardboard identical in size, four sheets of construction-weight paper which may be of the same color or two different colors, and several sheets of plain paper such as bond, typing, or newsprint for the pages.

In the example shown (figures 92 and 93), cardboards 5 by 7 inches and colored construction papers 9 by 12 inches in size are used. One of the cardboards serves as a measurement, eliminating the need for a ruler. It is laid on top of the horizontally positioned paper, as in diagram A, and a line is drawn underneath as the cardboard is moved across the paper. The bottom strip c is cut off. Two of the papers are cut this way and wrapped around the cardboards as in diagram B.

The same cardboard can be used for cutting the other two sheets; it is placed on the vertically positioned paper as in diagram C. A line is drawn down the side, and strip e at the side is cut off. Strip d (diagram D) is wrapped around the cardboard over strip b and tucked in at the top and bottom over the edges of the cardboard as in diagram E.

A folded piece 3 or 4 inches wide and the length of the cardboard can be made from strip e, as in diagram F. This strip is inserted in the

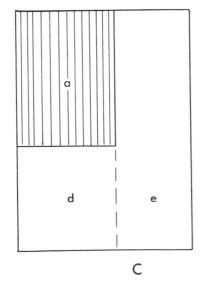

C

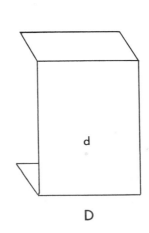

D

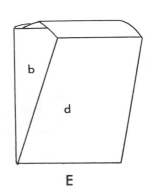

E

openings formed on the covered cardboards and joins the two covers together (diagram G).

The pages for the inside are cut ¹/₂ inch smaller than the covers and fastened by staples or other means to a piece of construction paper that is the height of the book and any convenient width up to the width of the book (diagram H). This piece of construction paper is inserted into the openings in each cover on the inside, where they are joined (diagram I). Although it appears complicated in construction, this book is easy to make. If the directions are followed step by step, the reasons for the procedures will become apparent.

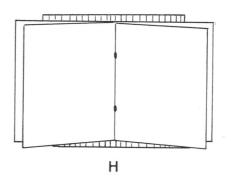

H

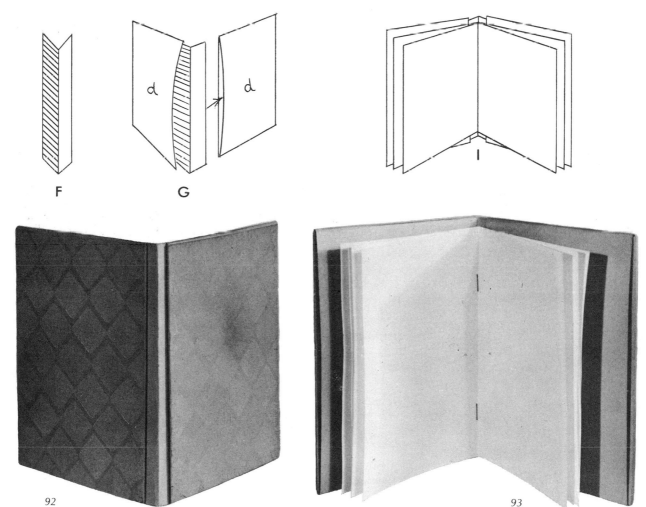

F   G

I

92

93

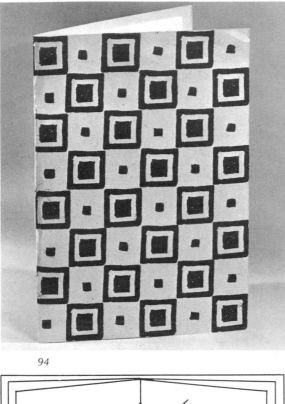

94

The process of bookmaking is introduced when several sheets of paper are folded, inserted one inside the other, and stapled or sewn in the center. This is an excellent way for young children to begin, as no measurement is necessary and they can experience some idea of book construction without technical hindrances. Either white or colored papers can be used for the pages, or they can be used together in alternation.

To sew the book, a hole is made through the center of the fold with a needle, and two other holes are made on either side at equal distances from the center. Children can measure by eye rather than with a ruler. The sewing is started with ordinary white or colored cotton thread through the center hole, on the inside, with a few inches of thread left projecting (diagram A). The needle is brought back up again through one of the other holes, down through the center once more, and up through the third hole. A knot is tied in the center, and the thread is cut off. The sewing can also be started in the center, brought up through the lower hole, then down through the top hole, and again through the center one.

The outside paper can be decorated in various ways, as with a potato or eraser print, cutouts, or other means. A previously prepared sheet can be used on the outside, sewn, and then cut or torn to size to fit the other sheets

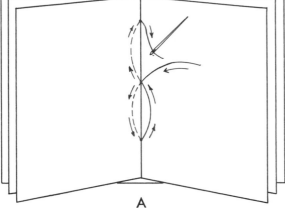

A

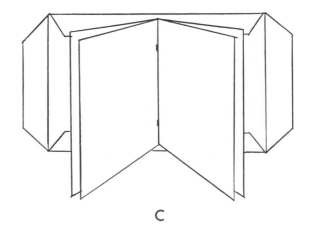

B

C

(figure 94), or it can be folded in on each edge as shown in diagrams B and C. Children can do this if they are shown how to cut off the corners of the larger outside sheet. The top is folded down and tucked behind the stapled or sewn sheets, the bottom is folded up, and then the sides are folded. These are pasted to hold them flat.

The book can also be made with the outside paper extending 2 or 3 inches beyond each of the two sides and then folded over to form flaps. If desired, the booklet can be strengthened with a piece of book cloth pasted over the back either before or after the sewing. The cloth should be the height of the book and extend over onto each side an inch or more, depending upon the proportion desired.

Single, unfolded sheets can be inserted into a pleated back for binding. A line is drawn down the center of the cover paper, and two equal spaces are marked off on either side (diagram D). The lines are scored or creased, the cover is folded along them into accordion pleats (diagrams E and F), and sheets of paper are inserted into the center fold and either sewn or fastened with brads (diagram G).

A child's pleasure is increased if he uses the book he has made for lists of words or numbers, for writing sentences, to hold drawings, or for mounting his work.

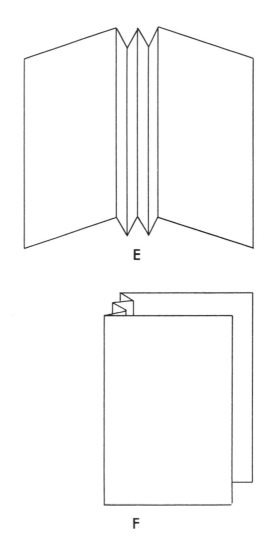

E

F

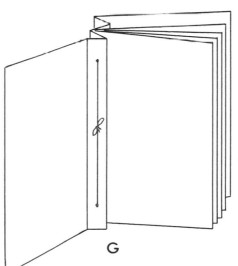

G

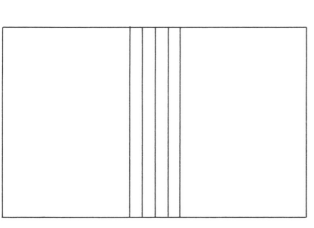

D

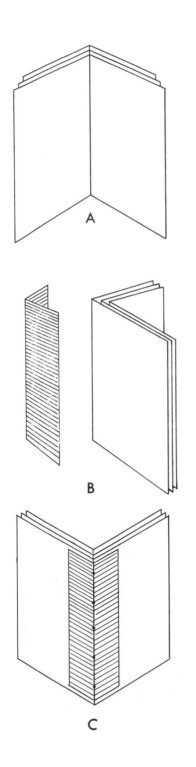

A

B

C

ONE-SIGNATURE BOOK

A single-signature book is similar to the booklet described on page 120, where folded sheets of paper are sewn together through holes in the spine. In this case the book is bound with a hard cover on the outside, and the principle of binding is introduced. Most books are composed of several signatures, but a book of one section is simpler to make and will help in learning binding methods (figure 95).

Several sheets of paper are folded in half and put together (diagram A). The paper used can be any lightweight kind, such as bond, typing, construction, or manila paper. If many sheets are used, and the paper is thick, the book may have to be trimmed after it is sewn (see pages 60-63). The outer sheet is the end sheet and may be of a different paper from the book pages.

A piece of book cloth or heavy brown wrapping paper is cut about 3 inches wide and an inch or so shorter than the book, to serve as a hinge. This strip is creased in the center and placed over the back of the signature; it can be pasted along the fold if there is difficulty in keeping it from slipping (diagrams B and C).

Holes are poked through both the signature and the strip with a needle or awl. If a cradle is available, it can be used for this purpose (see figure 125). One hole should be placed in the center and the others spaced about 2 inches apart. Either three or five holes are recommended. The sewing is done with a running stitch that passes through each hole and then returns. The knot is tied on the inside. Paper clips or a spring clothespin can be used to hold the papers in place and keep them from slipping while the sewing is being done.

Two pieces of cardboard are cut for the cover, $1/4$ inch longer than the book and either the exact width or $1/8$ inch less, depending upon how far from the spine the cover is to be placed. Paste is applied to the hinge strip sewn to the back, after a piece of wax paper or paste paper has been placed under it to protect the book (diagram D).

The paste paper is removed and a clean sheet is inserted before continuing. One of the cardboards is laid on the hinge, $1/8$ to $1/4$ inch from the spine and projecting $1/8$ inch beyond the book at the outside edge. The other cardboard is put on the back (diagram E).

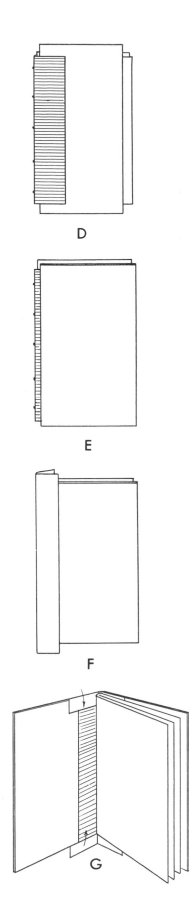

D

E

F

G

If a part binding is used, a strip of book cloth is pasted around the back of the spine. This should be cut at least 1 inch longer than the spine, and a width that is in good proportion to the cover (diagram F). Paste is applied to the board rather than to the strip, permitting the spine to be flexible between the boards.

The book is opened, and the top and bottom of the strip are pasted over the edge to the inside (diagram G). Cover sheets are cut, slightly overlapping the edges of the strip on the cover and extending at least 1/2 inch beyond the top, bottom, and front edges. Paste is applied to each board, the cover material is put on, and the corners are mitered. The first sheet in the book can be pasted down as a lining sheet, or a liner can be tipped in (see the section on pages 80-81 for end sheets).

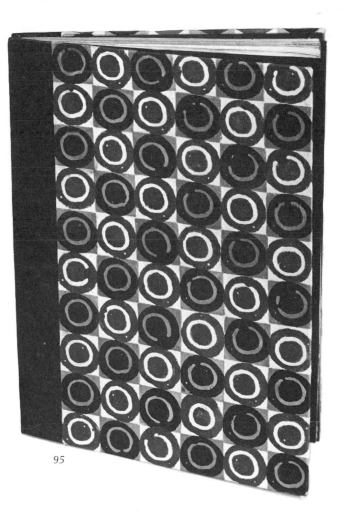

95

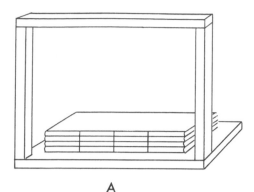

A

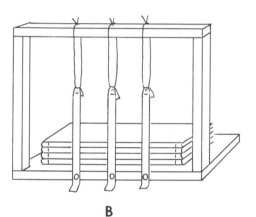

B

96

BOOK MADE ON TAPES

A multisignature book is composed of several sections, or signatures, sewn together and bound in covers. Commercially printed books can be rebound by the method explained here, or blank pages can be made up into a book and used for a sketchbook, to keep the record of a trip, or for any other desired purpose. If an old book is taken apart to be bound, it may need some repair (see pages 248-51).

Several sheets of paper are folded and inserted one inside the other to form a signature as shown in diagram A on page 122. Four sheets folded once and inserted together make eight leaves for a book. If the paper is quite heavy in weight, two or three folded sheets may be enough for each signature, but if it is unusually thin more sheets can be added. The number of sheets used in a signature can be observed by reference to a printed book.

The signatures are stacked one upon another and placed on a sewing frame with the fold edges forward (diagram A). Tapes are suspended from the top to the bottom of the frame; however, less tape is needed if a strong thread or string is looped over the top wooden strip and tied to the tape with a square knot (diagram B). The tape should extend at least 2 inches above and below the stacked signatures, and more should be allowed for looping and pinning the thread. The lower ends are thumbtacked to the wood below (figure 96). If a sewing frame is not available, a box with the front and back removed will serve as a substitute (diagram C), or a chair can be turned upside down and the rungs can be used.

If the signatures have a tendency to expand, a heavy book or a brick placed on top will keep them from slipping while they are being marked for sewing. The number of tapes used varies from two to five, depending upon the size and weight of the book being made. Their purpose is to help hold the book in the cover. Three are generally sufficient for medium-sized books, while five are needed for large ones. If three tapes are used, the spine is divided into four equal spaces (diagram A). One tape is placed over the center division line, and the other two are placed over the marks on either side. A line is drawn with a sharp pencil ½ inch from each end for the kettle-stitch marks, the purpose of which is explained below. Lines are drawn on either side of the tapes to mark the places for sewing, with signatures kept at

97

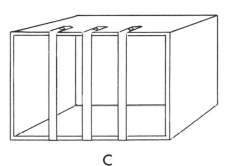

C

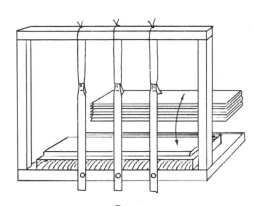

D

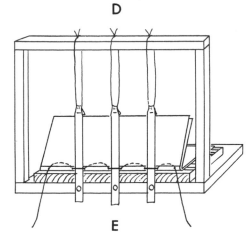

E

dead level so that the cuts will be the same depth.

The signatures are clamped in a finishing press or a vise, supported on each side with a press board or thick cardboard above which they extend 1/2 inch. The two kettle-stitch marks at the head and tail are cut with a fine hack-saw blade, a coping saw, a tenon saw, or a sharp knife. If a saw is used, it is pulled gently forward, or backward and forward, to a depth of about 1/16 of an inch, enough to go clear through the signature (figure 97). The other holes are pierced with a needle through the pencil marks on each side of the tapes to avoid making unsightly cuts which would show on the inside of the book. When sunken cords are used, as described in the section on making a book with cords, the marks are cut with a saw (figure 111) or nipped with a pair of scissors at the time each signature is sewed. When sawing the marks, do not saw the end-paper sections as the holes will show when the paper is pasted down to the cover. Marks are not cut for raised cords, since they are placed on top of the spine.

The signatures are removed from the press without being separated and are placed back on the sewing frame just as they were originally. Since the sewing is begun with the bottom signature, however, all the other signatures must be lifted off. They are turned over all at once, so that their order will be retained, and placed face downward behind the sewing frame with the open edges toward the frame as shown in diagram D, or they can be turned over to the right and kept beside the frame handy to be picked up when needed. As they are sewn, one at a time, they are flipped back over into position on top of the preceding signature (diagram B) until the last or top one is reached. A press board placed on the sewing frame under the signatures before the sewing is started will give the hand more room to handle each signature.

When the sewing is begun, the signature is held open in the center with the left hand while the needle and thread are put through the kettle-stitch cut at the far right end, leaving a few inches of thread protruding. If the other holes have not been cut, they can be pierced at this time. The thread is brought back out at the right of the first tape, then across it, and back to the inside again through the hole at the left side of the tape. The sewing continues in and out, across each tape, and the thread is brought out through the hole at the left end (diagram E).

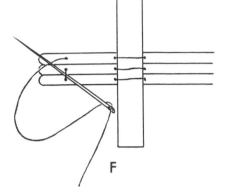

F

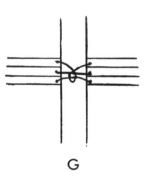

G

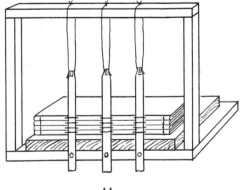

H

The second signature is flipped over from the pile into position on top of the first one, and the thread is brought up and put through the hole above at the end. The sewing is continued around the tapes, and when the thread comes out at the right end it is tied to the tail thread with a double knot. The third signature is flipped over on top, and the sewing is continued in the same way until the kettle-stitch hole at the left end is reached.

At the end of the sewing on the third signature, and from then on at the end of every signature, the kettle stitch is applied. This is used to link the signatures together, since otherwise they would not be fastened to one another at the ends. The kettle stitch is made by bringing the needle under the thread that links together the two signatures below through a loop made by the thread (see diagram F).

During the sewing, the thread should be kept at an even tension at all times, neither loose and sagging nor too tightly drawn. Thread can be added on as needed with a square or weaver's knot; if possible the knot should be put inside the fold of the signature in order to avoid a lump on the outside. This can be accomplished by tying the knot after a kettle stitch has been completed so that the knot can be pulled through the next saw mark above and will rest inside the signature. When the sewing is finished, two or three kettle stitches are made at the end, and the excess thread is cut off (diagram H). The signatures can be kept from swelling as they are being sewn if they are pounded down occasionally with a hammer, a mallet, the edge of a press board, or a piece of wood kept for this purpose. The swelling is caused by the thread's passing through the sections, and the heavier the thread the thicker will be the swelling. If the sections are thin, it is therefore advisable to use a rather fine thread, such as silk. If there are many signatures in the book, they can be caught up in groups about every three signatures. This is done by slipping the needle under the threads below, which cross the tapes (diagram G). After the sewing is completed, the tapes are cut about 2 inches above and below the back, and the book is removed from the frame.

Signatures can be sewn without the use of a frame if none is available. The tapes are cut and laid over the folds along the back, extending over the top about an inch or more, and are glued to the top sheet (diagram I). Marks are made on each side of

I

J

the tapes and $1/2$ inch from either end of the signatures, as already described. The end marks can be cut with a saw if the spine is held so that it projects over the edge of a table. For sewing, the top signature is turned over face down, parallel with and slightly protruding over the edge of the table, with the tapes swinging upward (diagram J). The sewing proceeds as already described, with each additional signature being turned back over onto the previous one in the order established so that, when the sewing is completed, all will be back in the original position. Each tape is then pulled snugly across the spine, and the loose ends are glued down on top of the last signature.

It is also possible to sew the signatures first and insert the tape afterward. The space left for the tape should be slightly wider than the tape itself; for instance, if the tape is $3/8$ inch wide, the space should be $1/2$ inch wide. When the sewing is completed, the tapes are pulled through the loops made by the thread on the backs of the signatures.

After sewing, the backs of the signatures are knocked even, and the book is kept as square as possible. It is screwed lightly into a press for gluing-up, with the back protruding a little above (figure 98; see also pages 66-67). If the spine is filled out from the sewing, cardboards the size of the book can be inserted on each side to fill in the gap. The book can be inserted vertically into the press, which is then screwed up and turned on its side, or the gluing press can be lifted up and the book pages dropped down into a finishing press with the gluing press resting on top. The finishing press is then screwed tight, the gluing press is removed, and the pages are left projecting.

It is not necessary to use a press for gluing. If none is available, the signatures can be placed with the spine projecting slightly over the edge of the table and held firmly with a ruler, a piece of wood, or a press board while glue is applied. This method is actually quicker and just as satisfactory. A little hot, thin, flexible glue is worked well between the signatures; it should be forced into the crevices with the fingers or a brush rather than allowed to remain on the top. If the glue is thick, the back will be too rigid. After a few minutes the book is taken out of the press, or released from other pressure, and laid on a press board to dry, with the back projecting slightly over the edge. A weight, such as a brick or a book, can be

98

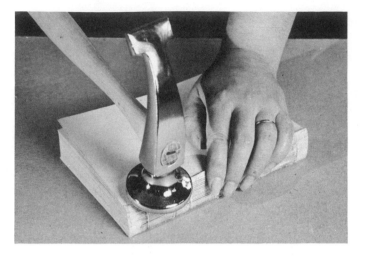

99

100

put on top for an hour or so, until the glue sets.

If the book is to be trimmed, as little as possible should be taken off. Some binders are reluctant to cut or trim edges, for a book can sometimes be ruined this way. They may use instead a little sandpaper for the uneven edges. The book can be cut either in the plow and press, between boards with a chisel, or with a commercial cutter as explained on pages 60-63. The fore edge is trimmed first. For this a pencil line is drawn along the outer edge, parallel with the back edge of the book, indicating the amount to be removed.

When the plow and press is used, the book is lowered into the press and placed between two wedge-shaped wooden cutting boards. The one to the left of the worker is placed level with the book edge. A cardboard is placed between it and the book to keep the cutter blade from jabbing into the cutting board and damaging it when the cutting is completed. The cutting board on the right side is placed at the level of the pencil line where the book is to be cut, level with the top of the press (diagram C, page 63). It is important to see that the bottom of the book is flat and square before the press is screwed tightly.

If the book is to be left with a flat back, as when there are only a few signatures, the head and tail are cut next. Otherwise the back is rounded first. As soon as the glue on the back ceases to be tacky, the book can be placed in a finishing press, extending about 2 inches above the top. If the glue is hard, it is softened and the surplus removed, making it easier to open the book and to round it. It is more important to have the glue between the signatures than on top of them. A moist sponge can be used, or, if the glue is difficult to loosen, the spine can be covered with a thin paste, which will moisten the glue so that it can be removed with a bone folder.

The purpose of rounding is to take care of the extra thickness produced by the sewing. The book is placed on the table with the fore edge toward the worker. It is supported by the left hand, with the thumb against the middle of the fore edge. The right hand pulls on the upper edge of the spine, or the closed fist can be used as a hammer. The book is turned over, the process is repeated on the other side, and this continues, first on one side and then on the other, until an even, rounded effect is produced. When a book hammer is available, it can be used

101

102

in place of the fist. The hammer is dropped onto the book with forward dragging motion (figure 99).

After the back is rounded, the head and tail can be trimmed. A pencil line is drawn where the cutting is to be; using a steel square will keep the book squared. The back of the book is always kept toward the worker when the plow and press is used.

When a book has been rounded, a groove is made on either side of the spine into which the cover board will fit, to give support and keep the back from caving in. This is called "backing." The book is placed between two backing boards made of wood or metal that slope downward on the top. These should extend a little way beyond the length of the book, and the distance from the edge of the spine should be the exact thickness of the cover board to be used. This thickness can be measured and marked at the head and tail ends.

The backing boards, with the book between them, are screwed tightly into the press, extending about 1/4 inch above the top. A hammer is used along the side of the spine with glancing blows in such a way that the edges of the first and last signatures are forced down over the boards to form a ridge (figure 100). This should be done repeatedly until the desired effect is achieved, without destroying the round effect of the spine. If the book slips during this process, lightweight cardboard or heavy paper can be put between some of the sheets.

After backing, the book can be given support by the placing of a cover board on each side up under the ridge that has been formed. If headbands are to be used they can be applied at this time (see section on headbands, pages 70-71).

A piece of bookbinder's super, or one of the substitutes suggested in the section on materials (see page 52), is used to cover the spine to help form a hinge to which the covers are attached. The super is cut about an inch shorter than the spine of the book and wide enough to extend across the back and project 2 inches on either side. A light dilution of glue is applied, and the super is laid on and rubbed well with a bone folder (figure 101).

A piece of brown kraft paper, cut the length of the book and the width of the spine, is applied over the super (figure 102). The paper is dampened with a small sponge on both sides; this will cause it to shrink later and fit tightly. Glue is applied directly onto the paper, which is then placed on the spine and rubbed

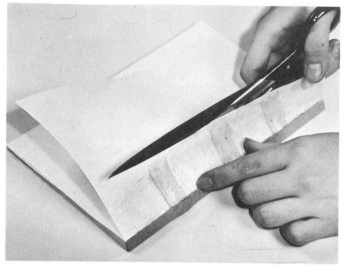

103

104

well. If the book is large and heavy, two pieces of paper can be applied.

There are other ways to build up a smooth back. Pieces of heavy wrapping paper can be cut and glued to fill in the areas between the tapes before the super is applied, or a hollow back can be made, as described on page 148.

After the spine is covered, the book is taken out of the press and the tapes are cut to fit the width of the super extending on either side. Paste is put under the tapes, which are then pressed down onto the outside sheets of the book (diagram K). Paste is put over them, as well as in the area between them, and the super is then pressed down upon them. If the book is bound with a prepared casing, as shown in diagram M on page 76, the pages to which the tapes are pasted can be left uncut and pasted into the cover board as a lining.

If the cover is made directly on the book, as explained in the following directions, these outside sheets, on the top and bottom of the book, to which the tapes and super have been pasted are cut off along the edge of the super to form hinges for attaching the cover boards (figure 103). About ¹/₂ inch of the hinge tabs should be cut off at the head and tail ends (diagram L) in order to facilitate turning the cover material over the edge at the back of the spine, or they can be slit with a knife, as demonstrated in figure 104. Waste paper is put under the hinge tab (diagram L) and after paste has been applied is thrown away and replaced with a piece of clean wax paper. The book is now ready for the cover to be applied.

The cover boards are cut ¹/₄ inch longer than the book and a width extending from about ¹/₄ inch from the spine edge to ¹/₈ inch beyond the outer edge, so that when placed on the pasted hinge they will

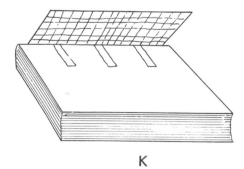

K

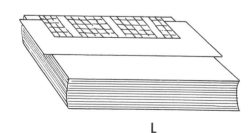

L

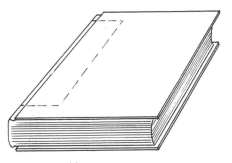

M

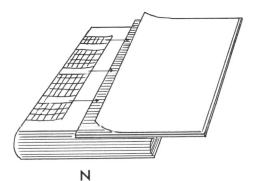

N

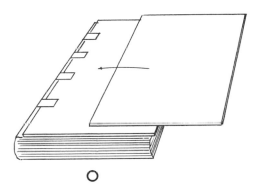

O

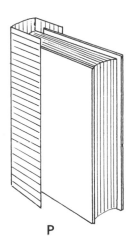

P

be ⅛ inch from all the outer edges of the book. The first cover board is laid onto the hinge tab and held down until the paste adheres to it; then the book is turned over, and the other cover is applied (diagram M).

A very rigid cover can be made by gluing two boards together. This is an advantage especially when the boards used are thin or very light in weight. If two boards of different weights are used, the thinner one is always placed underneath. They can also be different in type: for instance, one might be chipboard and the other a tar board. If the book is small, a sheet of heavy oak tagboard can be used for the underneath piece.

There are two methods of attaching this type of cover to a book. In the first, paste is applied to one of the boards to within 2 inches of one edge, and the other board is placed on top of it. They are clamped together or put in a press until dry. Two other boards are pasted together to form the other cover. When these are dry, the open edge is pried apart, paste is applied to the inside of both boards, and the hinge tab is inserted (diagram N). When both covers are on, the book is put to press until dry. This is called a split-board cover.

In the other method, the hinge tab is pasted down on top of the lower board, or if no super is used, the tapes are pasted down directly onto the board (diagram O). The upper board is then glued over this. This method is simpler, but care must be taken to get the covers on straight.

After the cover boards have been attached, a piece of book cloth is placed around the spine of the book over onto the boards, extending ½ inch or so beyond the book at the top and bottom (diagram P). The cloth is pasted to the boards, but not to the spine, and rubbed down with a bone folder (figure 105).

105

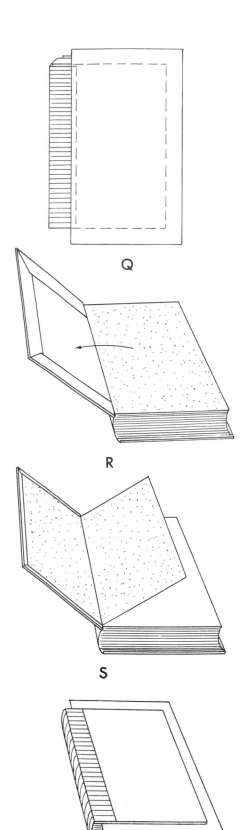

Q

R

S

T

If a stiffer back is desired, a lightweight cardboard, tagboard, or tough piece of paper can be glued to the book cloth before it is put around the spine. The projecting ends of the book cloth are folded over the edges of the cover board, slipped under the book contents, and pasted to the boards (figure 106).

To complete the cover, the cover paper is cut so that it slightly overlaps the piece around the spine and extends out beyond the boards about 1/2 inch on three sides (diagram Q and figure 108). The corners are mitered according to the directions on pages 78-79.

The top sheet is pasted down to the inside cover (diagrams R and S), or the end sheets are tipped in (see the section on end sheets, page 80). Tins or wax paper are put inside each cover to prevent the moisture of the paste from going through the entire book (diagram T), and the book is put to press until dry (see pages 68-69).

When the book is opened it will probably be noticed that there is a gap between the first two sections in the front and the last two at the back. This can be remedied by laying the book open where the second signature begins, placing a piece of wax paper

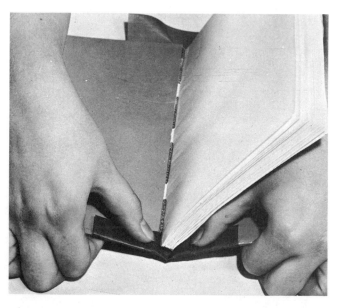

106

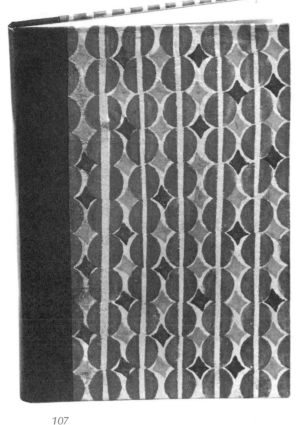

107

or paste paper about 1/16 inch from the fold edge, and applying thin paste very sparingly. The paste paper is removed, and the book is closed. The same process is repeated between the two last signatures, and a light weight, such as another book, is placed on top until the paste adheres. Examples of books made on tapes are shown in figures 107 and 109. Both have cover designs printed with shapes cut from potatoes.

In place of the method described here, a full binding can be used, with the cover material cut all in one piece, as shown on page 74.

108

109

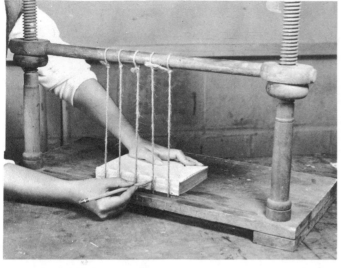

110

111

BOOK MADE ON CORDS

In the cord-bound book the signatures are sewn on cords instead of tapes. The cords are laced into the cover boards, permitting a more flexible type of cover. This method is preferred by the professional hand binder. Unlike tape, which lies flat, the cords can either be sunk in, level with the backs of the signatures, or left raised, standing on top. Many of the early books bound in leather had raised cords on the spine, sometimes built up with several cords, or with pieces of thick cardboard, to make them project more. A thinner cord is used for sunken cords, and the saw cuts are made a little deeper than the cuts at either end for the kettle stitch. Heavier cord is needed for very large books, or the cord can be used double to give more strength.

The signatures are assembled on the sewing frame, and the cords are tied to the rod at the top and around thumbtacks at the bottom in the same manner as the tapes in figure 96. If an adjustable frame is available, like the one in figure 110, the cords are tied to two-pronged brass keys and inserted through a slot near the edge at the bottom of the frame, where they rest underneath the frame bed. The number of cords used varies generally from three to five, depending upon the size and weight of the book.

A line is drawn with a pencil on the backs of the signatures next to each cord, and another about ½ inch from either end for the kettle stitch. The kettle-stitch marks are sawed first (figure 97). If sunken cords are to be used, the other marks are also sawed (figure 111). If raised cords are used, the marks are punctured with a needle. The end-sheet sections are put in place on the top and bottom, and holes are

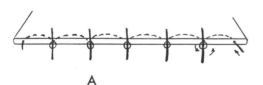

A

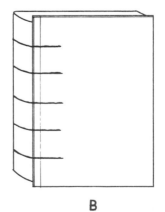

B

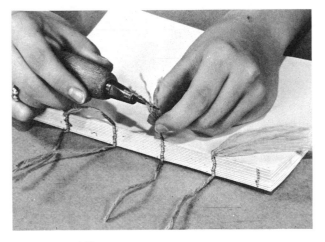

112

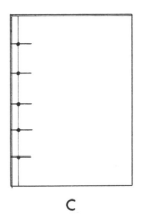

C

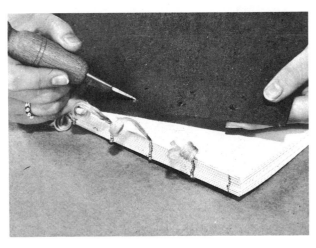

113

pierced in the same position as those in the other signatures. See pages 80-83 for the construction of end sheets.

The sewing proceeds as described for a book made on tapes, except that the thread encircles the cord rather than crossing straight over, as with the tapes. Starting with the hole at the far right end, the thread is brought to the inside of the signature and out again at the left of the cord, over it, and back through the same hole again on the right to the inside. The procedure is continued, each cord being encircled in the same manner, with the result that the thread cannot pull against the paper and cause it to tear (diagram A). When the second signature is sewn, from left to right, the thread is brought through on the right side of the cord first, encircling it by re-entering the hole from the left side.

The kettle stitch is employed at the end of the third signature, as explained in diagram F on page 126, and continued from there on, at each end, until all signatures have been sewn. The cords are cut off to about 3 inches. The book is removed from the sewing frame and put into a finishing press, where a thin solution of hot, flexible glue is applied between the backs of the signatures and left to dry for an hour or so. It is then trimmed if needed, rounded, and backed as described under the directions for a tape book. The strands of the cords are separated and frayed with a sharp point of an awl until they are soft and limp (figure 112).

If possible, the cover boards should be made of bookbinder's board. They are cut to extend 1/8 inch beyond the book at the top and bottom, and 1/8 inch beyond the fore edge when placed close to the joint that has been formed by the rounding and the backing process. A line is drawn or scratched into the board with a pair of dividers, awl, or compass point about 1/2 inch or less from the inside edge. When the board is put into position on the book, the frayed cords are laid on it, and a mark is made where the center of each touches the board (diagram B).

The board is removed from the book, and a line is extended from each of these center marks across the vertical line and at right angles to it. A mark is made where these lines cross the vertical line (diagram C), and a hole large enough for the cord to pass through is made at each mark with a round-pointed awl (figure 113). The board is turned over, and the roughed-up portion of the cardboard on the under-

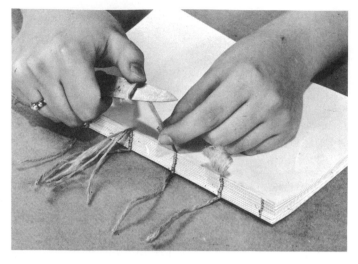

114

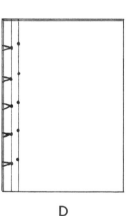

D

115

side made by punching the hole is cut or scraped off with a sharp knife or removed with sandpaper.

Next to these holes on the underside another vertical line is drawn about ½ inch over from the first. Another row of holes is marked on this line placed either higher up toward the head or down toward the tail of the book (diagram D). These are punched through with the awl from the inside, the board is turned over, and again the roughed-up part of the cardboard is taken off.

The frayed cords are now thinned to remove some of their bulk so that they will lie flat when joined to the cover board. This is done with a dull blade, such as that on a bookbinder's knife, which is pulled along the slip as shown in figure 114. The slip should be thinned from around all sides with a gradual tapering toward the end, and care must be taken not to sever it from its roots.

A wedge-shaped groove, in which the thinned cord will lie, is dug out on the cover board from the joint edge up to the first row of holes (diagram D). It is cut with a sharp blade to half the thickness of the board (figure 115). It tapers toward the hole, so that it is the width of the hole at one end and wider at the edge of the board. The slip is fitted into this V-shaped gouge to see if it is deep enough.

A thin dilution of paste is applied to the slips, and they are pulled into points at the ends before being laced into the boards. They are put through the first row of holes (figure 116). In diagram E the laced slips are shown with the board in position. The board is lifted up, and the slips are threaded through the second row of holes (diagram F). They are now again on top of the board and are pulled firmly with pliers or with the fingers to make the board fit snugly in place (figure 117).

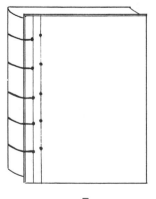

E

The cover on the back is attached to the book in the same manner. The cover is laid flat on a slab, pressboard, or table, and the rest of the book is held upright at right angles. The slips that have been laced into the board are tapped gently with a hammer or mallet in order to flatten them down as much as possible (figure 118). The book is turned over, with the cover lying on the edge of a table and the book suspended, and again the cords are beaten flat.

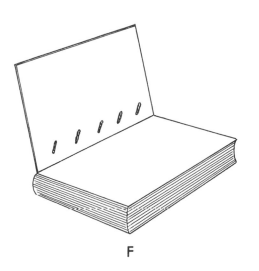

F

117

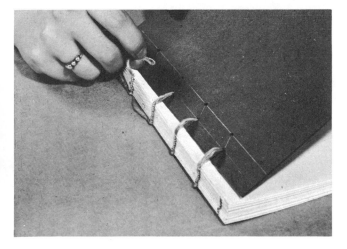

116

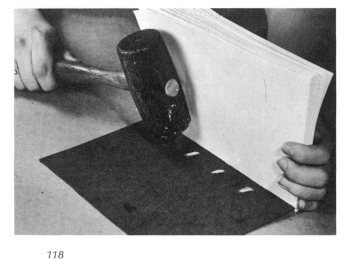

118

The ends of the slips are cut off to about ¾ inch, a little thin paste is applied, and they are fanned out as flat as possible on the cover. An awl and a bone folder can be used to help smooth down the fibers (figure 119).

Unless something like a thick leather is used on the cover board, the cord slips will probably make an imprint through the cover material. In some instances this may not be undesirable for it reveals a part of the structural quality of the book. If a lightweight leather or book cloth is used, however, the imprint may be too distracting. In this case a piece of brown kraft paper the size of the cover can be pasted over the cords before the cover material is applied. If they are still too prominent, the slips can be sandpapered down through this lining paper.

The book is returned to a press, and headbands are put on if desired (see pages 70-71). When the cords are sunken down into the backs of the signatures, a piece of brown kraft paper the exact size of the spine is glued over the back to give a smoother finish. If the cords are raised, smaller pieces of paper can be cut and fitted between them across the spine (diagram G).

The book is then completed as shown under the directions for covering a tape book on pages 131-33. If a leather cover is used, see pages 243-45. The edges of the pages may be colored or gilded if desired. For coloring, the book is put between pressboards and screwed tightly in a press. Water dyes or water color mixed with a little glue for size may be used. The color is applied very thinly with a brush or sponge. Gilding is a more highly specialized operation requiring special equipment, and information concerning this process can be secured from technical sources or professional binding texts.

119

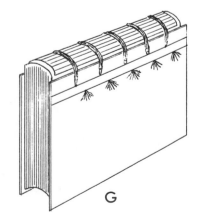

G

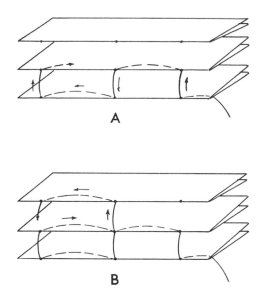

A

B

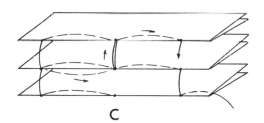

C

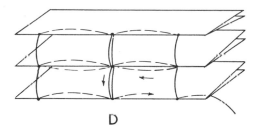

D

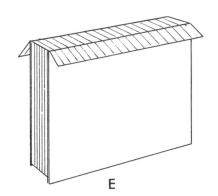

E

Thin books can be made without tapes or cords simply by sewing and catching the threads together as in making the kettle stitch (see diagram F on page 126).

Another method is shown in diagram A, where three or more holes are used with any number of signatures. After the holes are poked for the thread to go through, the sewing is started at the lower right following the position and direction marked by the arrows. The thread follows the fold on the inside, but the connecting threads between signatures are on the outside (diagrams B, C, and D). It is always necessary to move between the holes in the middle marks twice in order to return to the starting point, where the end thread is tied to the beginning tail that was left. The tying is done on the inside.

The example shown in diagram F is similar in plan except that more holes are used. There are an even number of holes, and each unit of two groups of holes is completed independently of the others, producing a neat appearance inside the book. A detail is shown in diagram G. When a book is sewn without tapes, the super is glued to the spine to form a hinge on which to attach the cover boards (diagram E).

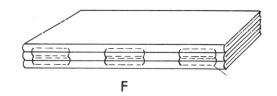

F

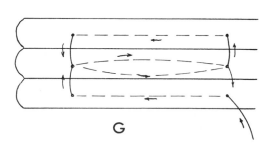

G

SIDE SEWING

Unfolded, single sheets of paper can be bound together by side sewing. A margin of 1 inch or more is desirable on the pages when there is written or printed material that might be blocked off by the sewing.

The stacked sheets, including end sheets (diagram A), are placed between two boards which are clamped in an upright press (diagram B) or a gluing press such as shown in figures 53 or 98. Glue is applied and worked well between the edges of the sheets, and the book is taken out of the press to wait for the glue to set.

Hinges are made with two strips of book cloth, cambric, or muslin cut 1½ inches wide and extending to ¾ inch from the head and tail ends of the book. One piece is placed on the top and the other underneath the glued sheets. A little glue applied along the edge of the sheets next to the back will hold the cloth in place and keep it from sliding. In this way the hinge is tipped on.

Holes are made ¼ inch or less from the glued back edge of the book. A mark can be placed about ½ inch from each end of the cloth flap and in the center, and the space between divided into halves or thirds, or any number of equally spaced divisions can be made. Holes can be stabbed with an awl, punched, or made with a hand drill through both the cloth hinges and the sheets of paper (diagram C). Liquid soap used on the awl or drill will make it go through the paper more easily.

If a drill-press sewing clamp is available, the sheets can be clamped in position and a hand drill used to make holes through the openings in the metal strip (figure 120). The book can also be held in position in the sewing clamp while it is being sewn, or it can be put into a gluing press with the back projecting an inch or so.

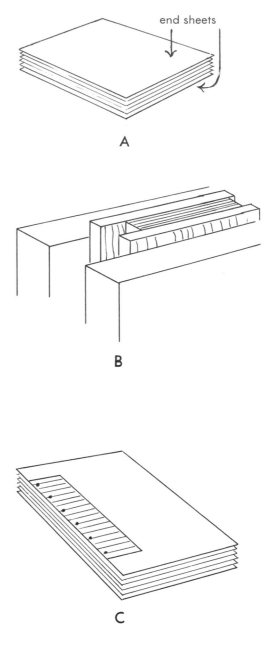

end sheets

A

B

C

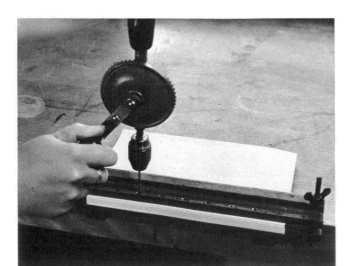

120

For sewing, linen thread or two strands of cotton thread are passed down through one hole and up through the next continuously, until the end is reached, and then returned through the same holes but in the opposite direction (diagram D). This binds the sheets together and makes a hinge of the cloth flaps.

The cover boards can be larger than the book, cut to extend 1/8 inch beyond the top, bottom, and fore edge, or they can be even with the edges of the pages as in diagram J. They are glued to the cloth hinge about 1/8 inch from the sewing (diagram E).

If cardboard is used over the sewing as in diagram F, a strip can be cut from the cover board piece. A strip about 3/8 or 1/2 inch wide is cut off and glued flush with the back to the hinge only, over the sewing. This leaves it free at the top and bottom where the cover material will be turned in (see figure 106). The larger board is glued to the cloth hinge, leaving a space of 1/8 inch between the two boards. If the cardboard is very thick, the distance between should be twice the thickness of the board to permit the cover to open freely. A paste paper is placed underneath the hinge to protect the book pages while the cover is being applied. The spine can be covered with a strip of tough, heavy brown wrapping paper, tagboard, or lightweight Bristol board.

If a cardboard strip is not used, a piece of heavy kraft paper or tagboard can be cut to cover the back with about 3/8 inch extending over onto the sides of the book to cover the sewing (diagram G). If a cardboard is used in this way it should be scored for easy folding with the point of a bone folder or a dull knife. The piece is then glued to the book (diagram H).

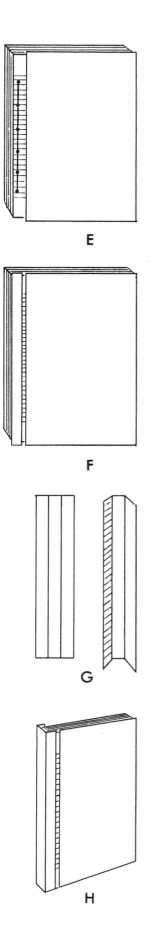

E

F

G

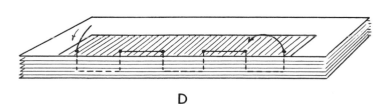

D

H

The cover material is applied as described on pages 74-77 and 131-35. The groove between the boards is emphasized by being gently rubbed with a bone folder. A lining sheet, matching or relating with the end sheet already sewn in, is glued to the cover board with a margin of 1/8 inch from each edge. The book is then put under a weight to dry.

Another way to bind single sheets is shown in diagram I. A piece of book cloth, cut the length of the book and 3 inches wide, is placed around the back and sewn through the side as illustrated in diagram D. A narrow cardboard strip is cut the exact height of the book and glued flush with the back edge, over the sewing. A space of about 1/8 inch is left between this strip and the large cover board, which is glued to the cloth hinge (diagram J). The cloth around the back is cut the same length as the boards and glued to them. It is not folded over at the top and bottom, since there is no room for this. The cover paper can be cut either the exact size of the board, overlapping the hinge cloth about 1/4 inch, or large enough to fold over the edges.

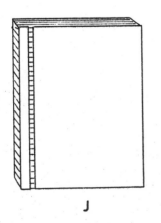

I

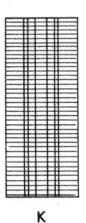

K

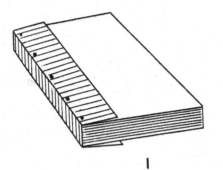

J

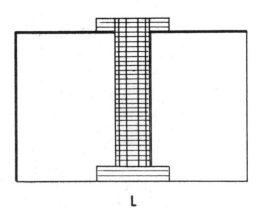

L

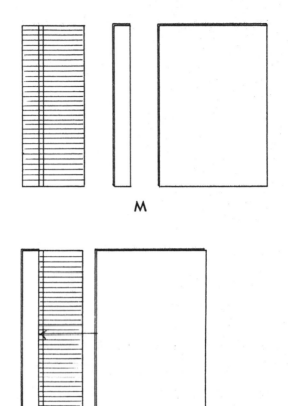

M

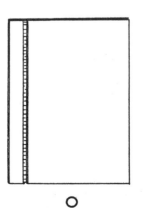

N

The cover can also be constructed like a casing and then attached to the book. A strip of book cloth is cut about 4½ inches wide and 1 inch longer than the book. The width of the spine of the book is drawn down the center of the cloth. The space left on each side should equal the distance from the spine edge to slightly over the line of the sewing on the book, plus an additional ⅛ inch to allow for the thickness of the cover board when the book is opened. These seven divisions are shown in diagram K. The cover boards are glued to the cloth along the lines on the outer edges of the strip (diagram L). The top and bottom edges of the cloth are pasted down, and the casing is glued to the back of the book and over the sewn hinge. It is smoothed down by being rubbed carefully with a bone folder. The cover paper is cut to extend ½ inch at the top, bottom, and fore edge and slightly overlap the cloth strip on the outside of the board. It is folded over, the corners are mitered, and the lining is pasted in.

A hinged cover can be made and attached directly to the book at the time it is sewn. Two pieces of book cloth are cut about 2 inches wide and the length of the book (diagram M). A narrow strip of board is glued to the edge of the cloth with a distance of ⅛ inch left between it and the larger cover board (diagrams N and O). Paste is applied for a width of about ½ inch on the top sheet of the group stacked to be sewn, and the hinged cover is attached to it. Holes are drilled or stabbed through the small board and the sheets (diagram P), and the sewing is completed through them (diagram G, page 144).

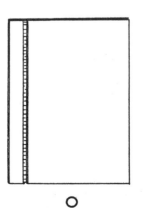

O

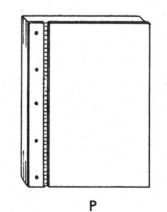

P

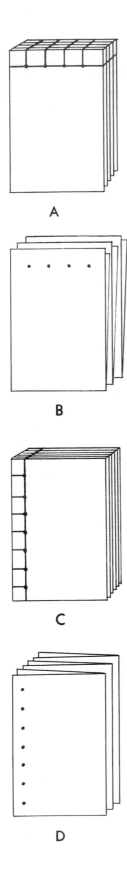

A

B

C

D

JAPANESE BINDING

In this method of binding, originally developed in China, the lacing that holds the sheets together serves also as a decorative unit. Thread, cord, string, yarn, tape, raffia, shoestrings, or rope fiber can be used. If the material is thin, several strands can be used together. The sheets of paper are folded, and the fold edge is placed on the outside opposite the sewn edge (diagrams B and D). This makes each page double and gives added strength; however, single sheets can also be used if desired. Holes can be pierced as close to the edge as $1/4$ inch or as far from it as $3/4$ inch or more, to fit the size and character of the book. They can be made with a darning needle, an awl, a small hand punch, or a hand drill, depending upon the thickness of the lacing material. In figure 121 the book is being punctured by twisting motions with an awl, while the pages are clamped with a clothespin to keep them from slipping.

The cover, which is also folded, can be of the same material as the sheets or somewhat heavier but still flexible enough to open easily. If a stiffer cover is desired, a piece of lightweight cardboard or oaktag can be inserted after the lacing is completed (diagram J). The lacing can be at the top (diagram A) or the side (diagram C), and the spacing of the holes can be equidistant or irregular.

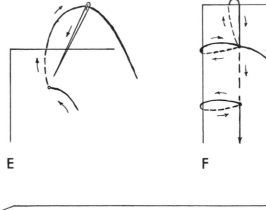

E   F

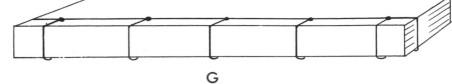

G

After the sheets are stacked and holes are made, the lacing is started near one of the ends. The needle is pushed through the hole, and the thread is brought up around one of the edges and pushed through the same hole again (diagram E). It is then brought around the adjacent edge and again pushed through the hole. The next hole is then entered, and as the thread encircles the outside edges it is continued along until the opposite end of the book is reached (diagram F). Dotted lines indicate where the thread passes underneath. It is then returned, moving in the opposite direction through the same holes again to the beginning hole, where it is tied two or three times (diagram G). The knot can be hidden on the back of pushed down into one of the holes.

A method for covering the spine is shown in diagrams H and I, where a stiff piece of paper is extended around the back of the book and over onto each side about 1 inch. This piece is inserted into a folded paper cover, and together they are laced in with the book pages (diagram H). It may also be slipped into the open ends of the folded cover after lacing, and pasted to it (diagram I). In this way two different papers of contrasting textures or colors can be used.

In diagram K the cover is made of a sheet of stiff paper folded so that one edge protrudes an inch or so beyond the other. This permits one edge to be sewn and the other to swing free. The first page of

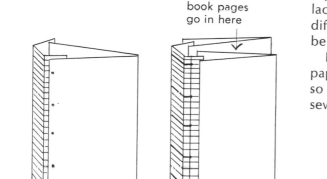

book pages
go in here

H   I

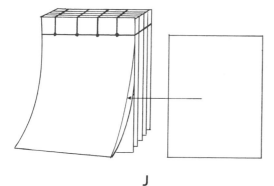

J

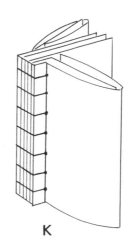

K

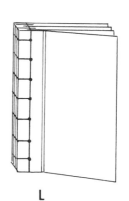

L

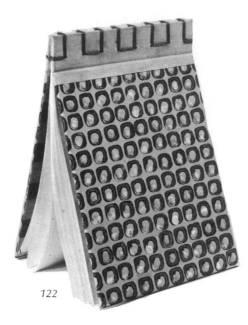

122

the book can be inserted within the opening if desired. The part that folds back can be cut to any width desired.

For a hard-cover book, refer to the procedures for making a scrapbook in which the cover is hinged with two pieces of cardboard (pages 104-5). Holes can be drilled or punched in the narrow cardboard strip, and the holes for the paper marked through these holes in the board so that they will coincide; or the book can be put into a drill press and the holes drilled through the board and the paper at the same time. The lacing is then completed as in diagram L. Finished examples with potato or eraser print designs on the covers are shown in figures 122, 123, and 124.

123

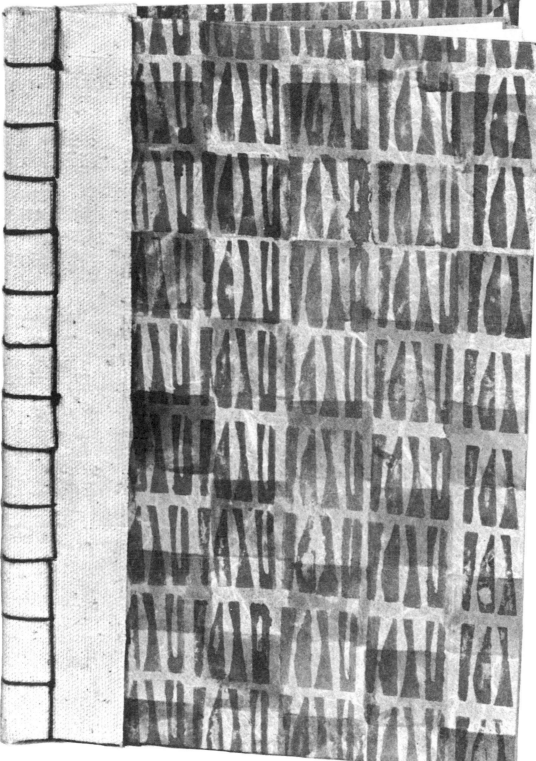

124

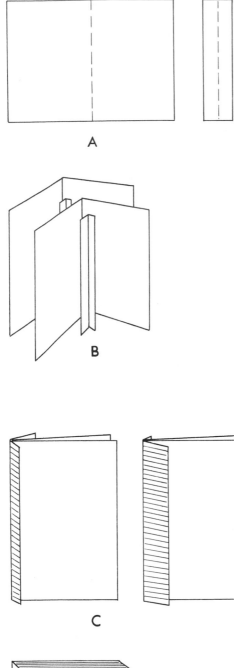

A

B

C

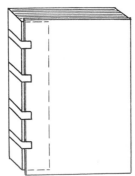

D

STUB BOOK

If a book is to be used for mounting material on its pages that will add to its thickness, stubs can be sewn between the folios to allow for expansion and prevent swelling at the open edges.

When a single-signature book is made, a stub can be inserted between every two folded sheets (diagrams A and B). If several signatures are used, the first one should have two sheets with one stub between them, and the next two sheets with a stub between and one behind, alternating all the way through, to avoid having two stubs come next to each other.

Instead of using super for a hinge, a piece of book cloth about 1½ inches wide and the length of the book can be wrapped around the first and last signatures and included with the other signatures as the book is sewn on tapes. This piece should extend about ¼ of an inch around the signature with the rest on the top or outer side, leaving enough for a hinge to which the cover boards can be attached (diagram C). The tapes can then be glued to the outside of the board, and the entire board covered with a piece of heavy brown kraft paper. The hinge is glued to the inside (diagram D).

For a flat, smooth appearance on the back of the spine, when the cover is made a piece of lightweight cardboard or paper can be cut the length of the spine and three times its width. It is folded in thirds vertically. The middle third is glued to the back, and the outer ones are folded over onto it, but not pasted. The cover is then finished in the usual way.

Short stubs can be sewn (diagram E) by the method described for a single-signature book on page 122. Single sheets can then be pasted to the stubs.

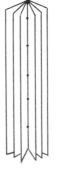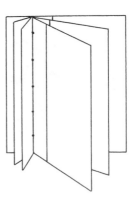

E

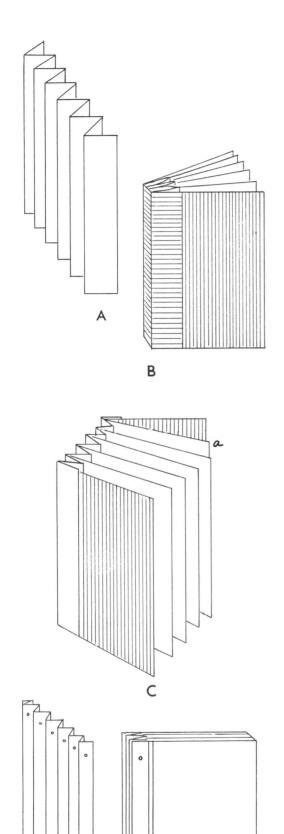

A

B

C

a

D

REVERSE-FOLD BOOK

Single sheets can be bound without sewing by being attached to stubs made from a strip of paper folded into accordion pleats. A piece of heavy wrapping or kraft paper is folded into strips approximately 1 inch wide. The paper is creased in half several times until the desired width is obtained, and the folds are reversed to make pleats (diagram A). A 12-inch sheet of paper folded into 1-inch strips will provide for the insertion of five single sheets or ten double ones.

When the pages are put in, each sheet is pasted to one side only of each of the pleats. If a folded sheet of paper is used, there will be twice as many pages (see *a* of diagram C).

To make the cover, a sheet of colored construction paper the same length as the pleats and the width of the pages is inserted into the end fold of each of the outside pleats (diagram C). The pleats are collapsed flat, and another piece of construction paper of contrasting color, approximately 4 inches wide, is put around the back and pasted to both covers (diagram B). This holds the book together.

If a hard cover is desired, the boards are cut ⅛ inch larger than the book pages at the top, bottom, and fore edge and covered with a plain or decorated paper. The paper is turned around the edges, and the corners are mitered. The cover is then pasted to the outside of the folded pleats, rather than on the inside of the fold as with the soft cover, and a strip of paper or cloth is put around the back as in diagram B.

For still another method of putting a cover on a reverse-fold book, a casing is made with a hinged cover, either extending around the back of the book or on the sides only (diagram D). To make a cover with a side hinge, refer to the directions for scrapbooks on pages 104-5. Holes are punched in the narrow strip of the cover board, continuing on through the fold stubs, and a cord is used to tie them together. In this way the cover can be fastened to the book without gluing or sewing.

Lightweight books composed of single sheets glued together at the back, like many of the inexpensive paperback books, can be bound simply by gluing super to the back to form a hinge. If the glue is strong, the hinge will usually hold sufficiently.

SAW-KERF BINDING FOR SINGLE SHEETS

The term "kerf" refers to a cut, and in saw-kerf binding cuts are made in the back edge of the book. This method can be used for old books that are in too bad shape to be sewn for rebinding, for paper-back books composed of single sheets glued together in the back, for old magazines, or for a group of single sheets. A gummed-back scratch pad purchased at a stationery store can also be bound in this manner. Books bound by this method will not lie flat when open as do those bound with sewn signatures.

If gluing is necessary, the book is placed between two heavy cardboards or book boards and clamped in a gluing press. The back is glued as previously explained for single sheets on page 140. End sheets can be included at this time or tipped in later. The book is removed from the press and left until the glue is dry.

When the cuts in the back are to be made, the book is returned to the gluing press and positioned so that it projects slightly above the edge of the press. If no press is available the book can be placed so that about ¼ inch of the back projects over the edge of a table and held in position by means of a board or strip of wood on top clamped to the table with a C clamp. Cuts are made with a small saw such as a coping saw, if thread is used, or a fine-toothed saw like a hack saw if cords are used. The cuts are made so that they are straight across the back at right angles but slanting as they go downward, to the depth of ⅛ inch. For this the saw must be tipped a little. These cuts are referred to as dovetails.

Cuts can be made as in diagram A, starting ¼ inch

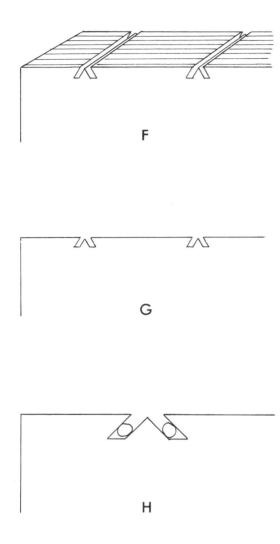

F

G

H

from the end and alternating ¼-inch and 1-inch spaces across. A cross section is shown in diagram B. Glue is put down into the cuts; then a strong linen thread is inserted and woven around the sections to hold the pages together. Each group of cuts is circled as shown in diagram E. Starting at *a* and leaving a tail projecting, the thread is brought through to point *b*, over to *d*, across to *c*, and back to *a*. It is returned to *b*, brought over to *h*, then to *g*, to *e*, to *f*, and over to *l*. It goes through *l* to *k*, to *i*, to *j*, and back to *l*. From there it goes through *k* and back to *e*, where it again circles around *f*, *h*, and *g*, and back to *a*, where it is tied. Glue is again put into the cuts where the thread has gone.

A piece of super is glued to the back, a casing is made according to the directions on pages 76-77, and the book is inserted. Cords can be used instead of thread, and the cuts can be spaced in various ways as in diagrams C and D. The cuts can also be made across the back as shown in diagrams F and G by starting ½ inch from each end and spacing about 1½ inches apart. At each mark two cuts are made, slanting in opposite directions. Glue is worked into the cuts, and two cords each 4½ inches long are worked into each cut opening so that approximately 2 inches of cord project on each side. Diagram H shows a cross section, and diagram I shows how the cords extend outward after having been laid in the glued cut. Glue is applied to the back, and a piece of super is put on. The cord slips are cut in even lengths, frayed out, and glued down to the top sheet or end paper (diagram J). The super is glued down on top of the slips as explained in the directions for the book made on tapes, and a cover is then applied.

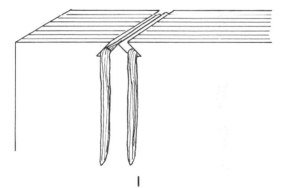

I

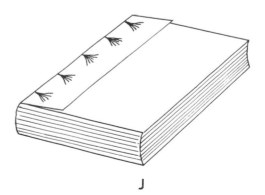

J

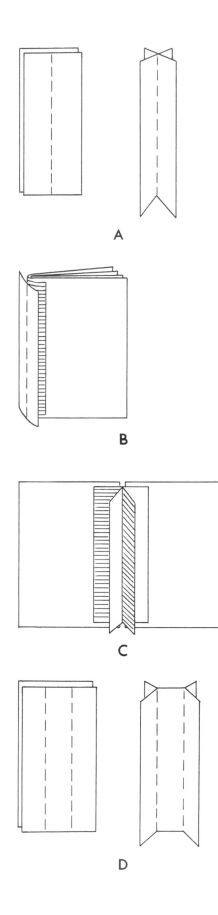

A

B

C

D

PAMPHLETS

Pamphlets, catalogues, music scores, and books of a similar nature can be bound with pamphlet binders made of hinged cloth tapes. Commercial binders are made of gummed cloth stitched down the center (diagram A) or on each side of the center (diagram D). Binders can also be constructed with two pieces of cloth like cambric, muslin, or book vellum stitched together on a sewing machine.

These hinged tapes are glued to the back of the pamphlet (diagram B), and cardboard covers are glued to the extra flaps. In diagram C the binder is glued to two cover boards, after which the pamphlet is inserted. Single-stitch binders are generally used for pamphlets up to 3/16 of an inch in thickness, and double-stitch binders for those 1/4 inch thick or more. The double-stitch binders are available in widths to fit the backs of books in 1/8-inch variations beginning with 1/4 inch up to 2 inches, and 1/4-inch variations from 2 to 3 inches.

A pamphlet can also be bound like a single-signature book, as shown on pages 122-23. The staples are removed from the back. End sheets are either tipped on with paste or cut double the size of the pages, wrapped around the back, and sewn in with the pages along with a piece of cloth to act as a hinge. The binding is completed with the addition of cardboard covers and whatever decoration or labeling is desired.

When a considerable number of pamphlets are being bound, a "cradle" (figure 125) can be used for making holes. After the staples have been removed, the pamphlet is laid in the trough and holes are stabbed with an awl.

125

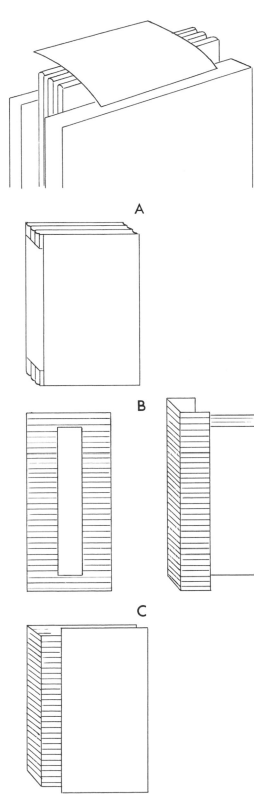

A

B

C

D

MAGAZINES

Magazines can be bound singly or together in a series to form a book. If a year's edition is desired, and the combined weight is too heavy, the series can be broken up into two or three parts and each part bound separately.

Covers and any advertising material not wanted are removed. The magazines are stacked in correct order and put into an upright press. If no press is available they can be laid on the edge of a table with the backs protruding slightly over the edge and a weight like a brick placed on top to keep them in position.

A strong, hot glue is applied to the backs and permitted to seep between the magazines to hold them together, or an adhesive called padding cement can be used for this purpose. While the glue is still moist, a piece of super about 2 inches shorter than the magazines and approximately 4 inches in width is put on the back (diagram A). If the magazines are rather heavy, a flannel-backed super or white outing flannel can be used for more strength.

When the magazines are of different sizes they may have to be trimmed before being bound. Cover boards are cut the same size as the magazines or slightly larger and are glued to the hinges made by the super. A space of ¼ inch is left between the edge of the spine and the cover board to allow the cover to open (diagram B).

To produce a smooth back, a piece of cardboard the width of the back and the length of the cover boards should be glued to the cover material (diagram C). If book vellum is used around the spine, another kind of cloth or paper can be combined with it and either decorated or left plain (diagram D). Directions for applying cover material are found on pages 74-77.

For a quick way to bind magazines together without a cover, stack them in order in a book press or on a table with a weight on top. Apply a good amount of hot glue, padding cement, or a plastic adhesive to the spine. After this has dried, apply another coat of glue. A label can be pasted on the back later if desired. If the glue remains tacky, a coating of wax can be put over it.

Decorated Papers

There are many ways of decorating papers that can be used for covers and lining sheets in the making of books, portfolios, scrapbooks, and similar projects. Such papers, whether simple or complex in plan, can be pleasing if they are considered from the standpoint of design. When shapes, colors, and values are organized in proportional relationships, and the units are repeated in some kind of directional plan, a pattern is produced. Patterns may be geometric and formal in organization or casual and free, but regardless of plan there must be evidence of some selectivity and ordering of parts so that pleasing relationships result.

Although the type of design that is applied to the flat surface of a book paper is primarily decorative in character, it should also be structural in the sense that it contributes to a well-organized whole. The making of decorative papers is more than a technical performance. It is an esthetic experience. If the papers are stilted or lacking in feeling for fine space relationships, they will serve no useful purpose in the design of a book.

Design is based upon a knowledge of the elements of art, for it is through a sensitivity to line, shape, color, and texture that artistic quality is achieved. Line is used to show direction and to define the contours of a shape. It should be limited in its movement so that unity will be achieved without producing monotony. Organization takes place as the artist limits and selects from the various elements, and he has to feel what is right for a given spot.

Color is one of the most important elements in the design of decorated papers, and there should be an opportunity to work with it so that various relationships can be tried. One hue can be mixed with another to produce a new one, values can be changed with white or black paint, and the brilliance of a color can be reduced by the addition of a complementary color or gray. A reluctance to put unusual colors together can be overcome if a spirit of adventure is allowed to prevail. It is helpful also to look at beautiful color relationships in the works of artists in order to develop an appreciation for the many possibilities of color usage.

Texture, a quality of the surface of a material, can be simulated in design so that a great variety of effects can be obtained. Examples of textural treatments can be seen in some of the decorated papers presented in this book.

A number of different processes for decorating papers are presented and described on the following pages, showing possible directions that can be taken for achieving original designs. An effort has been made to keep an awareness of esthetic qualities foremost at all times. Whether one is working with finger paint, printing with simple objects, mixing oil paint on top of water, or rubbing papers on rough surfaces, he needs to be conscious of rhythm and movement, dark-light contrast, pleasing color surprises, shape relationships, various textures, and all the factors that grow from personal expression into an organized form. Only from much experimentation and planning can creation take place. Any one of these methods can be explored to the fullest for interesting results, depending upon the imagination of the designer. A spirit of adventure and excitement must prevail as ideas are explored and developed or discarded. It is by this means that a real creative experience takes place and art values are grasped.

Although the principles of design are employed as the basis for creating, there is also a personal element involved in the process that makes a production a work of art. It is this personal sensitivity that is important in any creative work.

Time must be provided for experimentation with all kinds of materials such as those suggested under the various processes described. There should be opportunities to take these methods and explore their possibilities to the fullest degree to see what discoveries can be made. Teachers should provide students with the means for working and allow them freedom, within the limitations of the medium, to try their ideas. Many results will no doubt be discarded, but they should be considered as experiments and part of the process of creating. The best of what evolves can be chosen and applied to appropriate problems.

As the principles of design are put into practice and patterns are produced, the matter of scale must be considered. A large, overwhelming design would be out of proportion on a small book, whereas a small, subtle pattern might seem weak and be lost on a large surface. Large designs on small books often appear fragmentary.

Generally, when a decorated paper is used on the cover of a book, the lining sheet is kept plain or fairly simple but related in color or some other way to the outside. The reverse is true when a highly decorated paper is used as the lining sheet. This does not mean that both cover and lining cannot be decorated, but that they should have a complementary relationship and not compete or conflict in purpose or intent.

Various papers can be tried for this work. Perhaps the most generally serviceable is kraft or butcher paper. These come in rolls of which a plentiful supply can be kept available, and they are flexible and responsive without being deli-

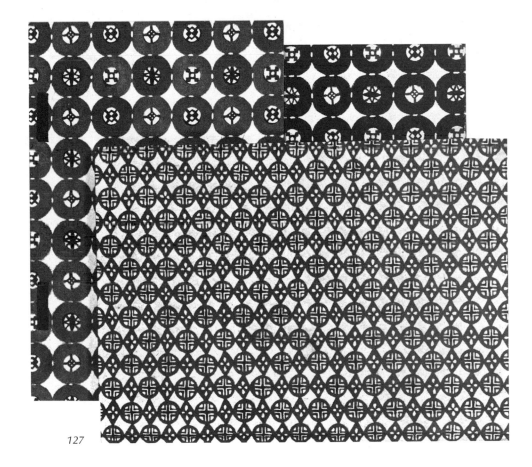

127

cate or easily destructible. Other papers should also be considered: for example, interesting and unusual results can often be obtained with vividly colored Japanese papers, rice papers, colored poster and construction papers. Even inexpensive newsprint can be used for many school problems.

Sometimes well-designed commercial papers will be found in stores or catalogue sample books, and occasionally good examples are seen among gift wrapping papers. Printed papers imported from Japan and Italy are generally attractive and distinguished by a restrained use of color and shape. If commercially made papers are used, discrimination in selection must be exercised in order to maintain standards of artistic quality. Such papers should be abstract in design, for pictorial elements are likely to be weak and distracting.

Hand-decorated papers can be waterproofed and protected from soil and fading by the application of a wax coating to the surface. The simplest method is to rub a small piece of paraffin (available at any food market) over the surface, covering a small area at a time. The finishing can be done after the paper has been applied to the book. Melted wax can also be applied to the paper with a brush, or the paper can be immersed in wax or paraffin and then pressed between several thicknesses of newspaper with a hot iron. Book lacquers are also available for this purpose, and shellac, any clear lacquer, varnish, or floor wax can be brushed or sprayed on. A protective spray called Krylon can be used on either paper or cloth.

Many of the processes described for paper can also be used on cloth with textile or waterproof paints or inks.

The designed papers in figure 126 are examples of the outstanding wrapping papers produced by contemporary Japanese artists. They are made by hand according to centuries-old traditions and have a style that is elegant yet simple, with designs that are timeless and beautiful in pattern. The colors used are both subtle and dramatic, often combining black or white with a brilliant orange red or purple blue, or with grayed versions of these as well as muted golds and browns. Simplicity is achieved by the use of geometric shapes based primarily on circles and squares, with some modifications and details provided for interest. A well-balanced dark-light contrast of values gives definition and strength to the entire pattern.

Such papers as these are available from art and Oriental stores, paper companies, and Japanese trade sources. They can be used effectively in many ways, such as on the scrapbook, writing case, and memo pad in figure 127.

The decorated papers in figure 128 are a composite grouping of examples explained in the processes described in subsequent pages.

128

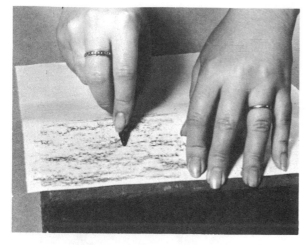

129

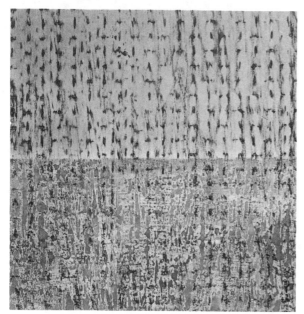

130

131

CRAYON RESIST

When crayon is applied to paper it forms a waxed surface that is resistant to a water medium. If the paper is placed over a rough or irregular surface, such as the brick in figure 129, and rubbed with a crayon until the markings show through, a textural effect is produced. Interest is increased by covering the rubbing with a water-color wash as in figure 130. A search will reveal many objects and materials with defined surfaces suitable for texture rubbings: a stucco wall, a floor, a piece of burlap or painter's canvas, markings on a paper cutter, cedar shakes, screening, bark, and leaves. Rubbings should be made on a number of surfaces so that differences in texture can be studied. Stronger impressions are obtained with lightweight papers like bond paper, kraft paper, or newsprint rather than with heavier or stiffer papers. A consciousness of texture and an awareness of the surface quality of materials develop from such tactile experiences as these.

Figure 131 shows a sheet of paper that has been folded into rectangles, opened up, and filled with a different rubbing in each space. To pull the various textures together, a brush full of paint has been applied across the sections, adding to the richness of the crayon rubbing. The part of the paper retaining the crayon will resist the paint.

Another type of rubbing can be produced with arrangements of cut or torn paper shapes placed in pleasing relationships with one another or overlapped to produce new shapes. A sheet of paper is placed over this grouping and rubbed with one or more colored crayons.

Crayon applied with considerable pressure, as in figure 133, will appear more brilliant when a wash of water color is applied over it. The paint slides over the crayon and adheres to the unwaxed areas of the paper, producing a pleasing and unified effect (figure 134). This method can also be used in combination with potato printing or other processes and media for different results.

In another method, poster paint is dropped or spread on a sheet of wax paper over which a piece of lightweight paper is pressed with an iron. The paint that adheres to the paper can be unified into a pattern with the addition of crayon lines.

In the two portfolios of figure 132 an allover repeat pattern was made with crayons in a controlled and planned design over which a color was applied. The way the paint adheres to the wax in spots in no way detracts from the effectiveness of the design but adds interest. The book in figure 135 is covered with a decorated paper of crayon and applied wash made with a line design that appears quite free and casual, yet has an organized plan.

Crayon shavings cut up into small pieces and dropped onto a sheet of paper can be melted into the paper if it is covered with a piece of newspaper and pressed with a warm iron.

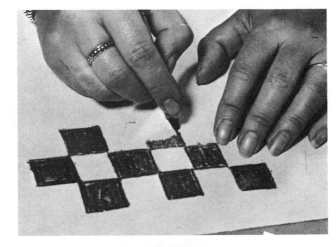

133

134

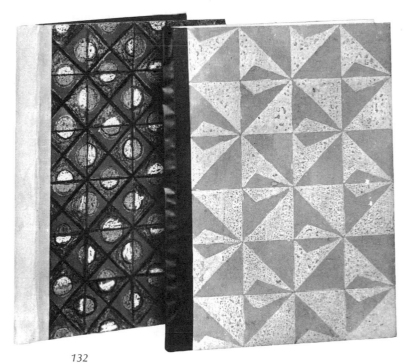

132

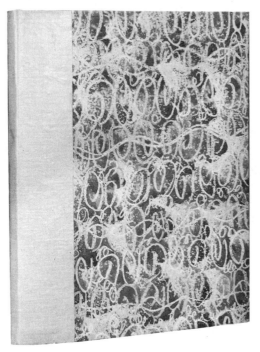

135

136

137

138

WAX RESIST

The wax-resist process is similar to the one used in batik, where hot wax and dyes are applied to cloth. The wax acts to stop out or resist the paint in the same way the crayon does in the crayon-resist process.

Approximately equal amounts of beeswax and paraffin are shaved off with a knife into a pan and heated over a hot plate (figure 136). If a crackled effect is desired, the wax should be more brittle, and in this case more paraffin than beeswax is used. The waxed paper can then be crushed in the hands and paint worked into the cracked areas.

After the wax is melted it is applied to the paper with a brush in lines, spots, and various shapes (figure 137). It spreads on the paper and dries almost immediately, making it necessary to work rapidly. With a little practice, however, designs can be controlled and can be made either casual and free or restricted. A water-color wash is applied over the entire paper, as in the crayon-resist process, and adheres to the part of the paper that is free from wax (figure 138). If more color is desired, part of the paint can be covered with wax again, and a darker color applied. To remove the wax, the paper is placed between protective sheets of old newspaper and pressed with a warm iron.

For colored wax, scrap crayons can be cut up and melted in a pan or double boiler kept on a hot plate. A little turpentine can be added to thin out the mixture if necessary.

Ordinary clear liquid floor wax works well also and is simpler for classroom use since it does not require heating. It can be either brushed on or applied with a shape like a cut potato or nails driven into a block of wood, as shown in diagram B on page 190, which is dipped into the wax and then stamped onto the paper.

Since wax is very hard on brushes, old or inexpensive ones that can later be discarded should be used for this work. Soap and hot water are sometimes effective in getting the wax out.

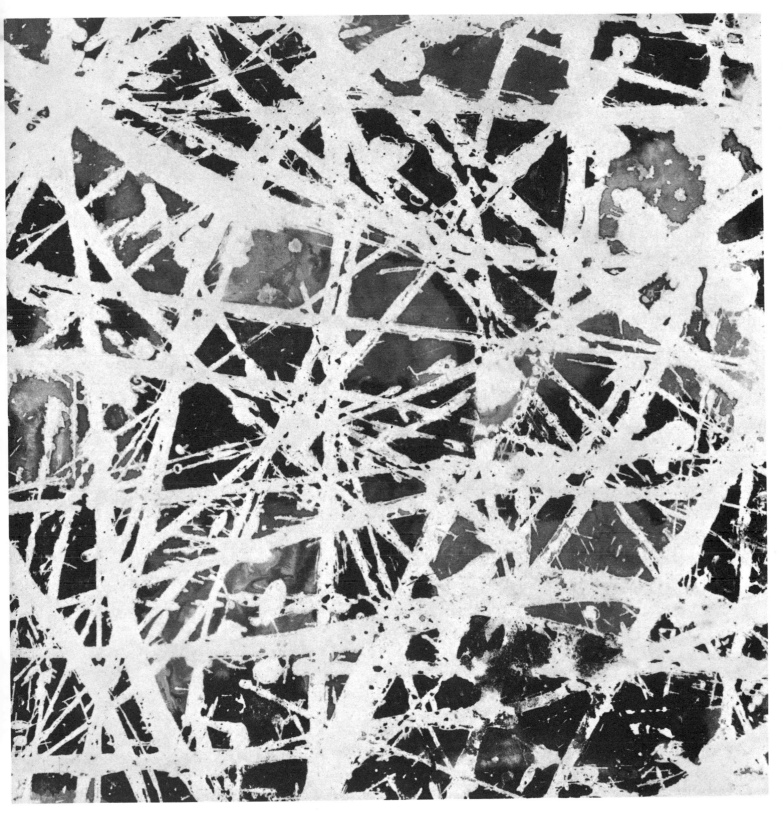

139

163

Wax-designed papers made for book covers are shown in figures 139 and 141, where casual patterns of lines and spots dripped from a brush form rhythmic arrangements. A book covered with a wax-designed paper is shown in figure 140. A more controlled type of design can be seen in figure 297, where the paper has been used in combination with leather. Here the pattern was drawn first on a light-colored poster paper, and wax was carefully applied with a small brush.

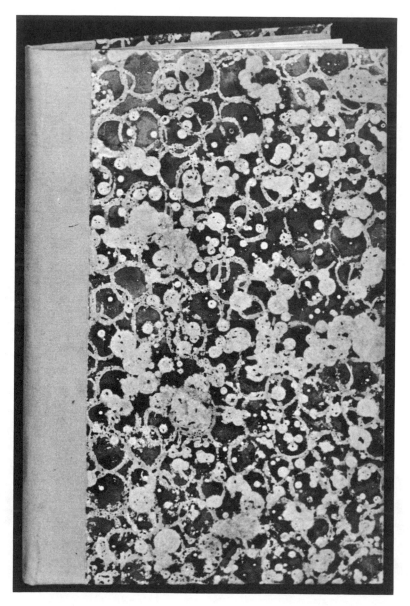

140

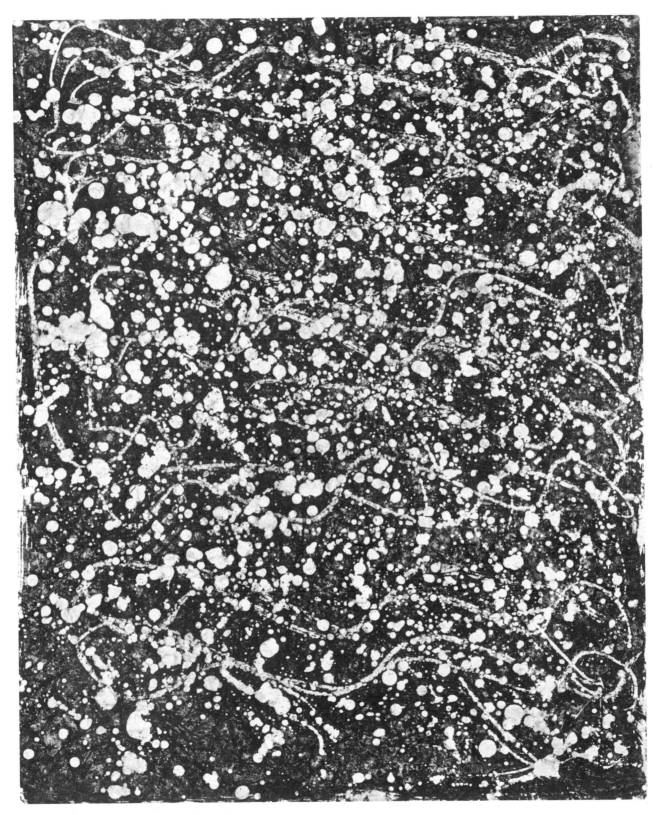

141

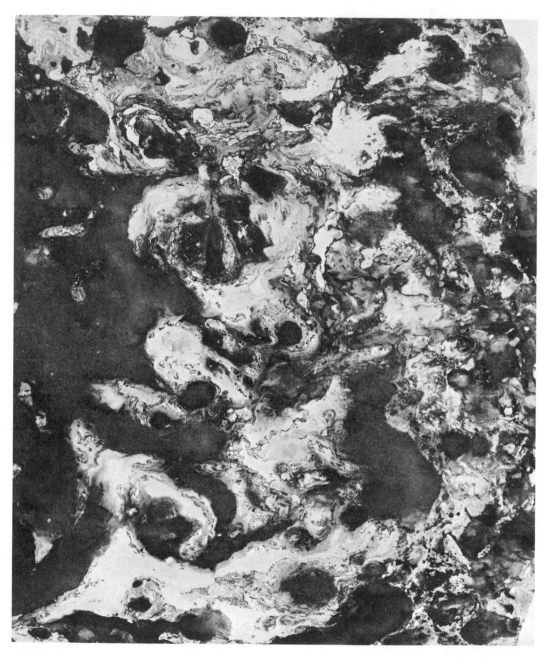

142

MARBLING

For marbled paper effects, colors not soluble in water, like oil paint or printer's ink, are mixed individually in small jars with turpentine to the consistency of thin cream and carefully dropped onto the surface of a pan of sized or plain water (figure 143). A brush can be used for flipping the paint on in small spots. Oil paint can be thinned with an oil medium instead of turpentine. Another type of mixture can be made with three tablespoons of powder paint, one tablespoon of turpentine or paint thinner, and enough varnish to make a solution like thin syrup, or bits of crayons can be shaved and combined with paint thinner or denatured alcohol, allowing thirty minutes or so for them to dissolve.

A shallow trough like a tray or cooky tin is used to hold the water, although a deeper pan can also be used provided it has a wide enough surface on which to lay the paper. If the paints are thinned too much, or not enough, they will either be absorbed by the water or drop to the bottom of the pan. A little experimentation will help determine the consistency needed.

The water is sized by spreading over its surface dissolved glue flakes, mucilage, or a solution of gum arabic or gum tragacanth. Gum arabic must be dissolved in water and cooked for two or more hours in a double boiler. It may have to be strained through a cloth and thinned with water before it is used. Gum tragacanth is soaked in water for several hours until it swells. It is then boiled for several hours in a double boiler, to prevent it from burning. If powdered size is available, it should be mixed according to directions.

The paint on the water is stirred slightly with a wooden stick, spatula, or brush to produce wavy lines and swirls and to form various changing patterns. A comb made by using a strip of heavy cardboard to which has been taped a row of pins with points extending downward about 1/2 inch can also be used for obtaining these effects. A sheet of paper, which may be dampened first if desired, is laid slowly on the water and, when the paint adheres, is lifted up carefully and set aside to dry (figure 144). It is better if the paper can be kept on top of the water so that it does not become engulfed with too much paint; it sinks quickly, however, and must be removed almost immediately. When the sheet is dry

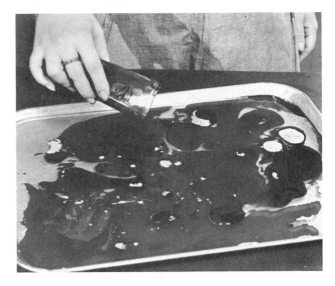

143

144

it can be pressed with a warm iron to flatten it.

Marbled papers can be produced without the use of size. Figures 142 and 145 were made this way, while the example on the facing page (figure 146) was made in a sized bath.

This method of paper design is called "marbling" because the swirls of colors resemble the patterns in marble. It was invented in Persia about five hundred years ago and developed to a high degree of technical perfection by French and English book-binders of the past generation. Examples of its use can be seen in many old dictionaries and other books which have marbled lining and end sheets. This type of paper was formerly used for covers on both commercial and hand-bound books.

The technique as developed is not much used in contemporary bindings, but it has possibilities that might be explored. New effects could be produced with this interesting process by using bold patterns of dark-light areas with one or more colors or super-imposing one color over another.

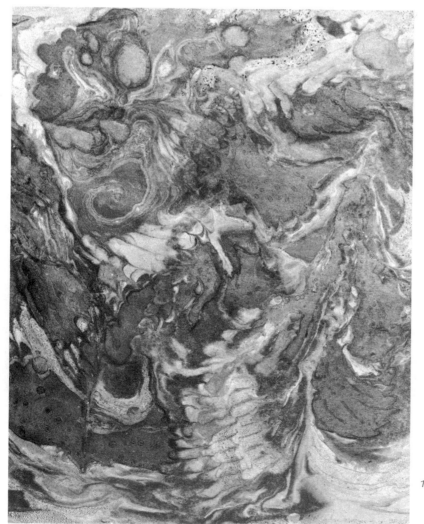

145

146

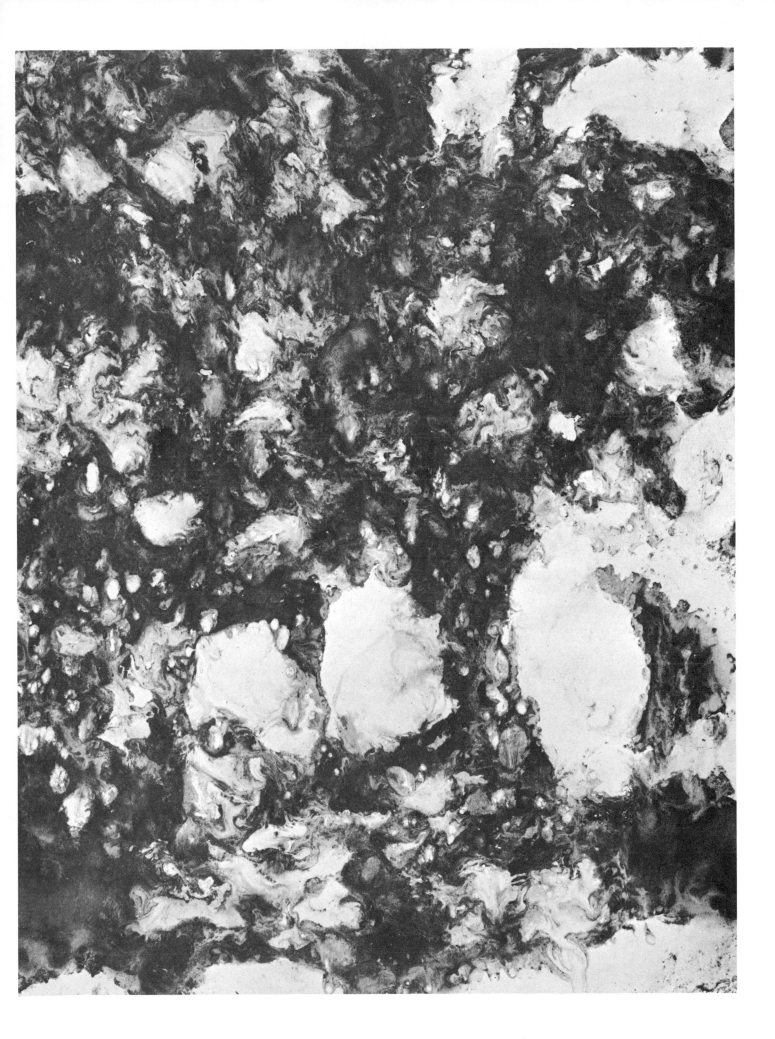

147

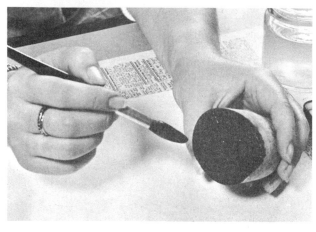

148

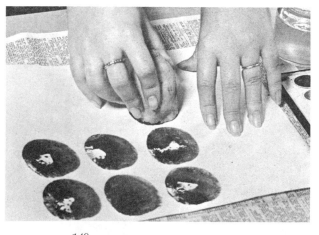

149

150

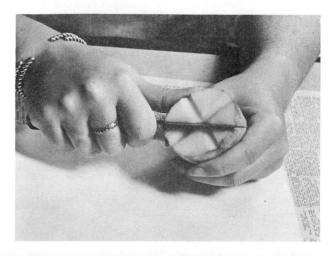

POTATO PRINTS

One of the simplest ways of applying design to paper is with a potato, which can be easily cut and shaped and does not require a great deal of pressure to make a print. A flat surface for printing is produced by cutting the potato straight across or lengthwise with a paring knife (figure 147). Water-color or tempera paint is applied with a brush to the surface (figure 148), which is then pressed firmly onto a piece of paper (figure 149). If a sharp outline is desired, the potato can be rocked a little in order to get pressure on the edges. A rounding shape will result which may be irregular in contour, with interesting textural qualities on its surface resulting from the cut. Do not fill in these spots but capitalize on their pattern, leaving them as they are, for it is important to retain a printed rather than a painted quality.

If the potato is printed in several rows so that the shapes touch one another on all sides, a pattern will be produced (figure 151). The spaces between the prints have a definite form and are referred to as negative shapes, while the print itself is the positive shape. All designs are made up of negative-positive areas. This is one of the most important concepts of art, for it means that all parts are important and there is no such thing as subject and background. The forms are integrated into a unified whole.

Movement and rhythm are created through the repetition of the shapes as the eye moves from one to the other. Dark-light contrast is produced by the tone of the print against the lighter value of the paper, making a pleasing balance of contrasting values.

The quality of texture resulting from the printed potato surface may add variety and eye interest to the design. Texture can also be produced by jabbing and scratching the surface of the potato with a knife, lino cutting tool, sharp pointed stick, back of a pen nib, nail, umbrella ribs, and so forth, and by gouging out parts in a free and casual manner, as in figure 153.

The designer also thinks of the shape of the forms with which he works. In all the examples on page 171 and in the book cover of figure 155 the original shape has been retained in the print, while on some of the following pages the basic shape has been modified and an entirely new form produced.

151

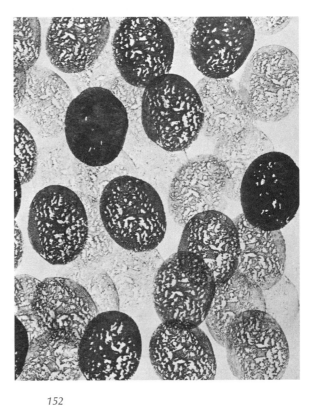

152

153

154

After the formal type of exercise just explained, a more casual approach can be tried by painting the potato and stamping it rapidly and freely several times without re-painting. This can be done in rows or in an informal arrangement, and shapes can be made to overlap one another if desired (figure 152). Instead of a limited dark and light contrast, there are now several tones, making gradations or transitions from dark to light. The effect is different from the more controlled type of pattern, yet rhythm is still experienced through movement and repetition of shape and tone. Simple shapes such as a triangle, circle, or square can be painted directly on the flat uncut surface of the potato, which is then pressed onto the paper, or the end of the potato can be cut in the shape of a square, rectangle, triangle, and so forth.

Parts of the potato can be cut away (figure 150), leaving raised areas upon which one or more colors may be painted and printed at the same time (figures 156-62). Prints may be used singly or in combination with different shapes cut from other potatoes.

Such vegetables as carrots, parsnips, and onions may be found suitable for printing also, with somewhat different effects. A print made with a carrot is shown in figure 154.

Interesting effects can be obtained when this type of printing is combined with other media, as with the wax design on the book in figure 160. The potato print might be combined with a string print or sponge print. Prints can also be decorated with pen and ink, crayon, or brush patterns. Ideas will evolve as methods are explored.

A padding of old newspapers or carpet felt provides a good working surface for absorbing the pressure of printing and reduces the noise resulting from pounding. Hard pounding is really not necessary for it is the pressure that makes the print. Teachers may want to demonstrate this fact to children who sometimes use a little more force than they need.

An inked pad, which can be used for printing in place of a brush, is made by soaking some folded absorbent paper towels or pieces of blotter paper in a small saucer in which there is a mixture of paint or ink, or two or three thicknesses of wool or flannel material may be placed on a tin lid or a plate, dampened with water, and saturated with a heavy mixture of dye, colored ink, or food coloring. A small synthetic sponge soaked in paint or ink will serve the same purpose. The potato is pressed against the pad and then applied to the paper.

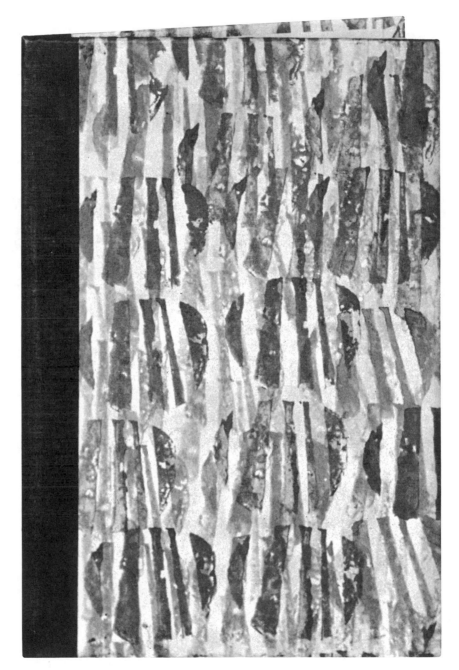

155

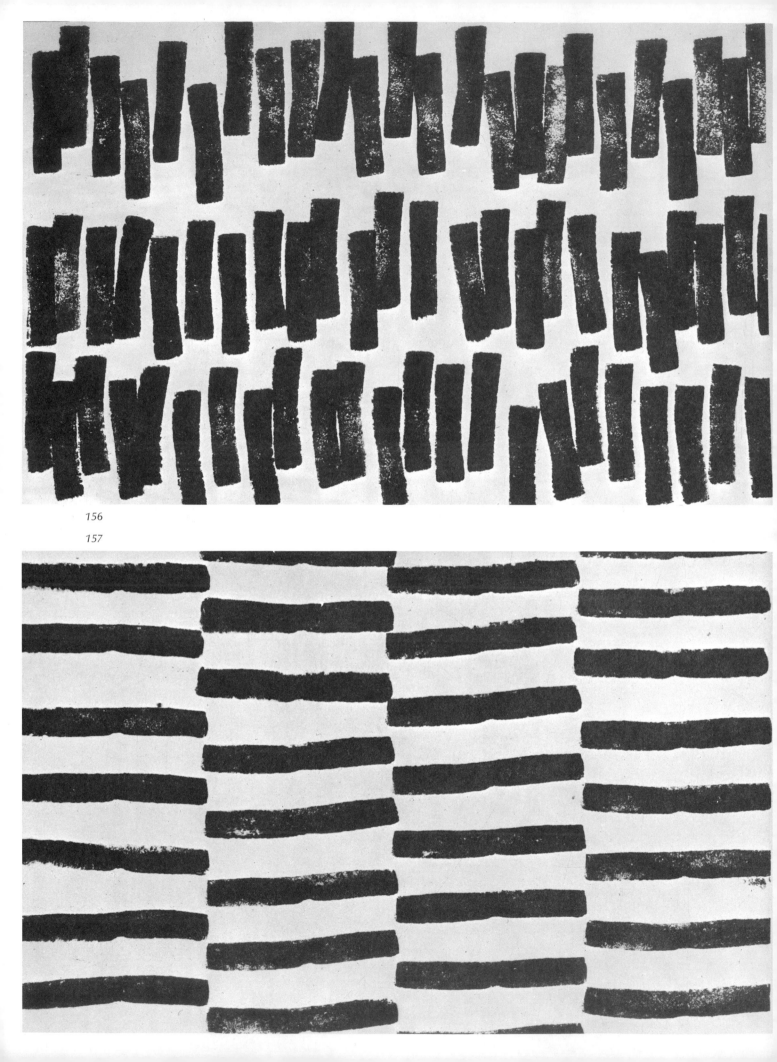

156

157

158

159

175

160

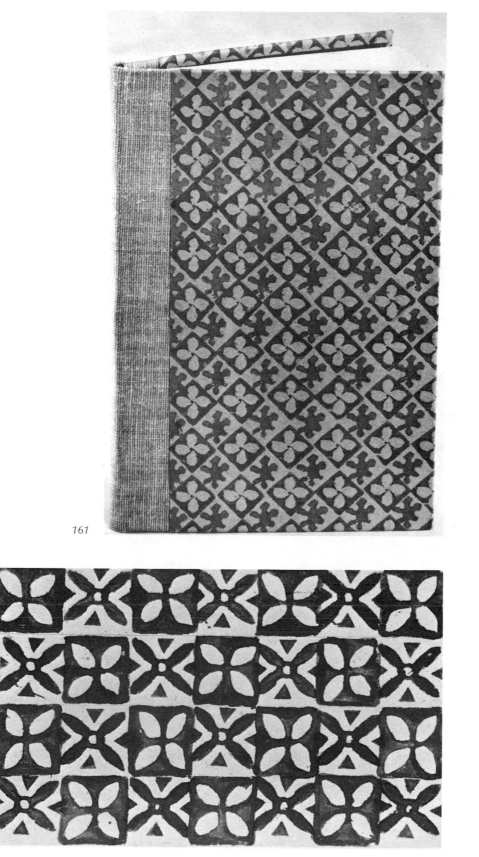

161

162

ERASER PRINTS

Rubber or artgum erasers provide good shapes to use for printing. Contrasts can be achieved with the round shape on the end of a pencil eraser and the square of an artgum eraser; if a long eraser is used, the sides will provide a rectangular shape, making possible more variety in developing patterns.

A small amount of printer's ink is squeezed from a tube onto a hard, smooth surface like a slab of marble, a piece of thick glass, linoleum, vinyl tile, a cooky sheet, or a sheet of tin. Either oil- or water-base ink can be used, but oil gives a richer finish. Inks come in black, white, and various colors.

The ink is spread out by being rolled with a brayer until it is smooth and silky in appearance (figure 163). If a brayer is not available a "dabber" can be made by placing a wad of cotton the size of a fist inside a square of oiled silk (available from pharmacies) or a piece of tightly woven cloth like muslin and tying it snugly with string at the top. This is used to pounce the ink around on the working surface until it has a smooth, even texture. If the ink is not well spread, the print will be uneven and sticky.

A substitute ink can be made by mixing powder paint and clear varnish with a spatula. Oil paint can also be used for printing.

The eraser is pressed onto the inked surface (figure 164) and applied to the paper (figure 165). Various groupings can be tried like those on the facing page (figure 167), where the eraser shape has been used in a number of different arrangements. Other ideas will develop as one experiments. Plain, uncut eraser shapes can produce beautiful patterns of dark-light areas with the use of either black or color.

For variations a sharp knife or razor blade can be used to cut out sections, as in figure 166. Designs

163

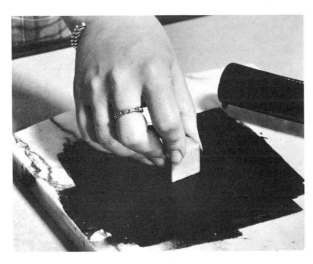

164

165

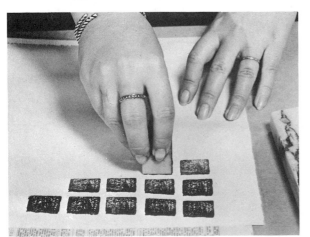

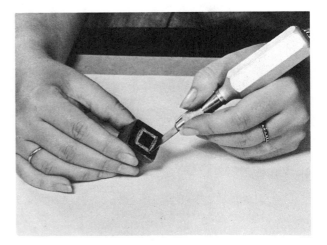

166

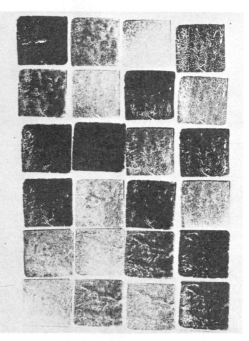

should be simple for the eraser chips easily. Such abstract shapes focus attention on line, color, and dark-light contrasts, with the emphasis upon pattern rather than subject ideas.

The booklets in figure 168 have covers showing the use of the eraser as a design and print medium. The effectiveness of the plain, uncut shapes is demonstrated in the two examples where a simple repetition of the form produces a beautiful result. In the third, a more complex pattern is achieved with shapes that have been cut on both the short and long sides of the artgum eraser. By this means the dark-light accents have been made more prominent. These books are made without sewing or pasting according to the directions presented on pages 118-19. Other eraser print designs made with cutout shapes are shown on the following pages, in figures 169-73.

168

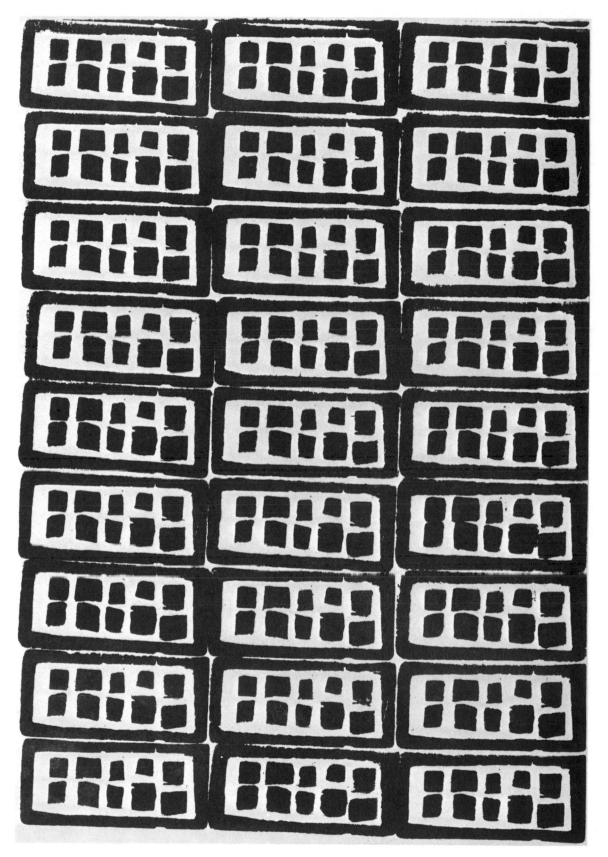

169

170

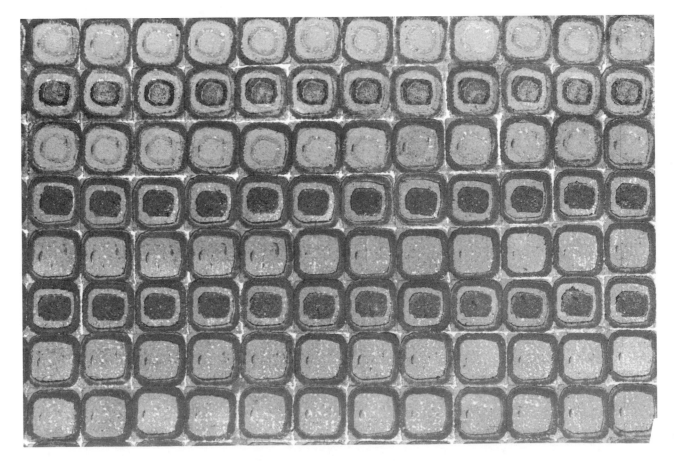

171

172

173

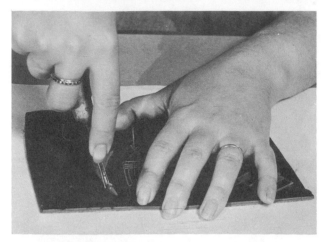

174

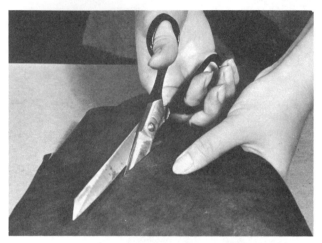

175

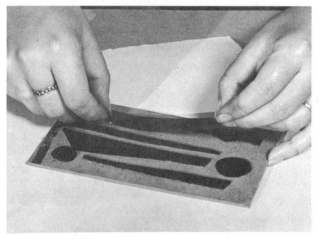

176

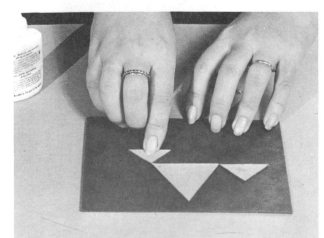

LINOLEUM PRINTS

A linoleum print is made by cutting a design with a gouge, knife, or razor blade in a piece of plain, unmounted linoleum, preferably of the type called "battleship" (figure 174). Oil- or water-base printing ink is rolled out on a slab with a brayer as shown in figure 163 and then rolled onto the linoleum, which is pressed firmly on the paper. The paper can also be placed on top of the linoleum and rubbed with the fingers, a brayer, a bone folder, the back of a spoon, or any hard, smooth object. If a small unit is used, the linoleum can be glued to a cork stopper or block of wood for greater ease of handling. The paper can be slightly dampened with a sponge or brush if desired. Two linoleum blocks with shapes gouged out are shown in figure 178. Prints made from linoleum blocks are shown in figures 180-82. The book in figure 181 is covered with a cloth stamped with a linoleum print.

INNER-TUBE PRINTS

Pieces of an old inner tube can be cut with scissors into various pleasing shapes (figure 175) and glued to a piece of cardboard (figure 176). If any shapes are cut from the center of the design, a sharp-pointed knife will have to be used. The design is printed with ink and brayer. Oil-base printer's ink works better than water-base ink because of the oiled surface of the inner tube. The print in figure 183 was made by placing a sheet of paper on the inner tube block and rolling over it with an inked brayer.

CARDBOARD PRINTS

Cardboard prints are made in the same way as inner-tube prints. If the cardboard is lightweight it can be cut with scissors, but if it is heavy a sharp-pointed knife will be needed. The shapes are glued to another piece of cardboard in a planned order (figure 177). When the brayer is rolled over the raised portions for inking, some of the ink may cover the background also. This can be effective, but if it is not desired the block will have to be inked with care, or the ink wiped off where it is not wanted. An example is shown in figure 179.

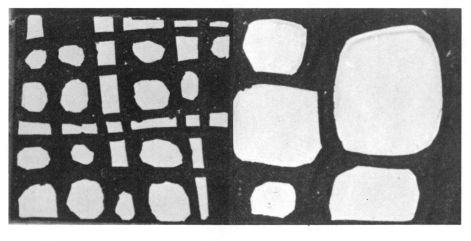

178

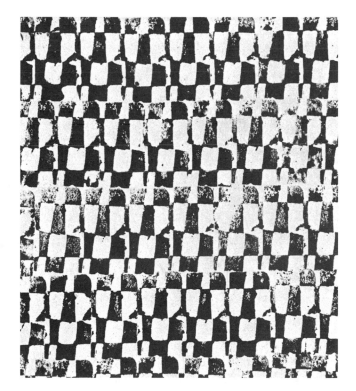

179

180

181

182

183

PARAFFIN PRINTS

Prints are made from paraffin by indenting the soft wax surface with a pointed tool like a meat skewer or pencil. Lines can be either pressed or dug out to produce a pattern leaving raised areas to be printed (figure 184). Only an oil-base printer's ink will work on the wax surface. It is rolled on the paraffin with a brayer, and a print is made by rubbing paper against its surface. The first prints are not always good, but the irregular effects sometimes achieved may be quite pleasing (figure 185).

184

185

SPONGE PRINTS

A fairly coarse sponge dipped in water paint or colored ink will produce a textured print (figure 186). The mixture can be put into a saucer into which the sponge is dipped. Variations are achieved when prints are overlapped or the color is changed (figure 187). Combinations with other media such as crayon, wax, or potato should also be considered; for instance, a block print can be stamped on top of the sponge print.

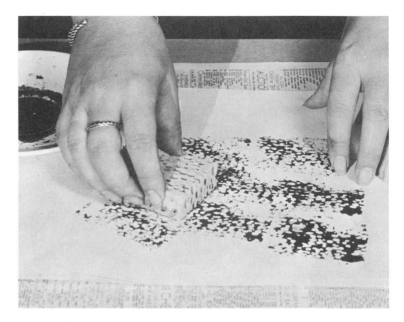

186

187

189

STICK PRINTS

Wooden doweling, spools, old pencils, ends of matches, bamboo, and wood scraps of all sorts are interesting materials to use for stick printing. Simple designs can be made on the end of the stick with a file. Poster paint to which has been added a little wheat paste, glue, or rubber cement is used for printing. This can be painted onto the stick with a brush. Another method is to make a pad with a sponge or small, torn-up pieces of blotter paper placed in a saucer containing paint of colored ink. The stick is pressed onto this for inking and then pressed onto the paper (figure 188). Results will be better if color is used sparingly and the stick is rocked slightly to get a good impression. A pattern using three different sticks is shown in figure 189.

Matchsticks glued to a block of wood form groups of lines that can be used to produce various patterns (diagram A).

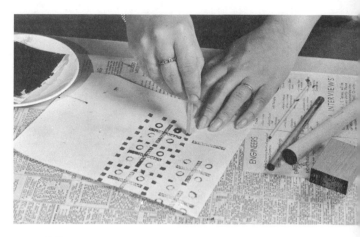

188

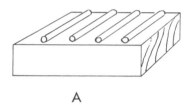

A

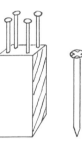

B

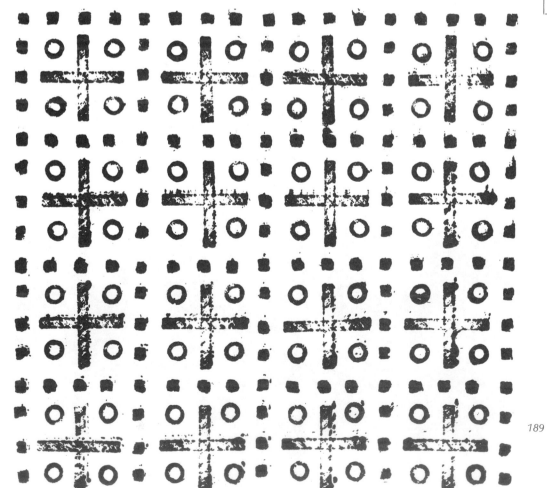

189

190

GADGET PRINTS

Man-made objects, varied in shape and structure, provide source material for many unusual print patterns. Bottle caps, buttons, cork stoppers, forks, and small kitchen gadgets like potato mashers and cream whippers are all good forms to use. They can be dipped into poster paint or into rolled-out printer's ink for printing. A bottle cap is being printed in figure 190, while a wooden fork was used for the pattern shown in figure 191.

Large nailheads can be printed singly or driven into a block of wood and printed as a group. If the nailhead is filed first it will produce a new shape (diagram B). Thumbtacks inserted into a block of wood can be stamped off to make a design.

190

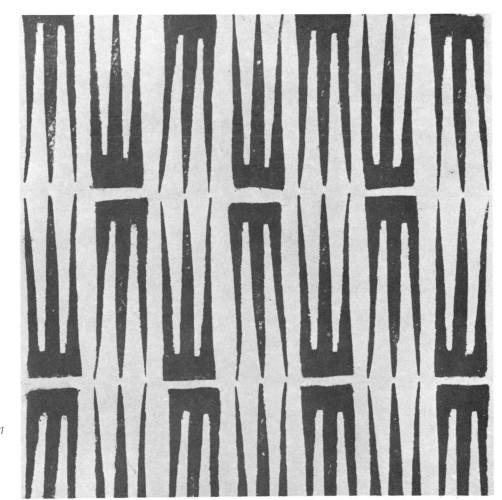

191

Interesting effects can be achieved when an inked brayer is rolled over a piece of paper under which flat objects have been placed. The shapes will be imprinted on the surface. This method is similar to that used for the rubbings on page 160. Such natural forms as leaves, grasses, weeds, and bark make pleasing patterns when used singly, arranged in groupings, or overlapped. One shape can also be printed on top of another.

An example of this method can be seen in figure 192, where a leaf has been placed under a sheet of paper and pressed with an inked brayer so the image comes through. The ink from the brayer will also produce various tones on the paper, resulting in interesting textural effects.

In figure 193 the leaf is being inked directly with the brayer. It is then laid face down on a piece of paper and pressed with either a clean brayer, the fingers, or a hard object like the bowl of a spoon (figure 194).

An inked brayer can be rolled over the surface of a plain sheet of paper first to give it tone, then objects placed underneath, and the paper again rolled with a different color. A leaf print is shown in figure 195, and books covered with leaf prints are shown in figures 196 and 197.

Objects other than natural ones can be used, such as wire screening or cut or torn pieces of paper grouped in arrangements.

192

193

194

196

197

195

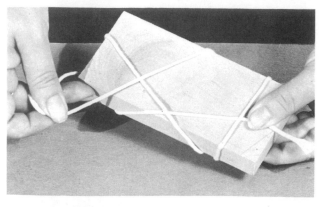

198

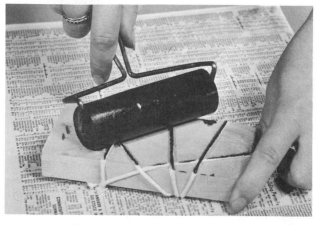

199

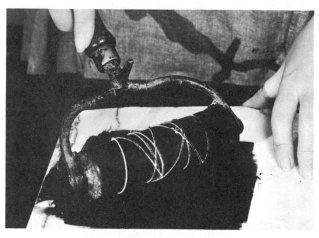

200

STRING PRINTS

With string as a medium for printing, a line pattern is emphasized. The string can be tied around a scrap block of wood as in figure 198, inked with a brayer (figure 199), and then pressed onto the paper, or the paper can be laid on the block and rubbed. The string can also be wrapped and tied around a brayer, which is rolled over printer's ink on a slab (figure 200) and then rolled on a sheet of paper. As the brayer rolls along, the print repeats itself (figure 201). Rolling in different directions and using more than one color result in variations in design (figure 203). In figure 204 the print was stamped from the block several times with each inking.

For more control in shaping the design in a formal arrangement, the string can be glued to a block of wood in the pattern desired and then inked and printed (diagram A).

Although not a string print, figure 202 illustrates a method that is similar in effect. A wooden stick such as a meat skewer, the stick from an ice-cream bar, or a pencil is used to dig out a design on the inked slab. A sheet of paper is placed on top of the slab and rolled with a clean brayer or pressed with the hands.

String prints can be combined with other media like crayon, wax, eraser, or potato prints. The paper can also be rolled first with one color and the string print applied over in a contrasting color.

201

202

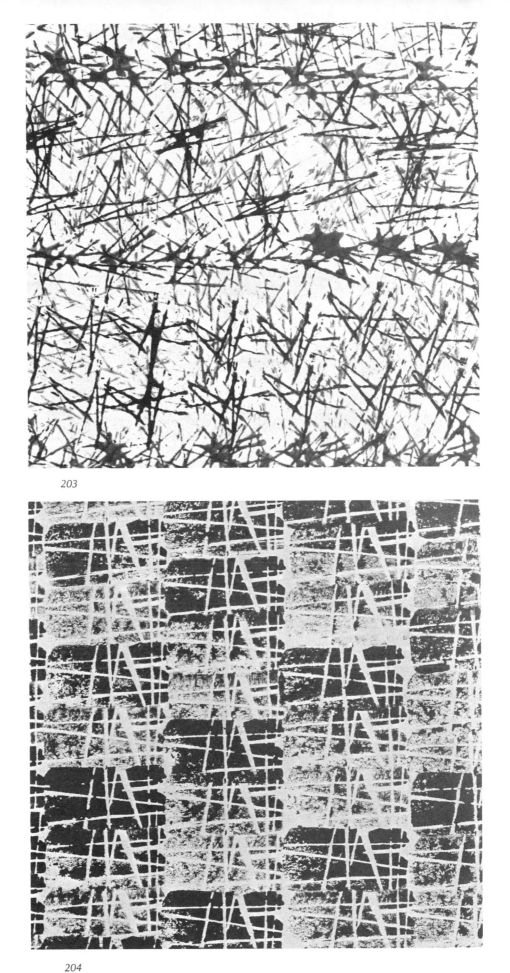

203

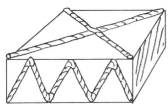

A

204

STENCIL PRINTS

A stencil is made by cutting a shape out of a piece of paper and applying paint through the opening. Lightweight papers such as butcher or wrapping paper can be used, but stiffer papers are easier to handle when printing. A prepared transparent wax stencil paper is available commercially and has the advantage that the design can be seen through it. Old mimeograph backing paper, waxed butter cartons, and tagboard are also recommended.

In figure 205 a stencil is shown being cut out with a sharp-pointed knife. If the paper is light enough in weight to fold, shapes can be cut with scissors as shown in diagram A. The paint is applied very sparingly with a stiff-bristled brush by starting at the edges of the cutout opening and working from on top of the stencil paper into the open area. This prevents the paint from seeping under the cut edge and leaves a sharper outline (figure 206). The paint can also be applied with a spray gun, or by rolling an inked brayer over the opening (figure 207). Either water colors or dyes can be used.

In figure 208 a strip of stiff cardboard is being used as a stencil edge, and a stiff stencil brush is being pounced up and down off the edge of the cardboard. If the paint is kept thin and used sparingly a stippled effect is achieved.

An example of a print made from a simple stencil cut is shown in figure 209.

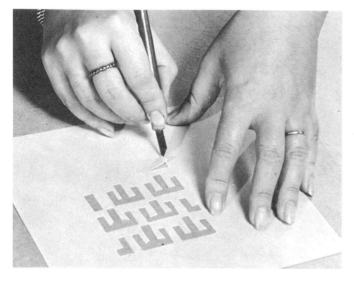

205

206

207

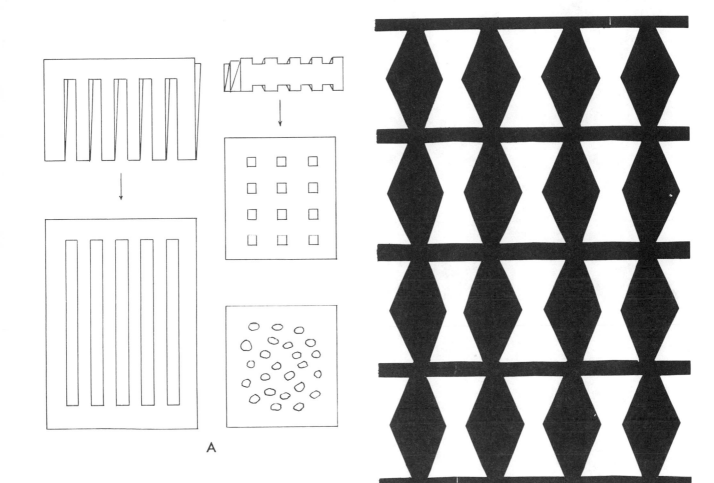

A

209

208

199

210

211

SILK-SCREEN PRINTS

The screen print is made according to the same principle as the stencil print, but the paint is forced through a cloth, producing a printed quality.

A simple method is shown in figure 212. An opening is cut in the center of a piece of rigid, thick cardboard or corrugated board; then across it is placed a piece of organdy, cheese-cloth, nylon stocking, tarlatan, fine mesh curtain, or similar material. This is stretched tightly and either glued or stapled to the cardboard around the edge, overlapping the opening at least an inch. Masking tape is placed around the edge of the cloth screen on the underside where it touches the cardboard. Painting the cardboard frame on both sides with lacquer helps to make it waterproof, thus keeping it from warping. A picture frame or canvas stretcher bar can be used in place of cardboard.

The pattern is cut with a sharp knife or scissors from a piece of lightweight paper like ordinary kitchen wax paper, tracing paper, kraft paper, newsprint, or bond paper. The cutout pieces can be used to form negative shapes if desired. The paper pattern is laid under the screen but on top of the paper on which the print will be made, with a padding of news-

212

213

papers underneath. When the paint is pushed through the screen, the paper pattern will stick to the cloth and form a stencil. Materials such as string, leaves, or any objects that will stick to the screen and not cause too great a change in the surface can also be used.

In place of a cutout paper stencil, a "stop-out" like rubber cement, Crayola, or melted wax (paraffin, beeswax, crayon, or candles) can be applied directly to the screen and will serve the same purpose.

Paint for printing can be made from a mixture of whipped-up ordinary wallpaper or wheat paste powder and water to which poster or powder paint has been added. It should be the consistency of whipped cream, but thin enough to flow freely so that it will not clog the screen. The less pigment used the more transparent the color will be. A regular silk-screen paint is also available.

Some of the paint mixture is put at one end of the screen with the aid of a tongue depressor or spatula and forced across the screen by being pressed firmly with a piece of stiff cardboard, preferably waterproofed, which serves as a squeegee. The print is made by the paint as it goes through the cloth onto the paper beneath. It is at this time that the paper stencil, or whatever object is used, will be attached to the screen by the adhesiveness of the paint as the first print is made. If the cardboard frame gets wet it will warp or become limp and will have to be discarded.

If different stencils are to be used to produce overlapping shapes or changes of color, the screen can be cleaned off and used again, or new screens can be made. Figure 210 shows a print from a paper stencil, and figure 211 shows a different one printed in another color. Both of these stencils are shown again in figure 213 with one printed over the other, producing a more complex pattern with a change of color and value.

The book in figure 214 has a silk-screen design on the cover. The print in figure 215 is the result of using two stencils and printing one over the other. The paper on which they are printed contributes to a contrast made up of three value tones.

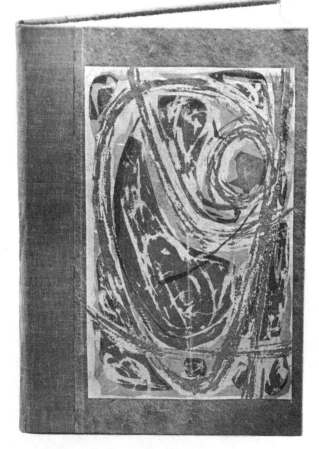

214

215

CUTOUT SHAPES

Covers can be decorated with shapes cut from paper, cloth, or leather and applied to a background material. Book vellum was used in the examples shown in figures 216, 217, and 218. It comes in a variety of interesting colors and can easily be cut with scissors.

Geometric shapes like the triangle, square, circle, half circle, rectangle, diamond, and modifications of these, are the basis of the forms used. Some proportional variations of the triangle are shown in diagram A to illustrate some of the ways a shape can be changed.

The filing case in figure 217 is an example of a design using various sizes of triangles. They are cut from book vellum and arranged in two shades against a background of a lighter tone. The spaces between are well related to the cut shapes, and the vertical and horizontal directions of the triangles are related to the shape of the case.

In figure 216 there is a vertical emphasis with angular shapes, and the spaces between are balanced by the positive shapes of the cut white forms.

Figure 218 was planned for the cover of a scrapbook. Shapes of white vellum are cut and arranged vertically and horizontally. There is a pleasing balance of dark and light with a good relationship of positive and negative space. The shapes combine both straight and curved lines and are modifications of parts of circles.

It is advisable, in planning, to cut shapes from paper first and use them as patterns, moving them around into various positions while trying out different arrangements. Value contrasts and color relationships should be kept simple and dramatic.

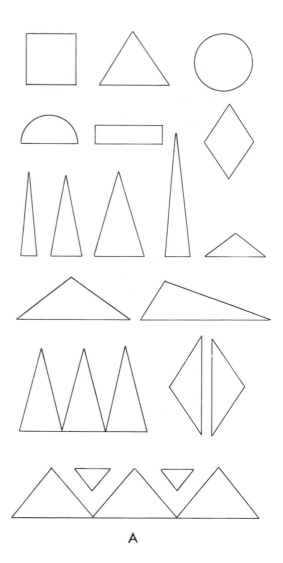

A

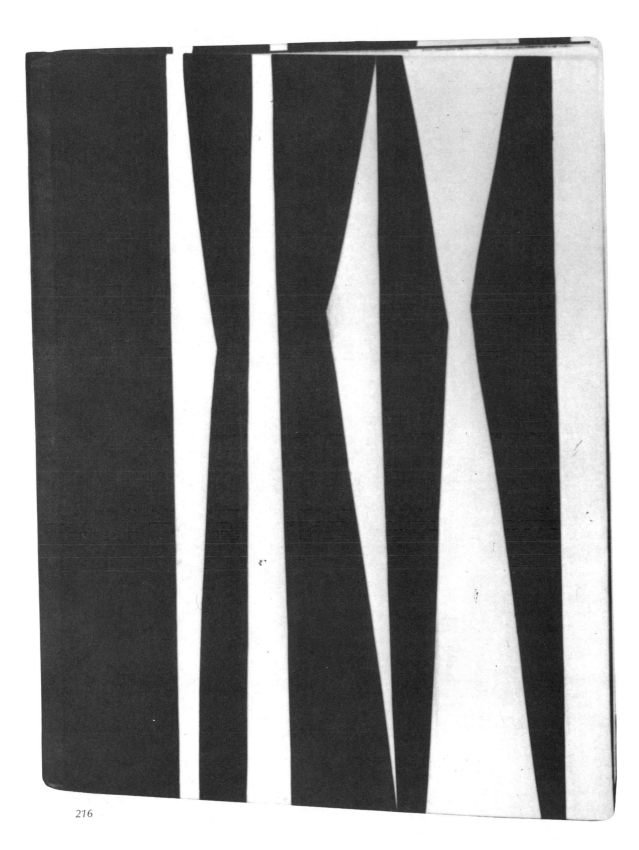

216

217

218

Positive-negative spaces, as important factors in design, can be observed in the examples of the counterchange method shown in figures 219, 220, 221, and 222. Areas are broken into divisions in which there is a reversal of the dark-light pattern, resulting in an alternation of tones. In figure 219, the circle and square shapes alternate on a checkerboard plan, and there is a continuous dark-light movement in either direction. What is light in one part becomes dark as it interchanges position. This makes for an equal emphasis of shape and a dark-light integrated balance.

In figure 220 the shape has been broken by a vertical line, in figure 221 by vertical and horizontal, while in figure 222 the division is diagonal. In each instance every space is important and background ceases to exist as such but becomes a part of the reversal plan.

A positive-negative space relationship based on a modification of the counterchange plan is shown on the cover of the scrapbook in figure 223.

Cut-paper designs are shown in figures 224 and 225. Those in figures 226 and 227 were cut from folded sheets of paper. This is an excellent way to study pattern and shape. While the design in figure 228 is painted rather than cut, it shows the relationship of the shapes to the spaces between.

219

220

221

222

208

223

224

225

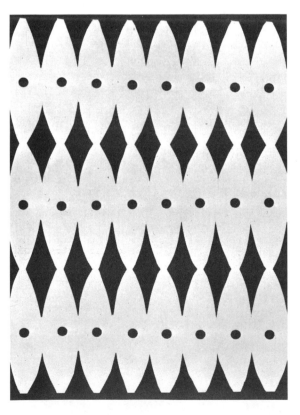

226

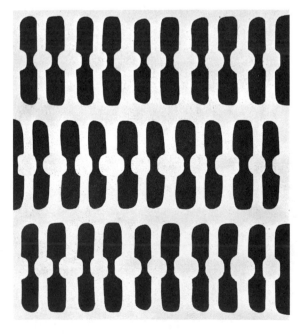

227

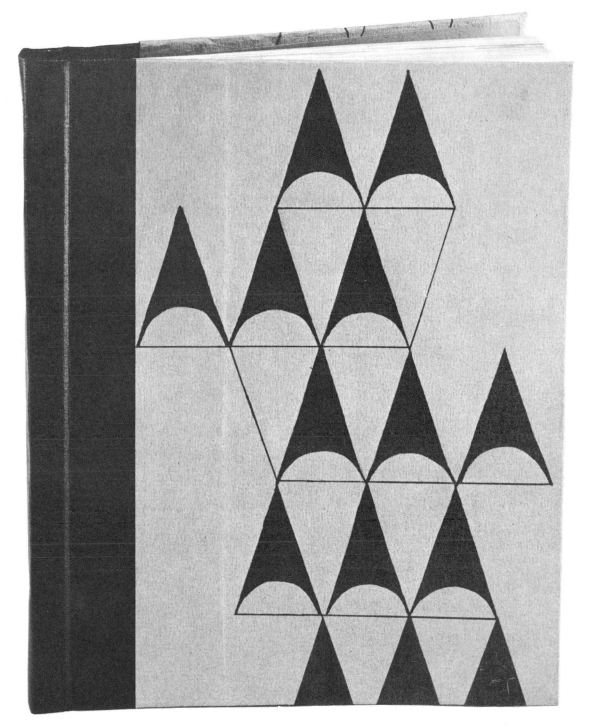

228

TORN PAPER

An exciting approach to design is through tearing shapes of paper, for here one can experience considerable freedom, controlled by an intuitive feeling for space. This method has appeal and value for young children and at the same time challenges the abilities of the mature designer. The possibilities are extensive.

A feeling for contour and shape results from experimentation by tearing various forms with the fingers. Irregular as well as geometric shapes should be tried.

The character of the paper used contributes to the effect produced, so it is advisable to try various kinds. In tearing, if the pull is equal on each side, the edges will appear similar, but if the paper is held steadily in one hand while the other does the tearing, a varied, ragged edge will result, similar to the deckle edge characteristic of distinguished handmade papers.

As the designer works he will develop an awareness of artistic qualities and will think of the importance of the spaces between the shapes, as well as the contrast of value tones made by the torn shapes against the paper on which they are mounted.

In the example shown in figure 229 the shapes were torn from a fairly stiff, grayed yellow paper. A horizontal rhythmic movement is emphasized, and there is a feeling of relationship between shapes. Such compositions as these can be used as cover designs on all kinds of books and portfolios. They are a form of the process known as collage.

229

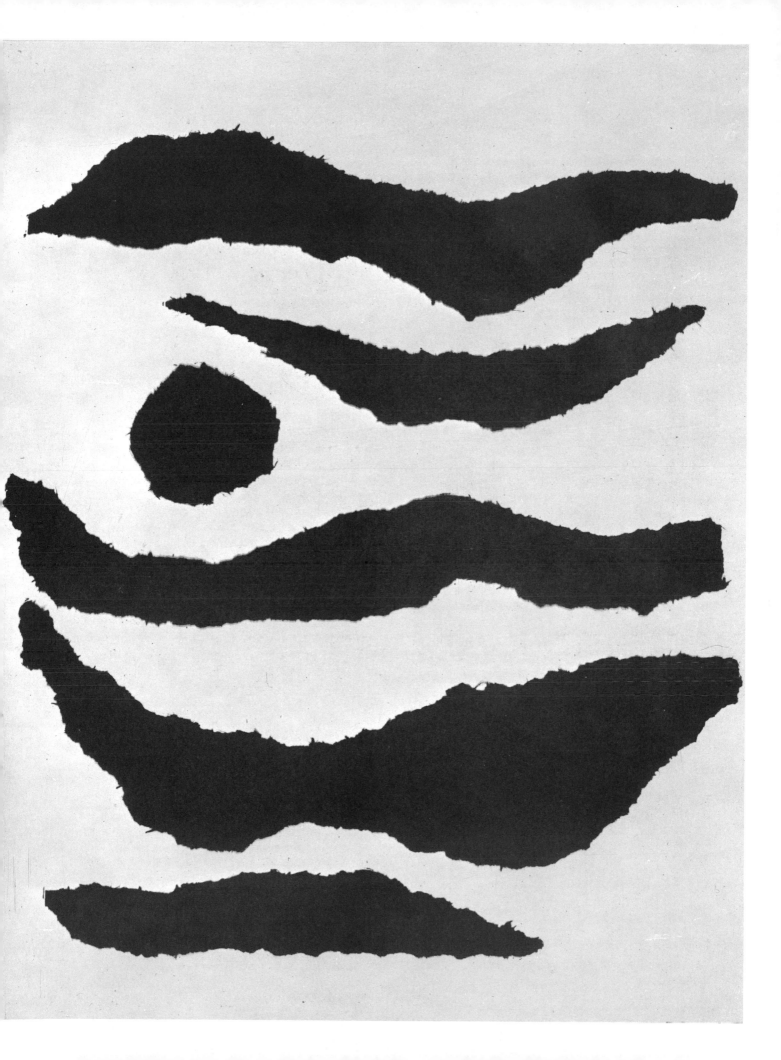

THREE-DIMENSIONAL APPLIQUÉS

Various techniques and materials can be explored, and ideas developed, for creating interesting textural and raised surface treatments on cover bindings. These may be in the form of collages, appliqués, mosaics, or sculptured forms. Common and inexpensive items such as string, yarn, cloth, and discarded costume jewelry are good possibilities for use, and a search of rummage and salvage centers will sometimes provide additional objects to stimulate the imagination of the designer. Fired enamels, glazed clay, metals, and glass are other suggested materials to be considered.

The raised effect on the cover in figure 230 is produced with cardboard shapes glued to the cover board, over which a soft paper covered with paste is molded. Such papers as Japanese rice paper, Silkspan (used for model airplanes and available from craft supply centers and hobby shops), or any that will permit some stretching are best to use. This technique is also successful when used with leather. A raised, textured surface is produced by the string glued in vertical strips on the outside of the cover paper in figure 231. The string can also be glued in other arrangements, for various patterned areas, and covered with clear varnish or shellac, with the areas between colored with enamel paint.

The patterns on the covers of the books in figure 232 were formed with heavy string glued to the cardboard over which a soft paper was pasted and molded. Additional interest is produced by the attachment of ten-cent-store jewelry and smooth, tough, colored papers on top of which small and large spots of thick white glue were dropped. The rich, luxurious effect produced is reminiscent of books of the Middle Ages when enamels, ivory, precious stones, and silver and gold metals were attached to leather-covered books.

Decorated cloth covers may make use of hand-woven textiles or of tapestry techniques, as in the stitchery example in figure 1. Hand-printed designs on fabrics may be combined with appliqués of cloth, sequins, and other objects, along with colored yarns. At one time in English history, hand-embroidered covers were much in vogue, with silks and velvets the favored materials.

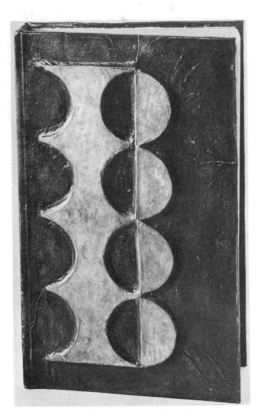

230

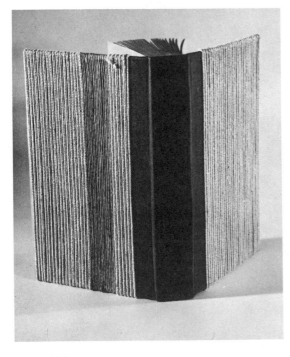

231

232

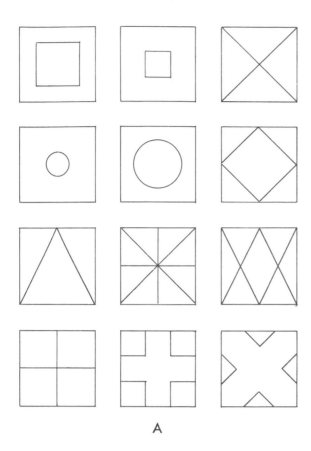

A

PAINTED PAPERS

Designs can be put directly on the paper with brush and paint either in a free and casual way or according to a highly controlled and carefully organized plan. To construct a formal type of design, a square can be used as the limiting area in which to build a unit which is repeated as an over-all pattern. Shapes about 4 or 5 inches in size are good to start with, and various ways can be explored of breaking up space within them. A feeling for the structure of the square is constantly maintained, and each line put in must have some relationship to the whole form.

In the examples shown in diagram A, a number of ways of breaking up the space are suggested, and many more can be developed. With these as the starting point to form the scaffolding of the design, modifications and detail can be introduced as personal inventive ability dictates. The design can be repeated as an allover pattern or alternated with another as shown in diagram B.

It is well to limit the value contrasts and to select colors that have some degree of excitement and interest, putting them together in

233

B

234

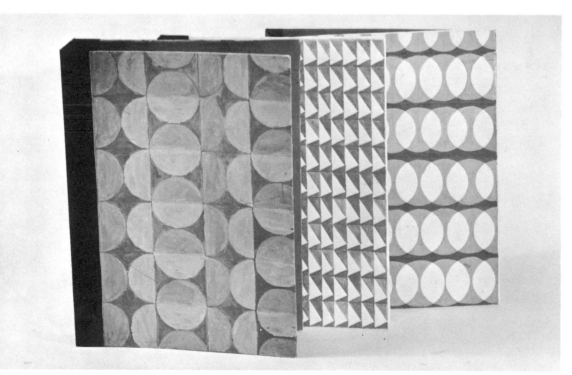

235

pleasing relationships based upon a knowledge of color functioning.

The examples in figures 233 and 234 show repeats based upon units formed from geometric shapes. The painted papers with geometric patterns on the portfolio covers in figure 235 were made by high school students.

Paper designs that are more casual in character can be produced by putting paint on wet or absorbent paper and letting it run over the surface to form a pattern of shapes. In figure 236 small puddles of several different colors of tempera paint were dropped in various spots around the paper and blown to force them to spread in different directions. In this way a rhythmic movement is established throughout the page, and a pattern of dark and light areas is formed. The cover on the book in figure 237 was made in a similar way.

Black or colored inks can be combined with paint. When these are applied with a pen over painted areas an interesting effect of line and mass is produced. Absorbent papers like Japanese rice papers, paper towels, and similar types should be tried; they can be dampened first if desired. For a mottled effect a pattern is created with a thick white poster paint over which is applied a waterproof ink that covers the entire paper. The white paint is then washed off under running water or scrubbed off with a wet, stiff-bristled brush.

Painting with a size produces a glazed paper. Powder paint is dissolved in water to which some size, like glue or mucilage, has been added. The paper is covered with this preparation and left until completely dry. It is then covered with another color, which is spread around in such a way as to reveal the color underneath and produce a pattern of lines, swirls, and masses. This can be done with a brush, the fingers, a comb, or a notched cardboard. The paper is again left to dry. If it curls, it can be pressed with a warm iron or left under weights.

236

238

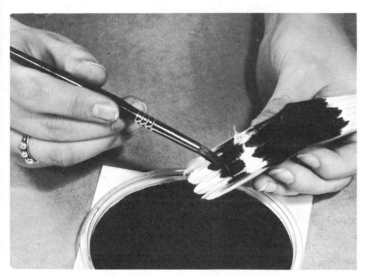

239

240

FOLD-AND-DYE PAPERS

For the fold-and-dye technique, a tough, absorbent paper, such as Silkspan, is the best material to use. Japanese rice papers are also acceptable, while newsprint and paper towels are good to practice on.

The paper is folded in half several times to form a strip and may be refolded into accordion pleats. The long strip is then folded several times with a reverse fold into a smaller shape, either diagonally or straight across (figure 238). For a center design, the paper is folded in both directions. All types of folds can be devised. A pattern is made by painting the edges and corners with a brush (figure 239) or dipping the paper into a dye or paint mixture (figure 240). The color will be more intense on the edges, shading off as it spreads into the absorbent paper. Colored inks and food coloring provide brilliant effects; poster paints, powder paints, dyes, and even bluing may be used. In addition to the example in figure 241, fold-and-dye papers used on book covers are shown in figures 242, 243, and 245. Figure 244 shows the inside of the book in figure 242, with student class notes and diagrams of bookbinding processes.

241

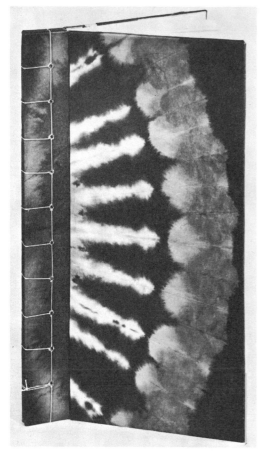

242

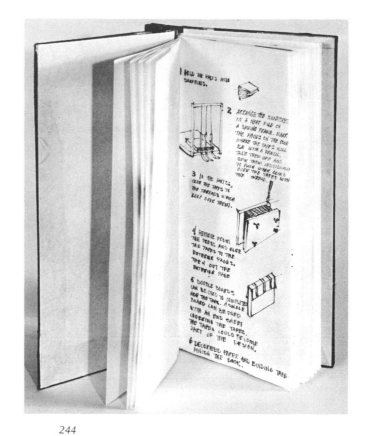

244

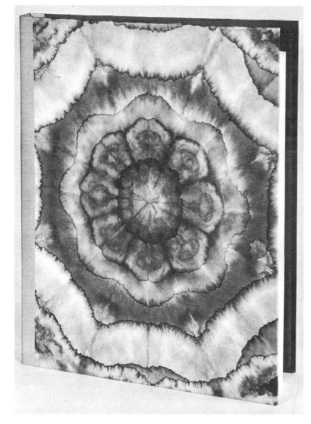

243

245

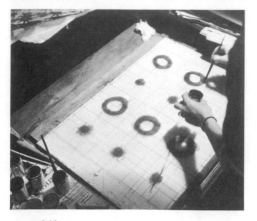

246

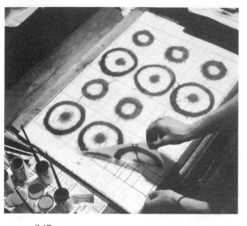

247

248

250

249

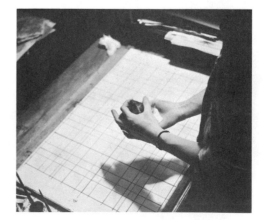

251

INK-AND-FOLD PAPERS

The ink-and-fold papers demonstrated here were made by laying a sheet of plain rice paper, 18 by 24 inches, on a glass surface under which can be seen guidelines drawn to aid the placement of the design. The glass can be wet before the paper is laid on, or the paper can be wet thoroughly with a sponge.

The design is laid on with Higgins colored drawing inks and a brush. In the example shown in figure 246, there are two rows of red dots alternating with two rows of violet circles. The red dots are encircled with dark blue (figure 247).

The two outer rows are folded over the two inner rows (figure 248), folded again into a single row (figure 249), and then folded into a square (figure 250). This square is tightly squeezed in the hands so that the colors blend somewhat and wrinkles are formed (figure 251). The sheet is then opened and spread to dry on newspapers (figure 253).

Another type of design is shown in figure 252, where blue stripes are shown being laid on. Yellow ones are then placed between them. The paper is folded into a strip (figures 254 and 255) and pinched together at each blue stripe (figure 256). When opened, the crushed paper looks like figure 257.

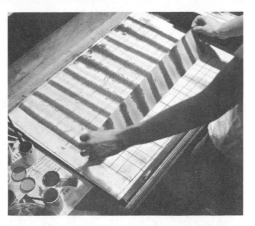

254

255

252

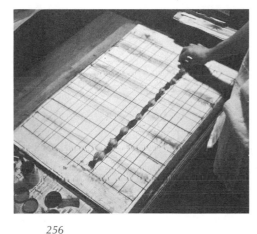

256

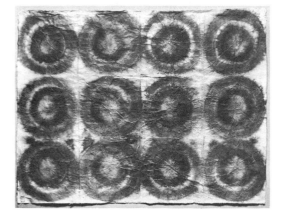

253

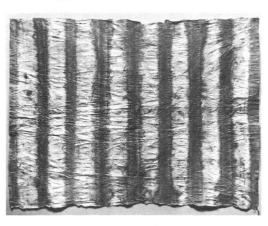

257

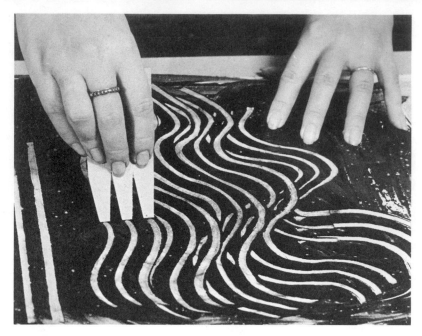

258

PASTE OR STARCH PAPERS

Rhythmic repeat patterns can be produced by pressing the fingers or objects into a paste or starch mixture that has been spread on paper. Lines or dabs can be free and casual in character, as in figure 258, or limited in direction (figures 259 and 260). Interesting effects can be obtained with a notched piece of cardboard, as shown in figure 258, a sponge, a brush, or a comb as well as the fingers.

A specially prepared commercial paper with a slightly glazed surface is available for this purpose, but other types like white shelf paper or butcher paper can also be used. The paper is placed on a table covered with protective newspapers and is dampened evenly with a sponge, brush, wadded-up paper towel, or piece of cloth dipped in water. A spoonful of the thinned-out paste or starch is put on the paper and spread with the hand over the entire surface. Then color in the form of powder or poster paints, dyes, colored inks, or food coloring is worked into the mixture.

A prepared starch paint can be purchased, or a mixture can quickly be made by adding water to a wallpaper powder paste until it reaches a creamy consistency. Liquid laundry starch can also be used, in which case the paper need not be dampened.

Many prefer a cooked paste made by mixing a cup of cornstarch with a cup of cold water and adding the mixture gradually to five cups of gently boiling water. This is stirred for a few minutes until it is cooked through and then set aside to cool. While it is still slightly warm, a cup of soap flakes is added to provide a smoother finish, and the mixture is stored in fruit jars or a pan until ready for use. The paint can be added at this time or later when the paste is to be used. A little water glass added to the colors will make the paper waterproof.

It is interesting to note that this method of decorating papers was used extensively in the seventeenth and eighteenth centuries.

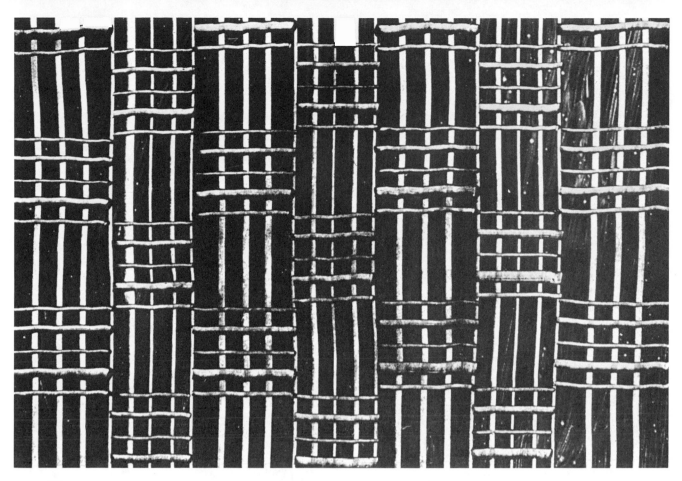

259

260

261. *Leather binding by Edgar Mansfield, African native-dyed morocco with recessed onlay dots and rings in white and various colors, and with blind, white, and red tooling*

Leather

Leather lends an elegance to the art of the book that cannot be obtained by any other means. It presents a pleasant sensation to both the touch and the vision. Until the nineteenth century this material was used more than any other on covers, for books were considered important and deserving of the best. Their rarity gave them more value, and methods of preservation had to be considered as well.

Now that books are available to all at moderate cost, methods of mass production and machine requirements are given first consideration. No longer is it practicable to use expensive materials limited to hand processes that require tedious and careful manipulation. Only occasionally, for some special purpose, is there any justification today for binding a book in leather. Bibles, important documents, and rare editions are sometimes given this distinction.

Many interesting leathers are available to the binder, and if he is not familiar with the different kinds a visit to a store that sells leather will furnish him with much worthwhile information. He will be able to make selections and see possibilities that will stir his imagination for working out ideas. If there are no shops in the immediate vicinity, mail-order sources are available through catalogue listings. These often include small sample pieces from which to order. A few such places are listed at the back of the book under "Supply Sources."

The leathers most preferred by binders are Cape levant and oasis goat. These are morocco leathers made from the skins of goats coming from the Cape of Good Hope in South Africa. Calfskin is generally quite popular but does not have the durability of morocco. It has a smooth surface that is good for dyeing and tooling. Other types of leathers come from the sheep, cow, steer, elk, seal, alligator, lizard, and other reptiles; more unusual types come from the shark, antelope, zebra, and kangaroo. Pigskin and ostrich skin have interesting textures. Suede leather, available in many beautiful colors, is made from a goatskin or lambskin with the outer grain shaved or peeled off. It has more character when combined with other leathers that contrast with its soft, dull finish (figure 295). Skiver is taken from the grain side of a split sheepskin and because of its thinness is less durable than other leathers. It does not, however, have to be skived for use, and it is easier to fold over at the edges and corners of a book.

Leather is sold by the hide, half hide, or foot. When less than a half or quarter hide is purchased the price is quoted by the square inch, thus making smaller amounts more expensive. To determine how much leather is needed to cover a particular book, a paper pattern is cut with an additional inch allowed on each side. This is laid on the leather to determine what part of the skin to select. Holes and blemishes should be avoided wherever possible, for they cannot be concealed. A paper pattern is cut when a quarter or half binding is used as well as for a full binding (see pages 74-77). Small skins or scrap pieces can often be used for part bindings. They can also be combined with other leathers, contrasting in texture, color, or tone, or they can be used in combination with decorative papers as in figure 297. Unusually small pieces can be used for inlay.

262

263

264

CUTTING AND SKIVING

Lightweight, thin leathers can easily be cut with scissors. Heavier leathers like cowhide and calfskin are cut with a sharp-pointed knife and the assistance of a steel square or metal-edged ruler (figure 262).

After the piece for the cover has been cut (figure 263), a pencil line is drawn on the underside (flesh side) to indicate exactly where the edge of the cover will come. Most leathers must be pared or skived around the edges on the underside to make them thin enough to fold over the edge of the cover board. The skiving begins at the outer edge and gradually extends over the pencil line.

Skiving knives are available from leather supply sources, or a shoemaker's knife can be used. It is important to keep the knife sharp at all times for good results as a dull knife will not work. A sharpening stone and a small can of oil should be kept at hand for this purpose.

A hard surface like a marble slab, a lithograph stone, a piece of heavy plate glass, or a hardwood block is needed for skiving. The leather is placed face down upon it, with the flesh side up, and held with one hand while the other grasps the knife and pushes it forward at an angle toward the edge. A small amount of the underside of the leather is shaved off at each stroke (figure 264). Considerable pressure is needed, but if the knife is pushed too hard into the leather it can easily dig a hole right through the piece. Practice on scrap pieces will help to give the feel of skiving and teach control. Some leathers will skive better if dampened slightly with a wet sponge.

Skivers with razor blade inserts are available from leather supply sources. To manipulate this type the worker pulls the blade toward him instead of pushing it away (figure 265). If no skiving knife is available, sandpaper should be tried as a substitute. This often works well on the edges of thin leathers.

Skiving takes time, and one should not expect quick results. The same area must be worked over patiently and persistently many times until sufficient shavings have been removed. These shavings should not be allowed to collect under the piece of leather as they will damage its surface or cause holes to be cut, so they should be continually pushed or blown away. The edge of the leather is tested frequently for thinness by being creased on the pencil line to

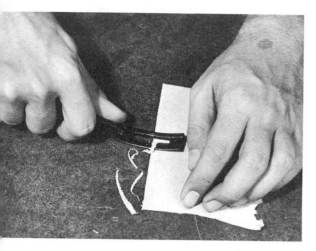

265

266

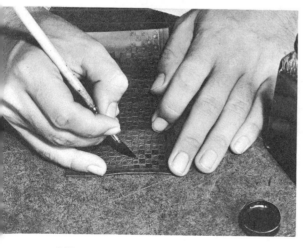

267

see if it is becoming thin enough to fold over the edge of the cover board.

If leather is used just over the spine of the book, it is skived at the top and bottom for turning in, and about ¼ inch on the sides that extend over onto the cover board. Otherwise the piece is skived evenly all around and also down the back at the places where it will fit into the joints. The head and tail should be made as thin as possible because of the double thickness that results when it is turned in.

DECORATING

The binder must decide whether he wants to leave the leather plain and undecorated with its natural color and finish or change it in any way. He has the choice of combining it with other leathers, using inlay or onlay, applying color, or adding a pattern by means of stamps and tooling. The decoration is usually applied to the finished book, but in some cases it is advisable to complete it before the leather is put on the cover. The decision is up to the binder. Designs should be conceived as decorative patterns that serve an ornamental purpose, and good space relationships and pleasing shapes should be kept in mind. Pictorial units should be avoided as much as possible for they bring in the element of illustration and storytelling, factors that tend to be destructive of good design principles and to violate the flatness of the surface, which it is desirable to retain. A design that emphasizes abstract qualities is more likely to result in a binding that is a work of art.

Leather can be purchased in different colors commercially dyed, or it can be colored by hand. It is advisable to experiment with small scrap pieces first, as different leathers react in different ways. Before the color is applied, the leather is dampened with a wet sponge on both the front and back. This helps to ensure an even job. A dry piece can also be tried, and the results compared—in fact, a considerable amount of experimenting should be carried out before the final piece is tackled.

Special dyes for leather are available, including shoe leather dyes as well as stains and colored inks. Even water colors are usable. The color can be applied with a sponge, swab, or brush either over the whole area (figure 266) or to specific units (figure 267); it can be sprayed on with a spray gun (figure

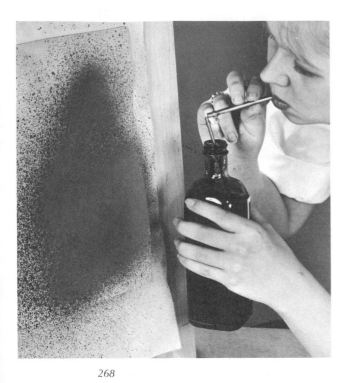

268); or the leather can be dipped into a dye bath in a pan (figure 269). A light tan leather can be darkened by being dipped in coffee. If only part of the leather is to be dyed, the color can be applied with a brush to the special areas desired for creating a pattern as on the cover in figure 279. This method is particularly effective for producing mosaic effects. A liquid "stop-out" or tape can be used as a stencil when the color is being put on. Sometimes it is necessary to go over the color several times in order to eliminate streaks and uneven application. If the leather already has a high glossy finish it may resist attempts to add color.

Printer's ink can also be used on leather as shown in figure 270. The design was cut in a potato, which was pressed onto an oil-base ink, rolled out as explained on page 178, and then applied to the leather surface.

268

269

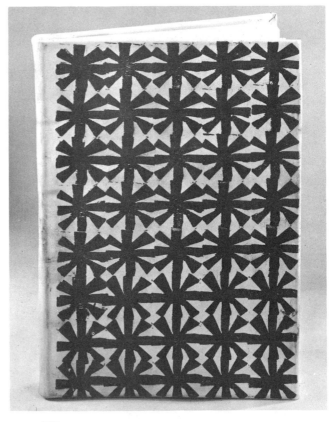

270

230

271

272

273

TOOLING AND STAMPING

Not all leathers can be tooled. Only those with a surface firm enough to hold a line, such as calfskin and goatskin, are suitable. Leather that is loose and stretchy will not retain a tooled impression.

Tooling can be applied to a leather cover either before or after it has been put on the book. If it is applied to a finished cover, a piece of tin such as is used in pressing can be inserted under the cover board to provide a firm working surface. If the book is small it can be clamped in a finishing press with its covers spread straight out, winglike, resting on each side of the top of the press.

A steel modeling tool is used for pressing lines into leather. The most common type has a turned-up point at one end and a flat, broad shape at the other. The pointed end is used for lines or stippled effects (figure 271), and the flat side is used for pressing larger areas (figure 272). To make the lines the tool is held with the point upward and is pulled toward the worker. Straight lines, if they are very long, should be impressed with the aid of a steel square or ruler to keep them smooth and even, unless a deliberately ragged effect is sought as part of the plan. Stippled effects are obtained by pressing the pointed end of the tool into the leather.

The design can be planned on paper or developed on scrap pieces of leather. If a geometric pattern with straight lines is used, it can be applied directly to the leather with ruler and modeling tool. A complicated design, or one with curved lines, should be drawn first on paper and attached to the leather with tape. Care must be exercised in using tape since it will leave marks on some leathers, as will a square or ruler if it is not kept clean and free from rust.

If the leather has dried out it can be given a paste wash to soften it up before it is tooled. A starch paste (see page 252) can be thinned down to a watery consistency and applied with a piece of sponge.

The design is traced through the paper pattern with a modeling tool that has been heated slightly on a hot plate. Care must be taken not to get the tool too hot, however. Only enough heat is needed to make a line impression. The leather is thoroughly dampened both on top and underneath, and the whole piece is kept damp, not just the parts being tooled. This prevents it from warping and drying un-

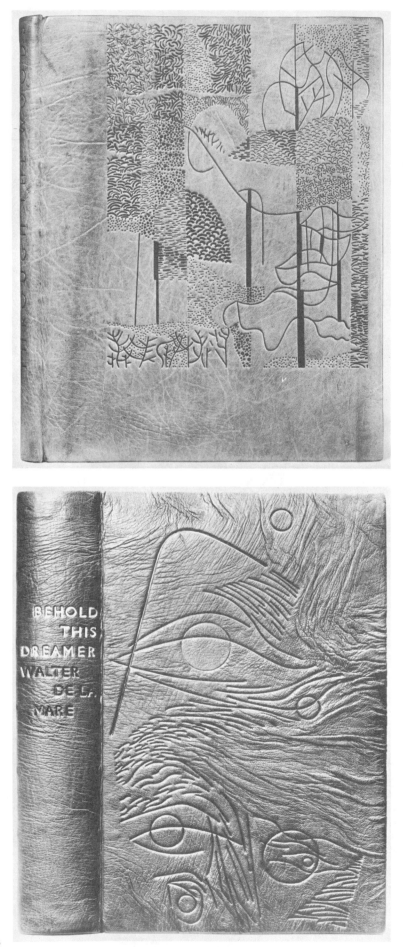

274. Leather binding by Edgar Mansfield, yellow native-dyed morocco with texture variations produced by curved and straight lines, with light, medium, and dark blind tooling

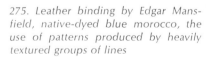

275. Leather binding by Edgar Mansfield, native-dyed blue morocco, the use of patterns produced by heavily textured groups of lines

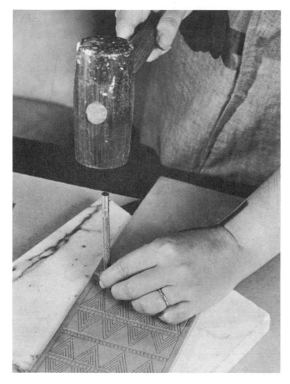

276

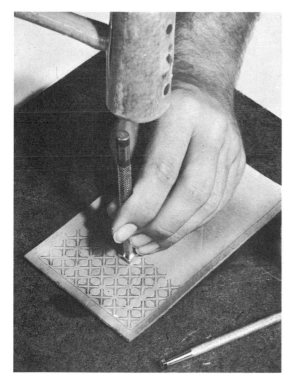

277

evenly. If it dries out while being tooled, it must be redampened. After the paper pattern has been removed, the lines are reimpressed with the modeling tool, heated no warmer than can be comfortably touched with the bare hand.

A tool called a fillet, a solid brass wheel guided by a handle grasped from above, is a handy means for making lines of any length. It produces a strong impression when it is heated and pressure is exerted.

Original effects can be achieved through experimentation and the imaginative use of tools as in Edgar Mansfield's work in figure 274, which shows a great variety of tooled lines, and in figure 275, where heavily inscribed lines form moving textural patterns.

Metal stamp tools for producing geometric designs on leather are available from leather supply companies and can be used effectively in combination with tooled lines. These stamps are engraved with simple forms, such as circles, triangles, sunbursts, crescents, half circles, and crosses, which are transferred to the leather by heat and pressure or by a gentle tap with a mallet (figures 276 and 277). Stamps can be made by using a small file across the top or on the edge of a large-headed nail or on a brass bar $1/4$ to $1/2$ inch in diameter (see diagram B on page 190). Even with a limited number of stamps a wide variety of combinations can be achieved. Plans should be tried out first on scrap leather pieces, or the tools can be inked and pressed onto paper and the results studied. If the tools are heated, the impressions will be deeper and the color of the leather slightly changed. If desired, the tools can be used hot enough to burn the leather and produce a much deeper tone. Otherwise they are used only after they stop hissing when touched by something damp.

A design combining tooling and stamping is shown in figure 273. The finished cover, which was made for a memo pad filler, is shown in figure 278. Note the effect of dark-light produced by this method. A pattern of textures can be created by using straight and curved lines in various widths combined with dots and other shapes. Figure 279 shows a tooled and stamped design in which the units have been painted with colored dyes as demonstrated in figures 266 and 267.

An embossed effect can be achieved by pressure which forces the leather to stretch and hold an imprint. Solid forms are constructed for pressing into the leather by gluing pieces of cardboard onto larger

233

278

279

pieces or by cutting areas out of a piece of linoleum such as is used in block printing, either mounted on a block of wood or unmounted (see figure 178). The forms are placed on top of the dampened leather, or underneath it, and pressure is applied with an etching or block print press. In this way a deep indentation is made, producing raised and sunken areas, as illustrated by the book cover shown in figure 280. The design for this cover was cut on linoleum which was then submitted to pressure. Cardboard shapes may also be glued to the cover board and the leather molded or pressed over them when it is glued to the cover. In this method the cardboard is retained within the impressed leather.

A similar effect with less depth can be obtained by recessing some of the design. Parts of the cover board are removed with the sharp point of a knife, and the dampened leather is forced down into the sunken areas with a bone folder and the fingers.

Plain or blind tooling can be combined with gold tooling in the same cover design. The leather is first washed with clear water and given a paste wash of very diluted commercial or starch paste. It is then slightly dampened with a moist sponge. If the design to be applied is fairly complex, it should be planned on paper and taped to the leather. The modeling or stamping tools are heated until they are warm, but not hot, and the design is pressed firmly through the paper to the leather. This is called "blinding-in"—the process of transferring the design to the leather so that it can be either blind tooled or gold tooled. The tools can be worked into the same impressions several times. If a straight edge is needed as a guide when the lines are tooled directly on the leather, a wooden ruler should be used since metal will stain damp leather.

280. *Binding of sheepskin hand-dyed in green, with embossed design made by pressure over raised forms*

281

282

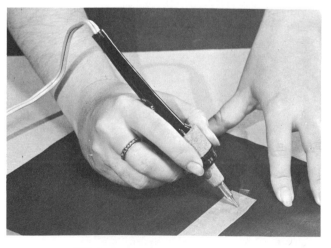

283

GOLD TOOLING

In the traditional process of gold tooling, an adhesive size called "glair" is applied to the leather, and pieces of gold leaf are laid on it and pressed down with heated tools to hold them to the leather. The size acts as a binder and causes the gold leaf to adhere to the leather when it is pressed with the heated tool. It is made by adding about ¾ teaspoon of vinegar to the white of an egg in a bowl and beating with an egg beater until the mixture stands up stiffly. The glair is the liquid that forms under the foam when it has been left to stand for several hours or overnight. This is poured off and saved. Unless it is kept in an airtight bottle, it will not keep more than two or three days.

The leather is freshened before it is gold tooled by being washed off with plain water. The glair is painted in the tooled impressions with a small camel's-hair brush. It is advisable then to leave the leather until the next day and apply a second coat of glair shortly before using the gold. This second coat should be allowed to dry enough so that it is not sticky. Before the gold is applied, the leather is rubbed lightly around and over the tooling with a piece of soft flannel greased with coconut oil, vaseline, or a similar oil. Care must be taken not to fill the depression with the oil. A piece of good quality absorbent cotton can be used in place of the flannel.

Gold leaf is difficult to handle. If possible it should not be touched with the hands, and it should be kept out of drafts, for even one's breath blowing on it can make it unmanageable. It comes in small sheets that lie between protective papers and can be lifted out with tweezers or a clean knife. The sheet is placed gently on a special velvet cushion or a piece of velvet, and strips or pieces are cut off with a knife or small sharp scissors in the approximate size of the areas to be covered. These are lifted with tweezers or a knife, or with a piece of slightly greased flannel, and laid over the tooled impressions. Several tooled

284. Leather binding by Dorothy Macdonald, gold tooling on crimson leather

285. Leather binding by Kurt Jungstedt, gold tooling on wine-colored morocco

lines can be prepared at once, or the whole book can be done at one time.

The tools are heated as needed on a hot plate or gas stove. They are kept quite hot, as more heat is needed for gold tooling than for plain tooling; in fact, the tool can be hot enough to sizzle when touched to a dampened sponge. The drier the leather, the more heat is required. The tool is held firmly, and pressure is applied as it is rocked from side to side in the hands or moved along the lines. If the results are not successful, more glair can be added and the job redone.

After the tooling, the excess gold is rubbed off with a piece of clean absorbent cotton or flannel and the tooled impressions are rubbed with a modeling tool. Then the whole book can be rubbed with cotton, and the leather can be washed off with pure gasoline if desired.

Examples of professional gold tooling, shown in figures 284, 285, and 286, illustrate the skill and exactitude necessary for this particular technique. Other examples can be seen in figures 14, 36, 38, and 43.

A much simpler method for applying gold than the traditional one just described has been devised, requiring less skill and bringing this phase of binding within the reach of the beginning student. Genuine gold leaf is now available at a reasonable price either in rolls 100 feet long and 1/2 inch or 2 inches wide, or in individual flat sheets 6 by 12 inches. Since the gold has already been properly sized, it can be applied directly to the leather of the cover without any additional preparation of the surface, and without the use of glair.

Tools are heated as previously explained (figure 281), quickly placed upon the strip of gold leaf which has been laid on the leather with the bright or shiny side upward, and held for a few seconds until the gold adheres to the leather. Pressure must be firm and applied quickly before the heated tool cools off, or the print will be imperfect. If the tool is given a forceful blow with a mallet or hammer the tooled impression and the gold application are achieved with one process (figure 282). There should be some experimentation first on small scraps of leather to determine the degree of heat and the amount of pressure required. Letters forming titles, as well as decorative lines and pattern units, can be applied in this way.

Hobby suppliers have small sheets of coated gold and silver papers that sometimes come in kits, along with an electric stylus tool that is plugged into a socket for heating. The coated paper is placed on the leather, and the heated tool is pressed firmly against it to form patterns or letters (figure 283). Gold pencils used by libraries for making title labels or numbers on books are also available for this purpose. Gold can be applied to various cover fabrics, including book vellum and other book cloths, as well as to leathers.

286. Gold-tooled leather binding by Dorothy Macdonald

INLAY AND ONLAY

Inlay refers to the insertion of different kinds and colors of leather within a larger piece, and onlay to the placement of smaller pieces on top of the larger one. It is simpler to put a section on the surface than to insert it in a cutout area. If the design is applied to the leather after the cover is on the book, there will be a smooth, well-stretched surface on which to work.

For inlay, the piece to be shaped and inserted can be laid on top of the larger piece, and both cut through at the same time with a sharp knife held at a slant to form a bevel, so that the edges in the leather of the larger piece will not show. If the piece to be inserted is thinner than the cover leather, it can be built up underneath with cardboard, or a layer can be removed from the top of the cover leather by cutting out an area that has been tooled, and another piece inserted in its place.

Leather used for onlay should be scraped or skived as thin as possible, unless a raised effect is desired. Sometimes it is possible to skin off the surface, or to peel a thin layer from the bottom. The complete design is first tooled on top of the large piece of leather, and the thinned pieces to be fitted on it are cut a little larger than the areas to be filled. The small pieces are moistened with water on both sides, pressed firmly over the design until the tooled lines show through, and cut out with small, sharp scissors. They are pasted to the leather, covered with a protective piece of paper, and rubbed firmly with a bone folder; then the cover is placed under a board with a heavy weight on top. Onlay pieces can also be set into scratched-out surfaces of the cover leather.

The term "inlay," through general usage, has come to include both inlay and onlay. Examples of inlay can be seen in figures 31, 35, 37, 39, and 41 (a detail of which is shown in figure 287). Onlay is illustrated in figures 289 and 291. The box cover in figure 290 has small pieces of leather appliquéd on gold paper and combined with stamped units, gold braid, and glass brilliants. A cover can also be formed by gluing small, shaped pieces closely together, much as a mosaic is constituted (figure 288).

A perforated design of holes with colored pieces inserted underneath can be made with punch tools of different sizes and a mallet. If larger areas or different shapes are desired, a sharp-pointed knife can be used for making the openings.

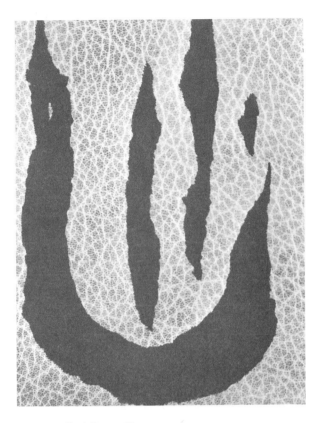

287. Detail of figure 41

288

290

292

APPLYING LEATHER COVER

Leather for covers may be cut all in one piece, used in combination with other leathers (figure 295), or combined with decorated papers (figure 297). When the leather is ready to be put on the cover boards, it is dampened all over on both sides with a sponge or cloth. A thick paste is applied with a brush to the underside and worked in thoroughly for several minutes until the pores are saturated. Commercial paste can be used, but some binders prefer a paste made with starch (see page 252). The leather can be folded over and left to soak for a few minutes, with more paste added as needed. Any excess can be wiped off later. This process makes the leather more pliable and easier to work with. If cords or other raised areas are used on the spine, the leather can be stretched or modeled right over them.

Some glues will discolor leather, so if there is any doubt the paste to be used should be tried first on a scrap piece. It may seep clear through the skin to the surface and cause patchy-looking spots that are unremovable. Rubber cement can sometimes be used with thin leathers like skiver on small books made in the classroom.

Plenty of paste is also put on the spine of the book, which is then laid down in position on top of the leather piece, where it has been marked (figure 292). Unlike cloth bindings, the leather binding is pasted to the spine. The other half of the leather is brought over onto the cover board, and the book is stood on its fore edge so that both sides can be smoothed firmly downward with the hands as though one were fitting on a glove. The part over the spine is rubbed with the hands and with a bone folder until it adheres to the book. If raised bands have been used on the spine, they should be nipped several times with a band nipper and the leather pressed down firmly between bands. It may be necessary to mois-

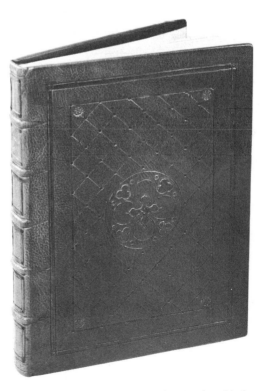

293. Leather binding by Dorothy Macdonald, detail of spine with raised cords

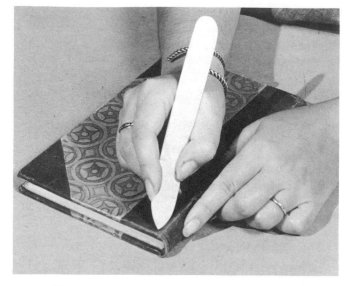

294

295. (Left) Book bound in suede and goatskin hand-dyed in yellow; (right) Bible bound in red calf with simple tooled line

ten the leather slightly to make it conform to the shape of the bands. They can be emphasized by using a piece of moist string and pulling it back and forth across the back, close to the band, to make an indentation. See figure 293 for finished bands.

The book is again laid on its side, and the leather is pushed gently into the hinged grooves on either side with the help of a bone folder. When the cover sticks sufficiently the book can be opened and the overlap of leather turned over the edge of the cover board. A convenient way to turn in the top and bottom is to stand the book upright on a wooden board with the spine extending over the edge and the fore edge toward the worker. After the leather has been turned in (see figure 106), a little paste is applied at the head and tail to make it adhere to the spine.

If the leather seems limp and crushes down at the head and tail of the spine, a thick string or cord can be inserted and glued to the inside of the leather next to the top and bottom edges at the back before the leather is brought over and glued to the boards. This will make the leather firmer, but care must be taken not to let the string slip.

The corners are mitered, and the overlaps are pasted down. If the leather is quite thick the corners must be handled skillfully so that they will look neat and trim. They can be cut so that they just meet, or if the leather is soft the corners can be gathered in as shown in diagram C on page 79. After the leather is turned in around the edges, the cover boards can be opened up, given a firm shove to push them well over into the joint next to the spine, and then closed again.

The groove joint is rubbed carefully with a bone folder so as not to mar the leather (figure 294). To retain its impression, a piece of string can be placed around the book in such a way that it lies in the grooves and goes over the top and bottom edges of the book, encircling it. This is tied firmly, left on while the book is drying under a light weight for twelve hours or more, and then removed.

When the book is in the press, tins are placed next to the inside of the covers to keep any moisture from going through the pages. Wax paper wrapped around the outside of the covers will protect them. The book is put between metal-edged pressboards in such a way that the back protrudes and the metal strips fit into the grooves (figure 296).

If there is a recessed area on the inside of the

296

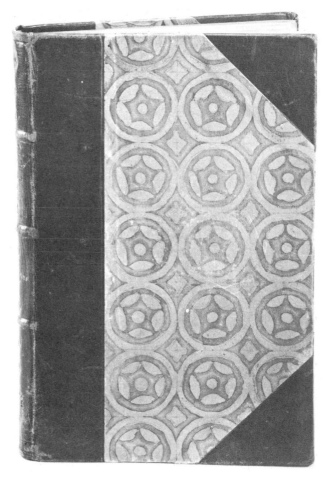

cover board produced by the thick ridge of the leather after it has been turned over the edge of the board, the leather can be trimmed even with the point of a sharp knife and a thick piece of paper or a thin cardboard that matches the thickness of the leather inserted and glued to the inside board. This is allowed to dry under a weight.

In making the book, the end sheets are put down either before or after the cover is decorated. The book is opened, and the covers are pulled straight back as far as possible. With the book lying on its side on a pressing board, paste is applied to the end sheet, which is then brought over onto the cover and pushed down into the joint with the fingers. After the other end sheet is pasted the book is left to dry for about half an hour, with the covers still open, until the paste starts to dry. Then it is closed and pressed lightly with tins and pressboards for several hours.

Some binders spread paste on the inside of the cover board, hold it at right angles to the book, and bring the end sheet up to it. Others prefer to close the book down on the end sheet after the paste is applied. It is important, with any method, to see that the end sheet fits into the joint.

Limp leather bindings are sometimes preferred for certain types of books, such as Bibles, prayer books, and special editions of poems, or where the leather seems too heavy to be put over cover boards. Flexible papers called "redboard" or "Newsboard" that are thin and tough and will bend without breaking are available from bookbinding supply sources. A flexible cover fits better on a tape-sewn book than on one made on cords. The casing method, as explained in the diagrams on pages 75 and 76, can be used for this kind of cover. Half bindings like that shown in figure 297 are explained on pages 76 and 77.

297. Half binding by Pauline Johnson, leather combined with a decorated paper

TITLES

When titles are placed on books the letters become part of the design. They can be put directly across the spine, spread lengthwise along the spine from tail to head or from head to tail, or arranged in any position on the front cover (figures 35, 38, 40, 42, and 298).

Three ways of composing titles to be applied to leather covers are: (1) by using single letters, made on the end of a brass tool with a wooden handle, which can be pressed into the leather one at a time to form words; (2) by using a typeholder or pallet in which the type is set and stamped with one operation; and (3) by using individual tools, each composed of a straight line of varying length, which can be combined with gouges of concentric curves made from various segments of circles (diagram A). The letters formed by lines and curves, used in combination, are geometrically structured and have great beauty and strength. The first and third methods allow for greater freedom and originality and permit the letters to be incorporated into the design pattern of the cover so that there is a harmonious relation between them. Titles can also be tooled freehand, with care, after considerable practice.

When the title is put across the spine, the book is placed in a finishing press with the spine upward and binder's board on each side for protection. The title is spaced on a piece of paper cut the exact height of the letters and 2 inches wider than the spine on each side. To test the printing, the tools can be blackened in a candle or with ink and stamped on the paper. The paper strip with the title is laid on the spine, which has been slightly dampened, and secured with Scotch tape to the binder's board on either side. If the title is to be put on the front cover, the paper can be taped or pasted to the edges of the book. The tools containing the letters are heated on a hot plate, but not to sizzling, and the title is pressed right through the paper. A firm pressure is applied, and the tool is rocked slightly back and forth. The letters can be impressed again after the paper is removed, and gold tooling can be applied later if desired. Gold strips are pressed firmly over the impressed letters so that they can be seen through the gold. The beginner may find it easier to print the title while the leather is flat, before it is put on the book.

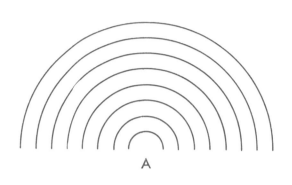

A

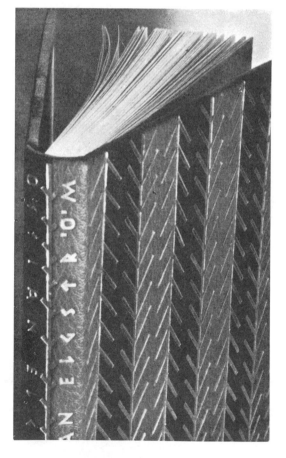

298. Leather binding by Swen Erik Skawonius, detail of spine showing letters stamped on calfskin

CLEANING AND PRESERVING

Other means of printing titles can be devised. Toy shops have little alphabet sets that can be mounted on the end of a cork or a block of wood. If they are strong enough, they can be stamped into the leather to make an impression. If they are too frail for this, they can be inked and used to print on paper or cloth covers. Individual letters can be cut reversed on the small end of an eraser, or groups of letters forming a word can be cut on the long side. Large letters can be cut from pieces of inner tube and glued to wooden blocks. Pieces of cork and cork stoppers might also be considered for this purpose. Titles for cloth and paper books can be printed on paper labels and mounted on the cover.

Most commercial leathers have a preparation on them that serves as a finish and produces a highly glossy appearance. When a leather needs cleaning, it can be rubbed on the surface with a small piece of moistened synthetic sponge dipped in saddle soap, which comes in the form of a congealed cream. The sponging should be done lightly but with a firm motion. The sponge is rinsed often in slightly warm water; the soap is not wiped off the leather, but is left on to dry. Grease spots can be removed with benzine on absorbent cotton.

A polishing iron is available for rubbing a leather cover and giving it a nice finish. The tool is grasped by the wooden handle and rubbed firmly over the whole surface.

When the leather is dry it can be oiled with neat's-foot oil, which is available from leather or sporting goods stores. The book is spread out on a table with its spine upward, or in a similar position on a book rack (figure 299), with newspapers placed underneath to catch any drippings. The oil is applied with a brush, generously and quickly, to avoid streaking. After the leather has soaked for an hour or so, any excess oil can be wiped off with a cloth. This can be followed with a sizing made with a very thin, watery solution of paste and again applied quickly to avoid streaking. The water soaks into the leather, and the surface becomes coated.

When the leather is dry, a French bookbinder's varnish applied with absorbent cotton will give a finish to the book and help prevent fingerprints from showing. A neutral leather cream or colorless paste shoe polish can also be used. It is applied with a slightly moistened sponge, and after a few minutes the leather is polished with a soft cloth.

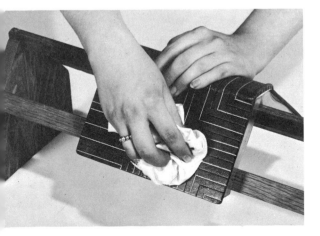

299

Book Repair

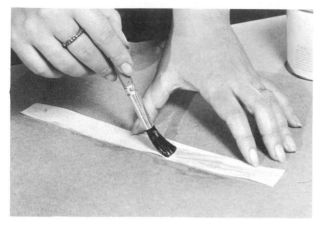

300

301

When a book is in need of major repair it is well to make certain it is of sufficient value to justify the time and effort required for its renovation. Often a few minor repairs are all that is needed rather than a complete rebinding; some books, however, have reached the point where they are beyond the possibility of any repair.

When the threads that hold the signatures together are broken, or the joints of the cover are split, a rebinding job is usually necessary. If the signatures are not too worn they can be resewn with tapes or cords; otherwise the single-sheet method, in which the book is sewn through the side, can be used.

Almost everyone has occasion to try to patch or mend a volume that for some special reason has personal interest and worth. It may be the family Bible, a well-used encyclopedia, sheet music, a valuable old book or rare edition, a textbook, or a child's favorite story book. Technical or legal books, or volumes of valuable records, may need to be rebound. If a book is out of print it may be desirable to extend its life as much as possible. Paperback books are given more permanence by the addition of a hard cover.

When a book is to be rebound, the end sheets and super are cut through at the joint with a sharp-pointed knife, and the cover is removed. The contents are lifted out, and the signatures are separated. This is done either by cutting the threads between them from the outside or by laying them open and snipping the threads inside with a knife or small scissors. The glue on the back should be gently scraped off with a knife or carefully pulled off with the fingers. If it is difficult to remove it can first be softened with a damp cloth. Care should be exercised not to tear the paper.

If the pages are in bad shape they may need to be cleaned and mended. A soft eraser is recommended for removing marks and dirt. Tears can be mended with paste applied with a very small brush to each of the torn edges (diagrams A and B). A paste made of cornstarch, laundry starch, or rice flour mixed with water and cooked until it thickens is the best kind to use (see pages 252-53 for recipes). The work should be done on a hard surface like a smooth wooden board or a thick piece of glass. A mending tissue is placed under the tear and another on top. A clean paper is placed over this and rubbed gently with a bone folder, after which a weight is put on top and the page is left to dry. When it is dry, the two tissues are carefully removed, leaving the tear pasted together. Available also is a prepared liquid for mending torn edges called "Bindry-Aid," or a transparent Scotch mending tape that comes on a dispenser can be used.

Packaged strips of Japanese mending tissues can be purchased from bookbinding supply companies for repairing folds in the sheets of signatures. If they are not obtainable, strips about 1/2 inch wide can be cut from white tissue or onionskin paper.

After a book has been taken apart for binding, the pages are opened out flat and examined for holes and weak spots in the crease from which the thread was removed. If they are in need of repair, a mending tissue is laid on a piece of paste paper, and a very thin solution of paste is applied with a brush (figure 300). The tissue is placed over the tear, covered with a clean paper, and rubbed gently with a bone folder or the fingers (figure 301), or a thin layer of paste can be put on a piece of glass and the mending strip pressed against it and then put on the book. If several sheets are to be repaired, a piece of wax paper is put over each one (diagram C), and they are stacked one on top of the other and placed under a light weight to dry. When they are dry, the tissue projecting at the top and bottom edges is trimmed off even with the edge of the page. Books taken apart and mended on the spine should be put into a press to flatten them before they are resewn.

Restraint should be exercised in mending for it can be overdone if attacked carelessly. If the pages are in bad shape, crumpled, or torn, the book may have to be discarded. If they are only wrinkled, however, they can be smoothed out, dampened, and pressed between wax paper or with a warm iron. Loose sheets and plates can be tipped in; paste is applied sparingly about 1/8 inch from the inner edge of the sheet, and it is attached to the page following.

Often the outside edges of the pages are soiled or have pencil markings on them. They can be cleaned with an eraser while the book is held firmly shut. A piece of medium sandpaper is useful for removing more stubborn stains and marks.

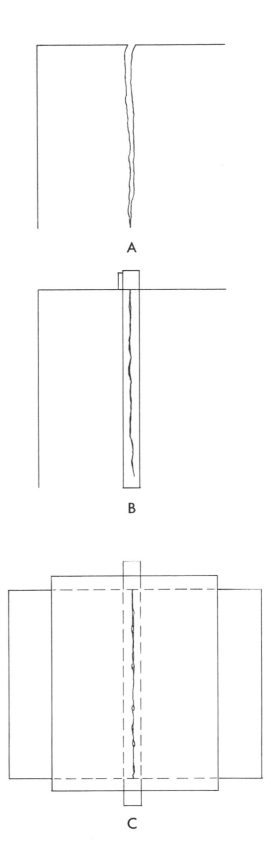

A

B

C

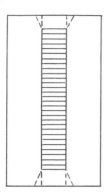

A

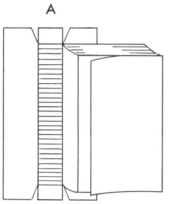

B

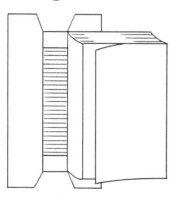

C

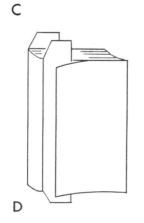

D

If resewing is needed, the signatures are put in order and stacked, and the directions for making a book on tapes or cords are followed (see pages 124-38). If the holes formerly used for sewing show a tendency to tear, new ones will have to be made between them.

When white paper is used for lining sheets in re-covering an old book, it should match or relate as much as possible to the tone of the pages of the book. Some whites are warm while others are cooler in shade. If thin papers are used they should be tough enough to be durable. Such types as light-weight drawing paper, brown wrapping paper, and various colored papers are recommended. When the paper is decorated it should be folded so that the design is on the inside and the outer side is pasted to the inside cover board. If the wrong side of the decorated paper has become soiled in the making of the design, it can be pasted to a plain sheet.

When it has been decided not to resew a book either because it is in excellent shape and does not need to be taken apart, or because the pages are so thin they do not warrant sewing, as with some Bibles, or there are single sheets only, as with most paper-bound books, care should be taken not to break the old stitches. Folded end sheets can be pasted in, super added, headbands applied, and a casing made and put on.

When the cover has come off or is partly torn off, a good plastic adhesive can be applied to the back of the contents and the inside of the cover, wax paper inserted between the cover and the contents, and the book put to press. A loose cover can be re-paired if the covers are bent straight back and glue is applied to the inside of the cover hinges. This is done by reaching in at the ends with a brush. When parts of the cover material of the book are torn they can be pasted down. The exterior hinge and worn edges can also be repaired.

If the cover is still attached to the book and only the cloth on the back needs to be replaced, this sec-tion can be cut out with a sharp knife and removed. A new piece of book cloth is cut, extending $3/4$ inch at the top and bottom of the book and 1 or more inches over on each side in addition to the width across the back. A lining paper is pasted in the cen-ter, the exact size of the book spine. Wedge shapes are cut at the top and bottom with a cut straight to the corners and then on a slanting line (diagram A).

The cloth or paper on the cover board next to the hinge is peeled back an inch or more so that the new back can be put under it when it is glued to the cover board. Paste is put on one of the cover boards under the cloth or paper, and the new piece cut for the back is inserted. The cloth or paper is pasted down over it (diagram B).

The flaps at the top and bottom of the new back piece are pasted down (diagram C), and the piece is brought snugly around the spine and inserted under the peeled-back portion of the other cover board (diagram D). The flaps left extending are folded down and pasted onto the inside of the cover boards. If the old back has printing on it and is still usable, it can be cut out and pasted over the spine portion of the new material.

When an old cover is in bad shape with broken corners, it is usually advisable to cut new boards, using the old boards for measurement. It is possible to mend bent corners, however, and this may be desirable when the cover material for some reason needs to be retained. This is done by separating the layers of the board with a pointed knife and inserting some paste between them. The cover is then tapped gently with a hammer on both sides. Care must be taken not to push the paste out.

Sometimes it is possible to repair old leather covers by gluing down parts that have pulled loose or by patching with newer pieces. Each case is an individual one, and the solution of the problem depends upon the judgment of the binder.

The book in figure 302 contains old architectural forms of an earlier period. When it was rebound, the design on the cover was suggested by some of the forms used in the illustrations. The rice paper used was very adaptable to the design. The lining was chosen because it contained the colors of the front cover (brown, gold, and beige) and yet provided a nice contrast. The feeling of texture is much the same as that of the building material used during this period of architecture.

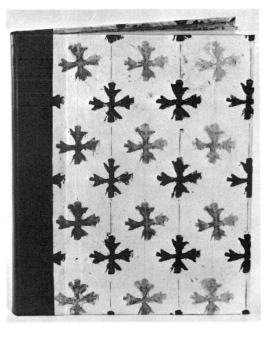

302

PASTE RECIPES

Cooked pastes can be made from any ordinary flour or starch, or with flour and starch combined. Rice flour makes a whiter paste than the others and for this reason is recommended for mending pages.

Recipes for pastes vary in amounts of ingredients used, and the binder may want to devise his own proportions. Paste thickens somewhat when it cools. If it is too thick it can be thinned with water.

A wooden spoon or stick is good to use for stirring.

Flour Paste

1 cup flour   1 cup cold water
4 or 5 cups boiling water

Put the flour in a saucepan or double boiler and gradually add the cold water, stirring well until all lumps are removed. The mixture should be runny like a thin cream. Slowly add the boiling water and cook the mixture for 3 or 4 minutes, stirring constantly. Let cool.

If the paste is to be kept several days a preservative can be used. Two teaspoons of powdered alum can be added to the flour when it is mixed with the water. A little powdered clove or three or four drops of oil of clove can also be added, if desired, to discourage mildew and mice and act as a preservative.

Cold-Water Paste

A wheat-flour wallpaper-paste powder is available in packages of 1 or more pounds. To mix, start with an inch or so of water in a saucepan and sift the powder with the fingers or spoon over the top until it begins to be absorbed. Then stir with a spoon or stick. If too thick add more water. For a smoother consistency the paste mixture can be whipped with an egg beater. Since this type of paste is quick and easy to make, only the amount actually needed should be mixed at any one time.

Flour and Starch Paste

1 teaspoon flour   2 teaspoons cornstarch
$^1/_2$ teaspoon alum   6 tablespoons water (about $^1/_3$ cup)

Mix all ingredients in a saucepan and boil for 4 or 5 minutes, stirring constantly. If the mixture becomes lumpy, it can be put through a kitchen strainer when cool.

Starch Paste

$^1/_2$ cup Argo gloss starch or any common laundry starch
$^1/_3$ cup cold water
A pinch of alum (if used with leather)

Mix the starch with cold water to form a mixture the consistency of thin cream. The boiling water is added quickly while the mixture is stirred constantly until it thickens and becomes smooth, transparent, and glossy. It should then be beaten hard.

GLUE RECIPES

Recipes for making flexible glues can be secured from a United States government bulletin.

Flexible glues are prepared from animal hide, cartilage, or bone, to which a softening agent like glycerin, diethylene glycol, or sorbitol sirup is added. The dry, ground, powder glue is added slowly to water in a steam-jacketed cooking kettle or double boiler and stirred and cooked until a smooth mixture results. Then one of the softening agents mentioned above is added. Beta-naphthol is used as preservative against mold, and terpineol to mask odors. The mixture is cooked at 150 degrees F. until it forms a homogeneous mixture, after which it is placed in a greased pan to solidify.

A flexible glue can be made quickly by adding a small amount of glycerin to a flake wood glue. The amount needed can be determined by experimenting. Flexible glue remains supple when dry.

Flexible glues in liquid or solid form can be purchased from bookbinding supply companies or from bookbinders. The liquid comes in bottles and is more convenient for general classroom use. A liquid plastic adhesive used by libraries for mending books comes in a white plastic squeeze bottle and makes a strong flexible film that dries quickly. It is so strong that several volumes of a periodical can be glued together with it without sewing.

Polyvinyl glue is a creamy white resin glue that becomes nearly transparent when set. It can be purchased ready for use under such commercial brand names as Cascorz and Mirade and is a good adhesive for paper, fabrics, and leather.

White liquid casein-base glues produce a caustic reaction and should be applied with a brush. Use of the hands should be avoided as much as possible to prevent skin irritation.

LEATHER DRESSING

(From United States Government Leaflet No. 69, 1933)
Preparation No. 6:
Lanolin, anhydrous, 40 per cent
Neat's-foot oil, pure, 60 per cent
Melt lanolin in double boiler; add neat's-foot oil.
The mixture is applied with a soft cloth, left overnight, and then wiped with a clean cloth.
Beeswax is added in some recipes to give a polish.

Supply Sources

(Many of the sources listed have catalogues and samples available.)

Arcon Coating Mills
3067 New Street
Oceanside, NY 11572
    Binding tapes (for reinforcement of spine or first and last signatures); end sheets

Basic Crafts Co.
1201 Broadway
New York, NY 10001
    Bookbinding tools and supplies; gold-stamping type, holders, foils, and stamps; leathers and cloths; end papers; how-to books; marbling supplies, kit, and how-to books

Dick Blick
P.O. Box 1267
Galesburg, IL 61401
    Table cutter for cardboard and leather

"Book Making Needs"
Bookbinding Supplies
665 Third Street, Suite 335
San Francisco, CA 94107
    Bookbinding tools; cloth; papers; thread; boards; PVA; pastes; how-to books

The Davey Company
164 Laidlaw Avenue
P.O. Box 8128—Five Corners Station
Jersey City, NJ 07306
    Binder's board

Demco Inc.
P.O. Box 7488
Madison, WI 53707
    or
P.O. Box 7767
Fresno, CA 93747
    General bookbinding supplies; manual and videotape on book preservation and repair; various book repair kits

Gane Brothers and Lane Inc.
1400 Greenleaf Avenue
Elk Grove Village, IL 60007
    also
Maryland Heights, MO; Dallas, TX;
Atlanta, GA; Vernon, CA; Conshohocken, PA
    General bookbinding supplies and equipment

Gaylord Brothers
P.O. Box 710
Stockton, CA 95201
    or
P.O. Box 4901
Syracuse, NY 13221
    Book mending supplies; manual on book-repair, *Bookcraft*

Guild of Book Workers Inc.
521 Fifth Avenue
New York, NY 10175
    Members receive a supplier directory and news about bookbinding

Hickok Bookbinders Equipment
W. O. Hickok Manufacturing
Ninth and Cumberland Streets
Harrisburg, PA 17103
    Large presses, cutters, and other heavy equipment for binderies

MacPherson Leather
519 12th Avenue South
Seattle, WA 98144
    Leather and leather tools

McManus and Morgan Inc.
2506 West 7th Street
Los Angeles, CA 90057
    Fine papers; extensive line of bookbinding supplies

Montana Leather
2015 First Avenue North
Billings, MT 59103
    Leather and leather tools

Oregon Leather Company
110 N.W. 2nd Avenue
Portland, OR 97209
    Leather and leather tools

The Tandy Leather Company
P.O. Box 791
Fort Worth, TX 76101
(184 stores throughout the country)
    Leather, leather tools; bone folders (nylon); linen thread; metal plates and rivets for telephone book covers

Zellerbach Paper Company
245 Spruce Avenue
San Francisco, CA 94080
    Chipboard, papers

Bibliography

Banister, Manly. *Pictorial Manual of Bookbinding.* New York: Ronald Press, 1958.

Bean, Florence O. *Bookbinding for Beginners.* Worcester, Mass.: Davis Press, 1931.

Bindery Glues. (Research Bulletin B-3, Bindery Series.) Washington, D.C.: U.S. Government Printing Office, n.d.

Bland, David. *A History of Book Illustration: The Illuminated Manuscript and the Printed Book.* London: Faber and Faber, 1958.

Bookbinding Leather. (Research Bulletin B-5, Bindery Series.) Washington, D.C.: U.S. Government Printing Office, n.d.

"Boxes Replace Bindings for Books," *Craft Horizons,* XLII (October, 1953), 10-15. A collection of limited editions incased by Gerhard Gerlach.

Boyce, George K. "The Pierpont Morgan Library," *Library Quarterly,* XXII (January, 1952), 21-35.

Brassington, W. Salt. *A History of the Art of Bookbinding: With Some Account of the Books of the Ancients.* London: Elliot Stock, 1894.

Bronze Stamping Leaf. (Research Bulletin B-6, Bindery Series.) Washington, D.C.: U.S. Government Printing Office, n.d.

Buffum, Clara. *Hand-bound Books: The Old Method of Bookbinding.* Providence, R.I.: published by the author; printed by Akerman-Standard Co., 1935.

Byrne, Brooke. *Mending Books Is Fun.* Minneapolis, Minn.: Burgess Publishing Company, 1956.

Chiera, Edward. *They Wrote on Clay.* Chicago: University of Chicago Press, 1938.

Cockerell, Douglas. *Bookbinding, and the Care of Books: A Handbook for Amateurs, Bookbinders and Librarians.* New York: D. Appleton and Co., 1902.

Cockerell, Sydney Morris. *Marbling Paper as a School Subject.* Hitchin, Eng.: G. W. Russell, n.d.

————. *The Repairing of Books.* London: Sheppard Press, 1958.

Collins, Archie Frederick. *Book Craft for Schools: The Approach to Bookbinding.* Leicester, Eng.: Dryad Press, 1934.

Combed Pattern Papers. (Dryad Leaflet No. 107.) Leicester, Eng.: Dryad Press, n.d.

Craig, Maurice. *Irish Bookbindings 1600-1800.* London: Cassell and Co., 1954.

Crane, Walter J. E. *Bookbinding for Amateurs: Being Descriptions of the Various Tools, and Appliances Required and Minute Instructions for Their Effective Use.* London: Upcott Gill, 1885.

Cushman, Eleanor. *Bookbinding.* (Merit Badge Handbook.) New York: Boy Scout Library. n.d.

Davenport, Cyril James. *The Book and Its History and Development.* New York: Van Nostrand, 1908.

Demcobind: A Practical Manual of Mending Books. Demco Library Supplies, Madison, Wis.; New Haven, Conn.; and Fresno, Calif. (This manual is now out-of-print.)

Devauchelle, Roger. *La reliure en France, de ses origines à nos jours.* Paris: Rousseau-Girard, 1959.

Diehl, Edith. *Bookbinding, Its Background and Technique.* 2 vols. New York: Rinehart and Co., 1946.

Diringer, David. *The Hand-produced Book*. New York: Philosophical Library, 1953.

The Dolphin. No. 2, "A Journal of the Making of Books." New York: Limited Editions Club, 1935.

Douglas, Clara, and Constance Lehde. *Book Repairing: New Ideas From the Mendery*. Seattle: University of Washington Press, 1940.

Evangeliorum Quattuor Codex Cenannensis (The Book of Kells). Facsimile. 3 vols. Berne: Urs Graf Verlag, 1950-51. Distributed by Philip C. Duschnes, 806 Lexington Avenue, New York 21, N.Y.

Evangeliorum Quattuor Codex Lindisfarnensis (The Lindisfarne Gospels). Facsimile. 2 vols. Oltun and Lausanne: Urs Graf Verlag, 1956-60. Distributed by Philip C. Duschnes, 806 Lexington Avenue, New York 21, N. Y.

Fahey, Herbert and Peter. *Finishing in Hand Bookbinding*. San Francisco, Calif.: printed and published by Herbert and Peter Fahey, 1951.

Fletcher, William Younger. *Bookbinding in France*. New York: Macmillan and Co., 1894.

Folmsbee, Beulah. *A Little History of the Horn-Book*. Boston: The Horn Book; printed by Thomas Todd Co., 1942.

Gaylord's Bookcraft: A Complete Manual on Book Repair. Syracuse, N.Y.: Gaylord Brothers, 1955.

Gibson, Strickland. *Early Oxford Bindings*. London: Oxford University Press, 1903. Printed for the Bibliographical Society. Contains photographs of beautiful old leather-covered books.

Goudy, Frederick. *The Alphabet*. Berkeley: University of California Press, 1940.

Groneman, Chris H. *General Bookbinding*. Bloomington, Ill.: McKnight and McKnight, 1946.

The Gutenberg Bible. Facsimile edition. Paterson, N.J.: Pageant Books, 1960.

Halliday, J. *Bookbinding as a Handwork Subject*. New York: E. P. Dutton and Co., n.d.

Harthan, John P. *Bookbindings*. (Victoria and Albert Museum.) 2nd ed. London: Her Majesty's Stationery Office; John Wright and Sons, n.d.

Helwig, Hellmuth. *Handbuch der Einbandkunde*. Vol. I. N.p., 1953.

Hewitt-Bates, James Samuel. *Bookbinding for Schools: A Textbook for Teachers and Students in Elementary and Secondary Schools and Training Colleges*. Peoria, Ill.: Manual Arts Press, 1935.

Hewitt-Bates, James Samuel, and J. Halliday. *Three Methods of Marbling*. (Dryad Leaflet No. 74.) Leicester, Eng.: Dryad Press, n.d.

The History of Bookbinding 525-1950. An Exhibition held at the Baltimore Museum of Art, November 12, 1957, to January 12, 1958. Baltimore, Md.: published by the Trustees of the Walters Art Gallery, 1957.

Hulme, E. Wyndham, J. Gordon Parker, A Seymour-Jones, Cyril Davenport, and F. J. Williamson. *Leather for Libraries*. London: Library Supply Co., 1905.

Hunter, Dard. *Papermaking: The History and Technique of an Ancient Craft*. New York: Alfred A. Knopf, 1947.

Ignatz Wiemeler, Modern Bookbinder. New York: Museum of Modern Art, 1935.

Johnson, Pauline. "Decorative Covers," *Craft Horizons*, XLV (August, 1954), 20-23.

Johnston, Edward. *Writing and Illuminating and Lettering*. London: Pitman, 1945.

Kepes, Gyorgy, and Others. *Graphic Forms: The Arts as Related to the Book*. Cambridge, Mass.: Harvard University Press, 1949.

Kitson, Edward. *Bookbinding*. New York: Dover Publications, 1954.

Klinefelter, Lee M. *Bookbinding Made Easy*. Milwaukee, Wis.: Bruce Publishing Co., 1935.

Kup, Karl. *A Fifteenth Century Girdle Book.* New York: New York Public Library, 1939.

Lewis, Arthur William. *Basic Bookbinding.* New York: Dover Publications, 1957.

Loring, Rosamond B. *Decorated Book Papers.* 2nd ed., edited by Philop Hofer. Cambridge, Mass.: Harvard University Press, 1952.

Lydenberg, Harry Miller, and John Archer. *The Care and Repair of Books.* New York: R. R. Bowker Co., 1960.

Mansfield, Edgar. "New Directions in Modern Bookbinding," *Graphis,* XV (July/August, 1959), 350-57.

Mason, John. *Gold and Colour Tooling.* (Dryad Leaflet No. 105.) Leicester, Eng.: Dryad Press, n.d.

Matthews, Brander. *Bookbindings, Old and New: Notes of a Book-Lover, with an Account of the Grolier Club, New York.* New York: Macmillan and Co., 1895.

McMurtrie, Douglas Crawford. *The Book: The Story of Printing and Bookmaking.* New York: Covici-Friede Publishers, 1937.

————. *Design in Bookbinding: As Represented in Exhibits at the Sixth Triennial Exposition of Graphic Arts at Milan, Italy, in 1936, with Illustrations of Eighteen Bookbindings There Exhibited.* Chicago: privately printed, 1938.

————. *The Golden Book.* Chicago: Pascal Covici, 1927.

————. *The Gutenberg Documents.* New York: Oxford University Press, 1941.

Miscellaneous Book Adhesives. (Research Bulletin B-4, Bindery Series.) Washington, D.C.: U.S. Government Printing Office.

Moseley, Spencer, Pauline Johnson, and Hazel Koenig. *Crafts Design: An Illustrated Guide.* Belmont, Calif.: Wadsworth Publishing Co., 1962.

Nicholson, James B. *A Manual of the Art of Bookbinding: Containing Full Instructions in the Different Branches of Forwarding, Gilding, and Finishing. Also, the Art of Marbling Book-Edges and Paper. The Whole Designed for the Practical Workman, the Amateur, and the Book-Collector.* Philadelphia: Henry Carey Baird and Co., 1902. Contains samples of marbled papers.

Ogg, Oscar. *The 26 Letters.* New York: Thomas Crowell, 1948.

Oldham, J. Basil. *English Blind-stamped Bindings.* Cambridge, Eng.: Cambridge University Press, 1952. Contains large photographs of beautiful tooled leather-bound books, and many rubbings of leather-tooled designs taken from books.

Orcutt, William Dana. *The Art of the Book: A Review of Some Recent European and American Work in Typography, Page Decoration, and Binding.* London: The Studio, 1914.

————. *In Quest of the Perfect Book: Reminiscences and Reflections of a Bookman.* Boston: Little, Brown and Co., 1926.

————. *The Kingdom of Books.* Boston: Little, Brown and Co., 1927.

————. *The Magic of the Book: More Reminiscences and Adventures of a Bookman.* Boston: Little, Brown and Co., 1930.

Palmer, E. W. *A Course in Bookbinding for Vocational Training.* Part I, Elementary Section. New York: Employing Bookbinders of America, 1927.

Percival, G. S. *Repairing Books.* (Dryad Leaflet No. 150.) Leicester, Eng.: Dryad Press, n.d.

————, and R. A. Graham. *Unsewn Binding.* Leicester, Eng.: Dryad Press, 1959.

Pleger, John J. *Bookbinding.* Chicago: Inland Printer Co., 1924. Contains section on marbling, edge gilding, and printed fore edges.

Plumer, John (comp.) *Manuscripts from the William S. Glazier Collection.* New York: Pierpont Morgan Library, 1959.

Portfolio: The Annual of the Graphic Arts. Cincinnati, Ohio: Zebra Press, 1951. Article on "French Marble Papers" shows methods of making the papers and includes an actual example.

Pratt, Guy A. *Let's Bind a Book.* Milwaukee, Wis.: Bruce Publishing Co., 1940.

The Process of Marbling Paper. (Research Bulletin B-1, Bindery Series.) Washington, D.C.: U.S. Government Printing Office, n.d.

Putman, George Haven. *Books and Their Makers in the Middle Ages.* New York: G. P. Putnam's Sons, 1896.

Rawlings, Gertrude Burford. *The Story of Books.* New York: Appleton, 1902.

Streeter, Burnett Hillman. *The Chained Library: A Survey of Four Centuries in the Evolution of the English Library.* London: Macmillan and Co., 1931.

Sullivan, Sir Edward. *The Book of Kells.* New York: Studio Publications, 1952.

Theory and Practice of Bookbinding. Washington, D.C.: U.S. Government Printing Office, 1950.

Town, Laurence. *Bookbinding by Hand.* London: Pitman, 1951.

Tuer, Andrew W. *History of the Horn-Book.* New York: Charles Scribner's Sons, 1897.

Watson, Aldren. A. *Hand Bookbinding: A Manual of Instruction.* New York: Reinhold Publishing Corp., 1963.

Weber, Carl. *Fore-edge Paintings.* Waterville, Me.: Colby College Press, 1949.

Wood, Stacy H. *Bookbinding.* (Merit Badge Series.) New York: Boy Scouts of America, 1940.

Woodcock, John. *Binding Your Own Books.* (Puffin Picture Book 104.) London: Penguin Books, n.d.

Index

Accordion book, 102-3
Alexandria: library of, 8
Appliqué, 204-15 passim, 239-41

Babylonian clay tablets, 3
Backing, 129
Band nipper, 243
Bands: raised, 138, 243-44
Beeswax, 162, 202, 253
Bible, 20-22, 24, 25, 35, 245, 248, 250
Binders: single-stitch, 152; double-stitch, 152
Bindry-Aid, 249
Blinding-in, 234
Blind tooling, 12, 35, 231-33
Block printing, 22
Boards: defined, 46
Bonet, Paul, 38
Bookbinders, 27-40 passim
Book box, 114
Book construction: single signature, 122-23;
    on tapes, 124-33; on cords, 134-38
Booklets, 118-21
Book of Hours, 18
Book of Kells, 20
Book of the Dead, 6
Brayer prints, 192-95
Byzantine books, 12

Calligraphy, 3, 20
Card: stand-up, 99
Cardboard: cutting of, 60-61
Cardboard prints, 184, 185
Carlyle, Thomas, 3
Casing, 60, 76 77, 113, 119
Caxton, William, 28
Cellini, Benvenuto, 27
Chained libraries, 26-27
Chaucer, Geoffrey, 29
Chinese printing, 22, 23
Clay tablets: Babylonian, 3
Cloth: decorated, 16, 214
Clovio, Giulio, 27
Cobden-Sanderson, Thomas James, 29
Cockerell, Douglas, 29
Collage, 214. See also Appliqué
Color, 155-56, 158, 216-18, 229-30
Coloring edges, 138
Coptic binding, 12, 13
Cord-bound book, 134-38
Corners. See Mitering corners
Cottage style, 28
Counterchange, 40, 208, 209
Covers: making of, 74-77, 130-33, 135-38,

141-43, 144, 145-46, 149, 152; leather, 243-45; flexible, 245
Cradle, 152
Crayon and crayon resist, 160-61, 167, 172, 189, 196, 202
Cuneiform, 2, 3, 4, 5
Cutout shapes, 204-11
Cylinder seals, 5

Dabber, 178
Design, 42-44, 155-58, 170-72, 204, 208, 212, 229
Desk blotter, 96
The Dictes or Sayengis of the Philosophres, 28
Diptych, 8
Donatus, 24
Dovetail cuts, 150
Drilling holes, 140, 144, 146, 152
Drill press, 140

Embossing leather, 233-34
Embroidered covers, 16, 214
End papers (sheets), 46, 47, 80-83, 245
Envelope-type folder. See Folders
Eraser prints, 178-83, 196, 247

Fahey, Herbert, 40
Fahey, Peter, 40
Files, 92-95; box, 114-17
Fillet, 233
Finder, 72-73
Fly leaf, 80, 82-83
Fold-and-dye papers, 220-21
Folders, 88-93, 112-13
Folio, 46, 47
Fore edge, 46, 47
Fore-edge paintings, 28
Full-bound book, 74
Fust, Johann, 23

Gadget prints, 191
Geometric shapes, 204-11 passim
Gerlach, Gerhard, 41
Gilding, 138
Girdle book, 22, 23
Glair, 236
Glue recipes, 253
Goffered edges, 28, 29
Golden oblong, 43
Gold leaf, 236-37
Gold paper, 238, 239
Gold pencil, 238
Gold tooling, 14, 15, 35, 37, 236-38

Gospel of St. John (St. Cuthbert Gospel), 20, 22
Grain: of paper and boards, 46, 64, 80
Grolier Club, 31
Grolier de Servières, Jean, 31
Gum arabic, 167
Gum tragacanth, 167
Gutenberg Bible, 24-26
Gutenberg, Johannes, 22-24

Half-bound book, 74, 76-77
Hammurabi, 5
Headband, 46, 47, 52, 70-71
Hereford Cathedral, 26-27
Hieroglyphics, 3, 5, 6
Hollow back, 148
Hornbook, 27

Illumination, 16-21, 24, 25, 27, 44
Ink-and-fold papers, 222-23
Ink pad, 172
Inlay, 31, 33, 34, 35, 37, 39, 239
Inner-tube prints, 184, 247

Japanese binding, 144-47
Japanese papers, 154, 157, 158
Job, 5
Johnson, Arthur, 37
Jones, Trevor, 33, 34, 35
Jungstedt, Kurt, 237

Kelmscott Press, 29
Kettle stitch, 124, 125, 126, 135, 139
Korean printing, 23

Lacquer: book, 158
Lahey, Marguerite Duprez, 40
Laurentian Library, 27
Leather: kinds of, 227; cutting, 228; skiving, 228-29, 239; decorating, 229-30; dyeing, 229-30; burning, 233; stamping, 233; embossing, 233-34; recessing, 234; covers, applying, 243-45; cleaning, 247; preserving, 247; dressing for, 253. See also Inlay; Tooling
Letters: for titles, 246-47
Lindisfarne Gospels, 20, 21
Lindisfarne Monastery, 20
Liner, 80-83 passim, 156, 250
Linoleum prints, 184, 185, 186, 189, 234

Macdonald, Dorothy, 237, 238, 243
Magazines: binding of, 109, 114-15, 117, 150-51, 153
Mansfield, Edgar, 30, 31, 32, 226, 232, 233
Manutius, Aldus, 27
Marbling, 166-69

Martin, Pierre, 40
Matchbox, 117
Mearne, Charles, 28
Mearne, Samuel, 28
Medici, Cardinal Giulio de', 27
Memo pad, 100-1
Mending. See Repair
Mending tissues, 249
Miniature painting, 18-20
Mitering corners, 74, 77, 78-79, 244
Morocco. See Leather
Morris, William, 28-29
Mosaic: leather. See Inlay
Museum of Modern Art, 40

Neat's-foot oil, 247, 253
Newsboard, 245
Niello, 11
Nineveh: library at, 5
No-paste book, 118-19
Note pads, 98

Oiled silk, 178
One-signature book, 122-23
Onlay, 239, 240, 242

Padding cement, 52, 153
Pads: note, 98; memo, 100-1
Painted papers, 216-19
Pallet, 246
Pamphlet binders, 152
Pamphlets, 113, 114, 152
Paper: invention of, 6
Paperback books: binding of, 149, 150-51, 248 ff.
Papyrus, 5-6, 8, 12; Prisse, 6
Paraffin, 158, 162, 202; prints, 188
Parchment, 7, 8
Paste-paper design, 224-25
Paste recipes, 252-53
Pasting, 64-67
Payne, Roger, 28
Persians, 20, 43, 168
Phillatius the Athenian, 27
Pierpont Morgan Library, 40, 41
Plow and press, 62-63
Polishing iron, 247
Polyvinyl acetate, 51
Portfolio box, 117
Portfolios, 106-13
Positive-negative shapes, 170, 204, 205, 207, 208, 209
Potato prints, 160, 162, 170-77, 189, 196, 230
Presses, 60 ff., 66 ff.; printing, 22-23; finishing, 66, 67; gluing, 66, 67; letter, 68; nipping, 68; standing, 68; drill, 140
Pressing books, 68-69, 244, 245
Printed papers, 170-203

Printers, 27-29
Printing: history of, 22 ff.
Proportion, 44-45
Pugillaria, 8

Quarter-bound book, 74-75, 123
Quarto, 46, 47

Rack: book, 247
Redboard, 245
Repair, 150, 248-51
Reverse-fold book, 149
Robinson, Ivor, 32, 33
Rosetta stone, 5
Rounding, 128-29
Rubbings, 160-61

Saddle soap, 247
St. Cuthbert Gospel, 20, 22
Saw-kerf binding, 150-51
Scrapbook, 102-5
Screen: folding, 97
Scriptoria, 8
Scroll, 5-6, 7, 8
Sewing, 120, 139; in one-signature book, 122; in tape-made book, 125-26; in cord-made book, 135; clamp, 140. *See also* Kettle stitch; Side sewing
Side sewing, 140-47
Signature, 46, 47
Silk-screen prints, 200-3
Single sheets: binding of, 140-46, 148, 149, 150-51, 248
Single-signature book, 122-23
Sizing, 167, 168, 218, 236, 237, 247
Skawonius, Swen Erik, 246
Skiver, 227
Skiving, 228-29, 239
Solander, Daniel Charles, 30
Solander case, 30
Spine, 46, 47
Sponge prints, 172, 189

Squaring, 60
Stahly, Claude, 39
Stamps: metal, 233
Stand-up card, 99
Starch-paper design, 224-25
Stencil prints, 198-99
Stick prints, 190
Stoneyhurst College, 22
String prints, 172, 196-97
Stub book, 148, 149
Stylus: electric, 238
Super, 46, 47, 52

Tags: gift, 99
Tailband. *See* Headband
Tape-constructed book, 124-33
Telephone book cover, 109
Texture, 33, 37, 156, 160, 170, 189, 192, 214, 227, 233
Titles: applying, 237, 246-47
Tooling: blind, 12, 35, 231-33; gold, 14, 15, 35, 37, 236-38
Torn-paper shapes, 212-13
Towneley Lectionary, 27
Trimming books, 60-63, 128, 129
Trinity College Library, 20
Typeholder, 246

Water glass, 224
Waterproofing, 158, 224
Wax, 189, 196, 202; floor, 162
Wax resist, 172, 176. *See also* Crayon and crayon resist
Wax tablets, 7-8
Westminster Abbey, 28
Wiemeler, Ignatz, 41
Wimborne Minster, 26
Wooden book cover, 9, 11, 12, 26, 113
Wood engraving, 22, 23, 30
World Judgment, 24
Wright, R., 36, 37